Working With Custodial Grandparents

Bert Hayslip, Jr., PhD, received his doctorate in Experimental Developmental Psychology from the University of Akron in 1975. After teaching at Hood College in Frederick, MD for three years, he joined the faculty at the University of North Texas, where he is now Regents Professor of Psychology. Dr. Hayslip is a Fellow of the American Psychological Association, the Gerontological Society of America, and The Association for Gerontology in Higher Education, and has held research grants from the National Institute on Aging, The Hilgenfeld Foundation, and the National Endowment for the Humanities. His published research deals with cognitive processes in aging, interventions to enhance cognitive functioning in later life, personality-ability interrelationships in aged persons, grandparents who raise their grandchildren, grief and bereavement, hospice care, death anxiety, and mental health and aging.

Julie Hicks Patrick, PhD, received her doctorate in Developmental Psychology/ Applied Cognitive Aging from The University of Akron (Ohio). She has held appointments as Project Director for three federal grants related to family caregiving in Cleveland, Ohio, and Peoria, Illinois (Bradley University). In 1998, she joined the faculty at West Virginia University as an Assistant Professor, Life Span Psychology. Dr. Patrick's research includes questions in social cognition, family caregiving, and successful aging. She teaches graduate and undergraduate courses in the areas of aging and cognition.

Working With Custodial Grandparents

Bert Hayslip, Jr.
Julie Hicks Patrick
Editors

Springer Publishing Company

Springer Publishing Company, Inc.
536 Broadway
New York, NY 10012-3955

Acquisitions Editor: Helvi Gold
Production Editor: Sara Yoo
Cover design by Joanne Honigman

01 02 03 04 05 / 5 4 3 2 1

Library of Congress Cataloging-in-Publication Data

Working with custodial grandparents / Bert Hayslip, Jr., Julie Hicks Patrick.
p. cm.
Includes bibliographical references and index.
ISBN 0-8261-1684-1
1. Grandparents as parents. 2. Grandparents as parents—Services for.
3. Grandparent and child. I. Hayslip, Bert. II. Patrick, Julie Hicks.
HQ759.9.W67 2002
306.874'5—dc21 2002070595
CIP

Printed in the United States of America by Sheridan Books.

For those whose examples continue to influence our parenting:

Velma and Darrel Hicks, Margaret Case, Martha and Richard Hicks, Kathryn Murphy, Bessie and William Sininger

Contents

Contributors

Annabel H. Baird, MA
University of North Texas
Department of Applied Gerontology
Denton, TX

Ana Begovic, MA
The University of Akron
Department of Psychology
Akron, OH

Denise Burnette, PhD
Columbia University
School of Social Work
New York, NY

Francine Conway, PhD
School of Social Work
Long Island University
Brooklyn, NY

Martha Crowther, PhD, MPH
The University of Alabama
Department of Psychology
Tuscaloosa, AL

Megan L. Dolbin-MacNab, MS
Purdue University
Department of Child Development and Family Studies
West Lafayette, IN

Jane Jooste, MS
University of North Texas
Department of Psychology
Denton, TX

Sally Keller, PhD
Gordon Derner Institute for Advanced Psychological Studies
Adelphi University
Brooklyn, NY

Susan J. Kelley, PhD
Georgia State University
School of Social Work
College of Health and Human Services
Atlanta, GA

Carolyn W. Kern, PhD
University of North Texas
Department of Counseling, Development and Higher Education
Denton, TX

Jennifer M. Kinney, PhD
Miami University
Department of Sociology, Gerontology, and Anthropology and Scripps Gerontology Center
Oxford, OH

Stacey R. Kolomer, PhD
University of Georgia
School of Social Work
Athens, GA

Karen Kopera-Frye, PhD
University of Nevada-Reno
Department of Human Development and Family Studies
Reno, NV

Jessica M. Lahner, MS
University of North Texas
Department of Psychology
Denton, TX

Philip McCallion, PhD
State University of New York (SUNY)
Center for Excellence in Aging Services
School of Social Welfare
Albany, NY

Kathryn B. McGrew, PhD
Miami University
Department of Sociology, Gerontology, and Anthropology and Scripps Gerontology Center
Oxford, OH

Ian Matthew Nelson, BA
Miami University
Department of Sociology, Gerontology, and Anthropology and Scripps Gerontology Center
Oxford, OH

Jenny Overeynder, MSW
Rochester University
Strong Center on Developmental Disabilities
Rochester, NY

Jennifer Pickard, MA
West Virginia University
Department of Psychology
Morgantown, WV

Sara Honn Qualls, PhD
University of Colorado at Colorado Springs
Department of Psychology
Colorado Springs, CO

Karen A. Roberto, PhD
Virginia Polytechnic Institute and State University
Center for Gerontology
Blacksburg, VA

Rachel Rodriguez, BA
The University of Alabama
Department of Psychology
Tuscaloosa, AL

Gregory C. Smith, PhD
School of Family and Consumer Studies
Kent State University
Kent, OH

George Stricker, PhD
Gordon Derner Institute of Advanced Psychological Studies
Adelphi University
Garden City, NY

JoNell Strough, PhD
West Virginia University
Department of Psychology
Morgantown, WV

Lisa M. Swenson, MA
West Virginia University
Department of Psychology
Morgantown, WV

Dena B. Targ, PhD
Purdue University
Department of Child Development and Family Studies
West Lafayette, IN

Deborah M. Whitley, PhD
Georgia State University
School of Social Work
College of Health and Human Services
Atlanta, GA

Richard C. Wiscott, PhD
Shippensburg University
Gerontology Program
Shippensburg, PA

Elizabeth C. Wohl, MA
University of North Texas
Department of Psychology
Denton, TX

Foreword

Social science research has now established epidemiological and sociodemographic characteristics of grandparent-maintained households, determined precursors and correlates of the rapid growth of this population, and established various sources of risk and resilience. According to the Census 2000 Supplementary Survey, an estimated 6 million, or 8.4% of the nation's children under age 18 live with nonparental relatives—a 173% increase in this household configuration since 1970, and a 78% increase since 1990 (U.S. Bureau of the Census, 2001). Between 2.3 and 2.4 million grandparents have primary responsibility for the care and upbringing of 4.5 million, or 75%, of these children. About three-quarters of these grandparents have provided this care for at least one year, as have 35% for 5 or more years. Also noteworthy, the steepest growth rates during the 1990s were for those households in which neither parent of the grandchild was present, figures that increased 53% between 1990 and 1997 and now account for about one third of all grandparent-maintained households (Bryson & Casper, 1999).

With respect to population characteristics, the Census 2000 Supplementary Survey shows that 62% of custodial grandparents are women, three quarters are married, over half are working, and 19% have poverty-level incomes (Bryson, 2001). However, an important breakdown of 1997 Current Population Survey data revealed marked variations in income by household type, with grandmother-only households averaging $19,750 per year and households with two grandparents plus one or both parents, $61,632 (Bryson & Casper, 1999). And, using the 1992–1994 National Survey of Families and Households, Fuller-Thomson, Minkler, and Driver (1997) estimated that grandparents of color are 2–3 times as likely as their white counterparts to be in a custodial role.

The combined influence of demographic changes in family structure and roles, social health problems of the 1980s and 1990s, and public policies that favor kin care for children in need of out-of-home placement on the growth of grandparent-maintained families is well documented (Burnette, 2000; Minkler, 1998). There is also a sizeable body of research on individual, familial, and environmental sources of risk and resilience. These studies consistently show that custodial grandparents face substantial health, mental health, and economic problems that are often compounded by the special needs of grandchildren, grief and ongoing concerns about their adult children, and various environmental stressors (e.g., Burton, 1992; Hayslip, Shore, Henderson, & Lambert, 1998; Janicki, McCallion, Grant-Griffin, & Kolomer, 2000; Minkler & Roe, 1993; Pruchno, 1999; Szinovacz, DeViney, & Atkinson, 1999).

Current knowledge on the scope, nature, and context of grandparent-maintained families has thus matured sufficiently to warrant initial investigations to address these and other identified problems. In keeping with prevailing emphases on translational research that aims to effectively move social science knowledge into applied practice with at-risk populations (NIMH, 2000), this timely volume advances the grandparent caregiving field into the critical areas of prevention and intervention research. The authors skillfully address the necessity for and complexity of working with custodial grandparents through theoretical, methodological, and substantive perspectives.

The developmental life course perspective, a widely used conceptual framework in the field of aging, offers a particularly promising approach to understanding the long-term, socially and historically situated experiences of grandparent caregivers. Hayslip and Patrick accurately note the significant but until now overlooked potential of this framework for identifying individual experiences within familial and societal contexts that could meaningfully inform social policy and service planning and delivery.

Other authors draw fruitfully on theoretical principles from developmental and social psychology and on practical standards of care from the robust literature on late-life caregiving. Conway and Stricker effectively apply tenets of human development and ecological systems theories to the development of an integrative, strengths-based assessment model for practitioners who work with grandparent caregivers. Kern emphasizes the centrality of child and adolescent development in parent skill training, and Keller and Stricker use attachment theory to illustrate the significance of grandparents in the healthy adaptation of preadolescent and adolescent children in their care. Similarly, Crowther and Rodriguez build on existing stress process theories of family care in proposing a four-stage model to discern the role of primary and secondary stressors and appraisal, social support, and coping tactics on African American custodial grandparents' well-being.

Regarding practical standards, Dolbin-MacNab and Targ distill a broad range of cross-disciplinary education and service literature on family care into a succinct set of professional guidelines. And, Roberto and Qualls's chapter skillfully extracts transferable elements of successful interventions for older adult caregiving, that is, educational programs, support groups, individual therapy, family counseling, and respite programs. They further recommend key methodological strategies to ensure high quality intervention research with grandparent caregivers.

Kelley and Whitley present data from the first two years of Project Healthy Grandparents, an ongoing community-based intervention designed to improve the well-being of grandparents who are rearing grandchildren in parent-absent households. They report specific findings from analyses of psychological distress and provide a detailed description of the program that will be of great value to program planners.

Two studies by Patrick and her colleagues and Hayslip's psychosocial intervention are noteworthy for their methodological approaches. Addressing the often disregarded dyadic features of caregiving, Patrick and Pickard observed a cooperative behavioral task to assess control and affiliation between grandmothers and their grandchildren. And, Strough, Patrick, and Swenson used vignettes to examine the impact of personal and vicarious experience with caregiving on problem solving. Hayslip's study is especially notable for its use of a more rigorous intervention design to assess the efficacy of a brief, standardized psychosocial intervention.

As several authors note, despite the rapid proliferation of support groups for grandparent caregivers, the content, structure, and outcomes of this widespread intervention remain underexamined. Three chapters address this gap. Wohl, Lahner, and Jooste describe an intervention that combines support and educational content to address parent training; adolescent sex; substance abuse; depression, grief and loss; special needs of grandchildren; and legal and financial issues. The authors provide a narrative account of major themes that focus largely on interpersonal relationships and phases of adaptation to the caregiving process.

Kopera-Frye, Wiscott, and Begovic interviewed 14 grandparents in the Grandparents as Parents Again support group in Ohio about eight general domains of their caregiving experience. They conclude that lack of institutional and fiscal support makes these groups unstable and that existing groups are inadequate for meeting the diverse needs of contemporary and future grandparent caregivers.

An essential feature of effective intervention design and implementation is the integral, ongoing involvement of consumers. Smith reports on an interesting focus group study in which 42 custodial grandparents report their views on major features of support groups such as content, activities, membership, and leadership. Important findings include a need for sufficient structure, a range of information and skills, balanced leadership, multimodal approaches to meet the needs of heterogeneous groups, and ongoing ownership in developing and conducting groups. Likewise, Kolomer, McCallion, and Overeynder's interview data identify underlying themes pervading raising grandchildren as well as documenting that needs for services are crucial in this respect. Baird's articulate autobiographical chapter further captures the importance of consumer narratives as a singularly valuable source of critical information for service providers.

Finally, intervention research with grandparent caregivers must be tailored to address the unique needs of special subgroups of the population. Kinney, McGrew, and Nelson report on their evaluation of Ohio's *Double Jeopardy* project, which aimed to support grandparents who are rearing children with special needs stemming from developmental disabilities and mental retardation in planning for the future and to increase professionals' involvement in assisting them with this process. The authors conclude that even a very brief training program can effectively increase knowledge and understanding of life planning for family members and professionals. They also provide sufficient guidance for others to replicate or adapt elements of the program for other groups of custodial grandparents who face permanency planning issues.

Together, the chapters in this volume are a significant contribution to intervention studies to address the needs of grandparent caregivers and the children in their care. The continued use of appropriate, robust theoretical models will help to extend and expand our understanding of the complex needs of these families. Future researchers should be able to build on foundational elements and key findings from these studies to design rigorous, evidence-based prevention and intervention studies that will enhance basic and applied knowledge for improving individual and family well-being and the quality of social and physical contexts for productive aging and childrearing.

Denise Burnette, PhD
Columbia University

REFERENCES

Bryson, K. (2001, November 17). *New Census Bureau data on grandparents raising grandchildren.* Paper presented at Annual Scientific Meeting of the Gerontological Society of America, Chicago.

Bryson, K., & Casper, L. M. (1999). *Coresident grandparents and grandchildren*: U.S. Bureau of the Census, Population Division Working Paper No. 26. Washington, DC: U.S. Bureau of the Census.

Burnette, D. (2000). Mental health of grandparent caregivers. *Journal of Mental Health and Aging, 6*(4), 263–267.

Burton, L. M. (1992). Black grandparents rearing children of drug-addicted parents: Stressors, outcomes, and social service needs. *The Gerontologist, 32,* 744–751.

Fuller-Thomson, E., Minkler, M., & Driver, D. (1997). A profile of grandparents raising grandchildren in the United States. *The Gerontologist, 37*(3), 406–411.

Hayslip, B., Shore, J., Henderson, C., & Lambert, P. (1998). Custodial grandparenting and the impact of grandchildren with problems on role satisfaction and role meaning. *Journal of Gerontology, 53B*(3), 164–173.

Janicki, M. P., McCallion, P., Grant-Griffin, L., & Kolomer, S. R. (2000). Grandparent caregivers I: Characteristics of the grandparents and the children with disabilities for whom they care. *Journal of Gerontological Social Work, 33,* 35–55.

Minkler, M. (1998). Intergenerational households headed by grandparents: Demographic and sociological contexts. In Generations United (Ed.), *Grandparents and other relatives raising children: Background papers from Generations United's Expert Symposium.* Washington, DC: Generations United.

Minkler, M., & Roe, K. (1993). *Grandmothers as caregivers.* Newbury Park, CA: Sage.

National Institute of Mental Health. (2000). *Translating behavioral science into action.* Report of the National Advisory Mental Health Council Behavioral Science Workgroup (NIH Publication No. 00-4699). Washington, DC: U.S. Government Printing Office.

Pruchno, R. (1999). Raising grandchildren: The experiences of black and white grandmothers. *The Gerontologist, 39*(2), 209–221.

Szinovacz, M. E., DeViney, S., & Atkinson, M. P. (1999). Effects of surrogate parenting on grandparents' well being. *Journal of Gerontology, 54B*(6), S376–S388.

U.S. Bureau of the Census. (2001). Available: http://www.census.gov/population

Preface

For nearly two decades, we have been seeking to understand grandparents who raise their grandchildren. For societal, cultural, and idiosyncratic reasons, the lives of millions of middle-aged and older persons have been altered by the responsibilities of the reassumption of the parental role to an infant, young child, or adolescent. In many cases, the parents of these children have divorced; abused drugs, alcohol, or one another; or have either abandoned their children or mistreated them emotionally, physically, or sexually, necessitating the grandparents' reemergence as surrogate parents. After perhaps hundreds of studies that have painted a thorough picture of the demands and rewards of custodial grandparenting, we are poised to move beyond such a descriptive approach to this new family form. The evolution parallels that which occurred in the field of gerontology, which at one time had been described in terms of simply "counting the wrinkles."

It is in this context that *Working With Custodial Grandparents* represents the efforts of many researchers, practitioners, and clinicians to move beyond a simple cataloguing of the differences between custodial and noncustodial grandparents and to document the impact of this comparatively new role on them and their grandchildren.

The chapters in this book reflect the view from many perspectives in framing—theoretical, empirical, and pragmatic helping efforts with grandparents who are raising their grandchildren. We believe that interventions that are not theoretically grounded may ultimately miss their mark because they fail to understand the phenomena they are attempting to change. Importantly, empirically based studies are necessary to document the impact of helping interventions, defined in the broadest sense, with such grandparent caregivers. Such work has important implications for the design and implementation of programs whose funding depends on evidence demonstrating their efficacy, and for the development of public policy and legislation upon which such programs' viability often rests. In light of our interest in the challenges that custodial grandparenting presents, it should not be surprising to learn that there are many well-formulated and thoughtfully designed programs that can be of immense pragmatic value to professionals who work with custodial grandparents.

Working With Custodial Grandparents brings together these resources in establishing a knowledge base for future cohorts of practitioners, policy makers, and researchers. It is for this reason that the chapters to follow are organized into those dealing with (1) Theoretical Perspectives on Custodial Grandparents, (2) Empirical Studies of Helping Efforts With Grandparent Caregivers, and (3) The Pragmatics of Working With Grandparents Raising Their Grandchildren.

Each chapter makes a unique contribution in helping to define an action-oriented stance toward changing the lives of grandparents and their grandchildren. This is what such grandparents want and expect from us as professionals who are charged with the development and implementation of knowledge that really makes a difference in peoples' lives. This is the least we can do for those grandparents who have made many sacrifices to improve the quality of their grandchildren's lives by taking on the immense responsibility of raising them, with its attendant frustrations, disappointments, joys, and satisfactions.

Bert Hayslip, Jr. and Julie Hicks Patrick

Part I

Theoretical Perspectives on Custodial Grandparents

CHAPTER 1

Custodial Grandparenting Viewed From Within a Life-Span Perspective

Bert Hayslip, Jr., and Julie Hicks Patrick

INTRODUCTION

In spite of the increase in research focusing on grandparents raising grandchildren, there has been little work in the development of theory that might guide such work. Perhaps most important from a life-span perspective (see Baltes, 1987, 1997), we advocate framing custodial grandparenting in light of both its antecedents and consequences. As grandparents and particularly grandmothers often assume caregiving under adverse and often unpredictable circumstances (Emick & Hayslip, 1996, 1999; Hayslip, Shore, Henderson, & Lambert, 1998; Hirshorn, 1998; Jendrek, 1994) and may be motivated to perform their newly acquired roles by a variety of concerns, attention to the multiple sociocultural, interpersonal, and intrapersonal antecedents of grandparent caregiving as well as to the multidimensional nature of such outcomes seems warranted.

Indeed, in spite of the tremendous attention to the stresses and demands of caring for a grandchild on grandparents and grandchildren, positive effects of custodial grandparenting have been noted, particularly among African-American families, where grandmothers are seen as buffers against the detrimental effects of insensitive mothers, and grandfathers can serve as role models for boys who do not often see their fathers (Burton, 1992; Burton & DeVries, 1992; Minkler, Roe, & Price, 1992; Minkler, Roe, & Robertson-Beckley, 1994; Wilson, 1986). In addition, younger children and adolescents are more likely to achieve in school, get off welfare, demonstrate more autonomy in decision-making, and engage in fewer deviant activities when residing with grandmothers (Wilson, Tolson, Hinton, & Kiernan, 1990). Recent work by the first author and colleagues suggests that there are two distinct groups of custodial grandparents: those who have difficulties in dealing with the new demands of the parenting role and those who have difficulties raising a problem grandchild (Emick & Hayslip, 1999; Hayslip et al., 1998). Each group of surrogate parents faces unique sets of difficulties that may undermine their personal, marital, social, and role adjustment.

We believe that studying grandchildren's perceptions of their grandparents as well as those of their grandparents in anticipation of their new roles (see Somary & Stricker, 1998) can further aid in the identification of the multiple antecedents and consequences of grandparent caregiving, and we believe that greater emphasis on the dynamic nature of grandparent-grandchild relationships as well as cohort differences in custodial grandparenting (to include such changes in the meaning of grandparenting) is warranted by existing data (see Hayslip, Henderson, & Shore, in press; Uhlenberg & Kirby, 1998). Likewise, attention to levels of intervention (Danish, 1981) and its proximal and distal effects is important in the design and implementation of specific parental skills training, and educational, therapeutic, and programmatic efforts for grandparent caregivers. Last, a more accurate picture of custodial grandparenting can be painted through attention to the societal context in which middle-aged and older persons raise their grandchildren.

LIFE-SPAN DEVELOPMENT AND CUSTODIAL GRANDPARENTING

Our own approach to late adulthood is grounded in life-span developmental psychology (Baltes, 1987). Life-span psychology embodies many principles, the first of which is that aging is a complex process. Thus, aging is best viewed along many dimensions (e.g., sensation, perception, intelligence, memory, personality). Each dimension exhibits its own unique pattern of change, of which growth and decline are but one type. With regard to custodial grandparenting, distinguishing between relationships with one's custodial and noncustodial grandchildren, spouse, service providers, and adult child might be valuable.

The antecedents of change in later life are also complex, and can be viewed as a joint function of age-graded influences (those that correlate highly with age and are generalizable across persons, such as age-related changes in biological/physiological functioning [see Whitbourne, 1999]), history-graded influences (those that covary systematically with historical change), or nonnormative influences (those that are idiosyncratic to persons and thus not generalizable in terms of their influence, e.g. natural disasters, unforeseen illness or unemployment; see Baltes, 1987). With these distinctions in mind, custodial grandparenting can be construed in biological terms; illness or death might affect one's relationship with grandchildren and possibly undermine one's ability to provide care (Shore & Hayslip, 1994; Solomon & Marx, 1995). Alternatively, viewing grandparent caregiving in sociocultural terms reflects the fact that changes in the incidence of divorce and sociodemographic shifts in the nature of caregiving have literally created the phenomenon of custodial grandparenting (Bengtson, Rosenthal, & Burton, 1990; Uhlenberg & Kirby, 1998). Increases in deaths from AIDS (for parents) or Alzheimer's disease (for grandparents), elder abuse, or child abuse will further change the grandparent caregivers of the future (Joslin, 2002). New family forms will therefore emerge in light of the changing nature of grandparenting to the extent that the stigma of being a custodial grandparent may lessen. Compared to the traditional grandparent role, grandparent caregivers often report isolation from peers and lack of social support (Burton, 1992; Minkler & Roe, 1993; Shore & Hayslip, 1994). Isolation, of course, impacts on the quality of their relationships with others and undermines their access to needed services of all types. This experience of being different from one's peers deserves more attention than it has received thus far in the custodial grandparenting literature.

The life-span approach maintains that aging is best understood in terms of the context in which it occurs (see Bronfenbrenner, 1977; Lerner, 1996). As cultures and/or more narrowly defined environments change, a certain degree of aging-related change can be attributed to changes in the context in which grandparent caregivers live, grow old, and die. In this context, Stroebe and Schut's (1999) dual process model of grief, that is, thinking about grief in both loss-oriented and restoration-oriented terms (see Baird, chapter 5, this volume), is consistent with a multileveled approach to coping with loss that confronts many grandparent caregivers.

Changes in longevity and life expectancy and changing expectations of the roles grandparents are expected to fill will create new cohorts of grandparent caregivers (see Uhlenberg & Kirby, 1998), consistent with the impact of cultural change on aging that is also reflected in the importance given to cohort or generational effects in aging (Rosow, 1978) within the life-span tradition. Historical shifts in the nature of grandparenting have been discussed by Uhlenberg and Kirby (1998), and such changes are no less likely to impact grandparents raising their grandchildren.

Another life-span factor involving aging is an emphasis on individual differences. Such differences increase across adulthood; older adults are more different from one another than are younger adults (Nelson & Dannefer, 1992). Such differences are evident with regard to custodial grandparenting along age, gender, racial, ethnic, or extent of care provision parameters. As those who have worked with custodial grandparents can attest, despite the commonality of their life circumstances, each grandparent caregiver's concerns are unique, and often change over time (see Wohl, Lahner, & Jooste, chapter 13, this volume).

A last dimension of the life-span perspective on custodial grandparenting is rooted in the dialectical perspective (Lerner, 1996; Riegel, 1976), which emphasizes the continuous dynamic between interdependent elements. Viewing the family as a dynamic system that copes with the loss of one of its members due to divorce, death, or incarceration, as well as responding to both normative and nonnormative changes in the persons' lives who define the newly formed family system, would be consistent with such a view. Likewise, viewing custodial grandparenting as an interpersonal experience, wherein the expectations of both grandchildren and grandparents are continually modified as their relationship deepens, is essentially a dialectic view of custodial grandparenting. Such grandparents, dialectically speaking, are active processors of information and decision makers in response to changes in their physical and mental health, their legal status as custodians or guardians of their grandchildren, retirement-related concerns, and changes in their marital relationship as a function of the maturation of their grandchildren. Changes in the dynamics of custodial grandparenting can therefore be understood in terms of relationships between forces at intrapersonal, interpersonal, biological, and sociocultural levels.

NOVEL THEORETICAL PERSPECTIVES ON GRANDPARENTS RAISING THEIR GRANDCHILDREN

Because little attention has been paid to the development of theory that might properly frame both research and applied work, it is instructive to explore the multidimensional and diverse nature of theory-driven processes that might operate to either enhance or undermine the adjustment of grandparents who are raising their grandchildren. For example, one might predict on the basis of Role Theory, as discussed by Burnette (1999), that roles that are unanticipated and/or ambiguous, such as custodial grandparent caregiver, might require more social resources for these individuals to cope with their demands. In this light, what often complicates custodial grandparenting is that typically grandparents have previously endorsed the norm of noninterference, wherein mothers, especially those separated or divorced, emphasize the utility of grandparents' practical and moral support in childrearing, while expecting grandparents to avoid interfering in the upbringing of their grandchildren (Thomas, 1990). As a result, grandparents are often reluctant to interfere, only doing so when a crisis develops. Moreover, in view of recent work by Somary and Stricker (1998), which suggests that persons anticipate their roles as grandparents while their grandchildren are still in utero, it seems likely that assuming responsibility for a grandchild is both continuous and discontinuous in light of its relationship to the previous traditional grandparental role. Significantly, custodial grandparents, who may be especially prone to either role conflict or role strain have indeed reported social isolation and lessened social support from family and age peers (Burton, 1992; Jendrek, 1994). As reliable social support has been demonstrated to provide many health-related and psychosocial benefits to older adults (Unger, McAvay, Bruce, Berman, & Seeman, 1999), workable social convoys of support (see Antonucci, 1990) may help some grandparents to adapt to their surrogate parental roles. Also crucial to this process can be the identification of critical "significant others" under stressful circumstances through a process of socioemotional selectivity (Carstensen, 1995), as well as an accurate assessment of role demands and one's own resources to deal with the requirements of grandparental caregiving (see Pearlin, Mullan, Semple, & Skaff, 1990). Attachment theory (Ainsworth, 1989) might also be fruitful in framing variations in adjustment to this newly defined family system, viewed from both the grandparent's and the grandchild's perspective. Likewise, theoretical developments in the psychology of grief and loss (Stroebe, Hansson, Stroebe, & Schut, 2001) might also hold keys to understanding grandparents' ambivalence, guilt, or hostility directed to the adult parent whose child is being raised by the grandparent, or to the grandchild's relationship to the parent who has abandoned him or her (Hayslip & Shore, 2000). For example, the Stroebe and Schut (1999) dual process model of grief mentioned above is consistent with a multilevel approach to coping with loss, and might be utilized in this regard.

INTERVENTION RESEARCH AND CUSTODIAL GRANDPARENTING

Significantly, in light of the theoretical void that has characterized custodial grandparent research, it is not surprising that there has been little properly designed intervention research to document the effects of both formal and informal community-based programs on grandparent caregivers and their grandchildren. What is available often fails to include control groups, fails to utilize random assignment to treatment or control groups, is often based on small samples of convenience that are not generalizable to the larger population of grandparent caregivers, and does not incorporate even short-term, to say nothing of long-term, follow-up efforts to document their efficacy. Such work might be best understood in terms of the construct of levels of intervention (see Baltes & Danish, 1980; Danish, 1981), wherein efforts to effect the adjustment and well-being of custodial grandparents could be targeted to the culture at large, the community, and the interpersonal system that incorporates the grandparent, his or her spouse, and the grandchildren who are and are not being cared for by the grandparent (see also Gottesman, Quarterman, & Cohn, 1973). Of course, the impact of such interventions would vary with individual differences in both grandparent and grandchild characteristics such as health status, age, gender, race, and ethnicity. In this context, it is significant that many states are enacting responsive and supportive public policies for these families (Beltran, 2000; Butts, 2000). Yet, challenges remain to educate more states about the need for such policies and to inform policy makers of the informal caregivers in their jurisdiction and the particular obstacles they face.

Longitudinal research, especially of a prospective nature, may also yield important understandings about the antecedents of parental styles and coping mechanisms custodial grandparents employ, as the dynamics of such relationships are likely to be in flux. To date, only a handful of such studies exist (Hayslip, Emick, & Henderson, in press; Strawbridge, Wallhagen, Shema, & Kaplan, 1997). Such data may provide important insights for the targets of psychosocial interventions with custodial grandparents.

Interventions that target both grandparent caregivers and grandchildren may also be effective in generating knowledge about the impact of grandparent caregiving on each generation. For example, it is noteworthy to observe that in a developmental sense, we know little about the consequences in adulthood of having been raised by one's grandparents. Such persons may hold more positive attitudes toward aging or may be more effective parents. Moreover, we know little about cultural variations in custodial grandparenting (see Toledo, Hayslip, Emick, Toledo, & Henderson, 2000). Information that speaks to these issues will be valuable in the design and implementation of helping efforts directed to grandparents and the grandchildren they are raising.

Our view is that a life-span developmental perspective can both frame research leading to a greater understanding of custodial grandparenting as a nonnormative life event, and impact the development of services and social policy that are especially relevant to custodial grandparents. It is in this context that we argue that greater attention to the multidimensional nature of outcomes linked to interventions with grandparent caregivers is warranted, wherein both the grandparent and the grandchild are studied, and the role of the culture in framing the experience of changes in grandparent caregiving outcomes can be better understood.

REFERENCES

Ainsworth, M. (1989). Attachments beyond infancy. *American Psychologist, 44,* 709–716.

Antonucci, T. (1990). Social supports and social relationships. In R. Binstock & L. George (Eds.), *The handbook of aging and the social sciences* (3rd ed., pp. 205–226). San Diego, CA: Academic Press.

Baltes, P. B. (1987). Theoretical propositions of life span developmental psychology: On the dynamics of growth and decline. *Developmental Psychology, 23,* 611–626.

Baltes, P. B. (1997). On the incomplete architecture of human ontogeny: Selection, optimization, and compensation as foundation of developmental theory. *American Psychologist, 52,* 366–380.

Baltes, P. B., & Danish, S. J. (1980). Intervention in life span development and aging: Issues and concepts. In R. Turner & H. Reese (Eds.), *Life span developmental psychology: Intervention* (pp. 49–78). New York: Academic Press.

Beltran, A. (2000, Summer). Grandparents and other relatives raising children: Supportive public policies. *The Public Policy and Aging Report, 1,* 3–7.

Bengtson, V., Rosenthal, C., & Burton, L. (1990). Families and aging: Diversity and heterogeneity. In R. Binstock & E. Shanas (Eds.), *Handbook of aging and the social sciences* (pp. 267–287). New York: Academic Press.

Bronfenbrenner, U. (1977). Toward an experimental ecology of human development. *American Psychologist, 32,* 513–531.

Burnette, D. (1999). Social relationships of Latino grandparent caregivers: A role theory perspective. *The Gerontologist, 39,* 49–58.

Burton, L. M. (1992). Black grandparents rearing children of drug-addicted parents: Stressors, outcomes, and social service needs. *The Gerontologist, 32,* 744–751.

Burton, L., & DeVries, C. (1992). Challenges and rewards: African-American grandparents as surrogate parents. *Generations, 17,* 51–54.

Butts, D. (2000). Organizational advocacy as a factor in public policy regarding custodial grandparenting. In B. Hayslip & R. Goldberg-Glen (Eds.), *Grandparents raising grandchildren: Theoretical, empirical and clinical issues* (pp. 341–350). New York: Springer.

Carstensen, L. L. (1995). Evidence for a life-span theory of socioemotional selectivity. *Current Directions in Psychological Science, 4,* 151–156.

Danish, S. (1981). Life span development and intervention: A necessary link. *Counseling Psychologist, 9,* 40–43.

Emick, M., & Hayslip, B. (1996). Custodial grandparenting: New roles for middle aged and older adults. *International Journal of Aging and Human Development, 43,* 135–154.

Emick, M., & Hayslip, B. (1999). Custodial grandparenting: Stresses, coping skills, and relationships with grandchildren. *International Journal of Aging and Human Development, 48,* 35–62.

Gottesman, L., Quarterman, C., & Cohn, G. (1973). Psychosocial treatment of the aged. In C. Eisdorfer & M. P. Lawton (Eds.), *The psychology of adult development and aging* (pp. 378–427). Washington, DC: American Psychological Association.

Hayslip, B., Emick, M., & Henderson, C. (in press). Temporal variations in the experience of custodial grandparenting: A short term longitudinal approach. *Journal of Applied Gerontology.*

Hayslip, B., Henderson, C., & Shore, R. J. (in press). The structure of grandparental role meaning. *Journal of Adult Development.*

Hayslip, B., & Shore, R. J. (2000). Custodial grandparenting and mental health services. *Journal of Mental Health and Aging, 6,* 367–384.

Hayslip, B., Shore, R. J., Henderson, C., & Lambert, P. (1998). Custodial grandparenting and grandchildren with problems: Their impact on role satisfaction and role meaning. *Journal of Gerontology & Social Sciences, 53B,* S164–S174.

Hirshorn, B. (1998). Grandparents as caregivers. In M. Szinovacz (Ed.), *Handbook on grandparenthood* (pp. 200–216). Westport, CT: Greenwood.

Jendrek, M. (1994). Grandparents who parent their grandchildren: Circumstances and decisions. *The Gerontologist, 34,* 206–216.

Joslin, D. (2002). *Invisible caregivers: Older adults raising children in the wake of HIV/AIDS.* New York: Columbia University Press.

Lerner, R. (1996). *Concepts and theories of human development.* New York: Random House.

Minkler, M., & Roe, K. M. (1993). *Grandmothers as caregivers: Raising children of the crack cocaine epidemic.* Newbury Park, CA: Sage.

Minkler, M., Roe, K. M., & Price, M. (1992). The physical and emotional health of grandmothers raising grandchildren in the crack cocaine epidemic. *The Gerontologist, 32,* 752–761.

Minkler, M., Roe, K. M., & Robertson-Beckley, R. J. (1994). Raising grandchildren from crack-cocaine households: Effects on family and friendship ties of African-American women. *American Journal of Orthopsychiatry, 64,* 20–29.

Nelson, E., & Dannefer, D. (1992). Aged heterogeneity: Fact or fiction? The fate of diversity in gerontological research. *The Gerontologist, 32,* 17–23.

Pearlin, L., Mullan, J., Semple, S., & Skaff, M. (1990). Caregiving and the stress process: An overview of concepts and their measures. *The Gerontologist, 20,* 583–592.

Riegel, K. (1976). The dialectics of human development. *American Psychologist, 31,* 689–700.

Rosow, I. (1978). What is a cohort and why? *Human Development, 21,* 65–75.

Shore, R. J., & Hayslip, B. (1994). Custodial grandparenting: Implications for children's development. In A. Gottfried & A. Gottfried (Eds.), *Redefining families: Implications for children's development* (pp. 171–218). New York: Plenum.

Solomon, J. C., & Marx, J. (1995). "To grandmother's house we go": Health and school adjustment of children raised solely by grandparents. *The Gerontologist, 35,* 386–394.

Somary, K., & Stricker, G. (1998). Becoming a grandparent: A longitudinal study of expectations and early experiences as a function of sex and lineage. *The Gerontologist, 38,* 53–61.

Strawbridge, W. J., Wallhagen, M. I., Shema, S. J., & Kaplan, G. A. (1997). New burdens or more of the same? Comparing grandparent, spouse, and adult-child caregivers. *The Gerontologist, 37,* 505–510.

Stroebe, M., Hansson, R., Stroebe, W., & Schut, H. (2001). *Handbook of bereavement research: Consequences, coping and care.* Washington, DC: American Psychological Association.

Stroebe, M., & Schut, H. (1999). The dual process model of coping with bereavement: Rationale and description. *Death Studies, 23,* 197–224.

Thomas, J. L. (1990). The grandparent role: A double bind. *International Journal of Aging and Human Development, 31,*169–177.

Toledo, R., Hayslip, B., Emick, M., Toledo, C., & Henderson, C. (2000). Cross-cultural differences in custodial grandparenting. In B. Hayslip & R. Goldberg-Glen (Eds.), *Grandparents raising grandchildren: Theoretical, empirical and clinical perspectives* (pp. 107–124). New York: Springer.

Uhlenberg, P., & Kirby, J. (1998). Grandparenthood over time: Historical and demographic trends. In M. Szinovacz (Ed.), *Handbook on grandparenthood* (pp. 23–39). Westport, CT: Greenwood.

Unger, J. B., McAvay, G., Bruce, M. L., Berman, L., & Seeman, T. (1999). Variation in the impact of social network characteristics on physical functioning in elderly persons: McArthur studies of successful aging. *Journal of Gerontology: Social Sciences, 54B,* S245–251.

Whitbourne, S. (1999). Physical changes. In J. Cavanaugh & S. Whitbourne (Eds.), *Gerontology: An interdisciplinary perspective* (pp. 91–122). New York: Oxford University Press.

Wilson, M. N. (1986). The black extended family: An analytical consideration. *Developmental Psychology, 22,* 246–258.

Wilson, M. N., Tolson, T. F. J., Hinton, I. D., & Kiernan, M. (1990). Flexibility and sharing of childcare duties in black families. *Sex Roles, 22,* 409–425.

CHAPTER 2

Intervention Strategies for Grandparents Raising Grandchildren: Lessons Learned From the Caregiving Literature

Karen A. Roberto and Sara Honn Qualls

The United States Census Bureau (2001) estimates that 5.6 million grandparents maintain households that include grandchildren younger than 18 years of age. Approximately 2.4 million of these grandparents have primary responsibility for their grandchildren, 840,000 of whom have been caring for their grandchildren for five or more years. The majority of grandparents raising grandchildren are married (73.1%) and women (62.2%). More than one half (56.8%) of grandparents responsible for their grandchildren are in the labor force and one in five (18.9%) has an income below the poverty threshold. When these grandparents assume responsibility for raising their grandchildren, they often confront several personal and social challenges as they make adjustments in their daily lives to accommodate their acquired parental roles. Many grandparents perceive themselves as having to manage their situation alone and report feeling judged, criticized, and abandoned by their family, friends, and society (Poe, 2001).

Grandparents take on the parenting role for a variety of reasons including teen pregnancy, parental illness, divorce, incarceration, and substance abuse. Although more grandparents are assuming responsibility for their grandchildren, it is not the relationship that they typically foresee when they imagine themselves as grandparents. Few grandparents plan, anticipate, or prepare for a second parenthood. The context of the family situation influences the amount and type of care provided by grandparents as well as the impact on their lives and their well-being. Research on grandparents raising their grandchildren suggests that these grandparents are at higher risk for physical and mental health problems than their same-age peers (Hirshorn, 1998). As more grandparents assume the parental role, they will need greater support from community services to assist them in providing for their grandchildren, and from educators, practitioners, and clinicians to help them cope with the physical and emotional challenges of an altered family life.

The issues and challenges faced by grandparents raising grandchildren parallel another group of family caregivers—persons caring for older adults with physical health problems and cognitive decline. Professionals have developed a variety of programs and interventions to support family members who assume responsibility for caring for their older relatives (for detailed reviews see Bourgeois, Burgio, & Shultz, 1996; Farran, 2000; Knight, Lutzky, & Macofsky-Urban, 1993). The purpose of this chapter is to describe different intervention strategies used with caregivers of older adults and discuss how educators, practitioners, and clinicians can transfer and transform elements of these strategies as they develop and implement programs and interventions for grandparents who are now in a parenting role. We introduce the topic of caring for caregivers with a brief overview and critique of the late-life caregiving intervention literature. Then, we discuss strategies for transferring and building upon what we have learned from the aging caregiving literature to develop and implement successful programs and interventions for grandparents raising grandchildren. We end the chapter with suggestions and recommendations for the evaluation of supportive strategies and intervention research.

SUPPORTING CAREGIVERS OF OLDER ADULTS

Nearly 73% of persons over 65 needing assistance with daily activities rely exclusively on informal caregivers (Institute for Health & Aging, 1996). Most family caregivers are spouses or middle-aged daughters who are caring simultaneously for children or adolescents and parents. Eighty percent of caregivers for elderly family members provide help seven days a week, spending an average of four hours daily. Housekeeping, meal preparation, and shopping are common tasks, and over 60% of caregivers also regularly help with feeding, bathing, dressing, and using the toilet (Stone,

Cafferata, & Sangl, 1987). Most communities have programs and services to support families providing care for aging relatives and to help alleviate caregiver distress.

Intervention Programs

Family caregivers who seek support from professionals present a wide array of issues and concerns, including responding to feelings of guilt and inadequacy, meeting the older person's emotional and behavioral needs, providing for the physical well-being and safety of the older adult, handling legal and financial affairs, maintaining the quality of relationship with the care receiver, needing to develop appropriate or more effective coping skills (e.g., time management, stress management, communication skills), resolving family conflicts, eliciting informal and formal support, and engaging in long-term planning (Smith, Smith, & Toseland, 1991). Intervention strategies designed to support family caregivers include educational programs, support groups, individual therapy, and family counseling.

Community educational programs are a common, low-cost means of providing information to individuals faced with the challenges of providing care for aging relatives. Most programs are designed for spouses and adult children who have assumed the primary responsibility for a family member experiencing physical or cognitive decline. Programs typically focus on topics such as normal aging, chronic illness, behavior management, communication skills, coping and problem-solving skills, living arrangements, and community resources (Roberto, 1990). Among the few education program descriptions or evaluations found in the caregiving literature, there were several commonalities. First, the presentation formats are similar. A two-hour session offered over several weeks is the most popular model. Second, almost all programs use a multiple topic approach. Third, although the majority provided similar content, most programs are designed for a specific target population. Fourth, most participants evaluate the educational programs positively and demonstrate increased knowledge applicable to their individual situations (Brubaker & Roberto, 1993).

Support groups, a popular form of caregiver intervention, are also widely available and generally well attended by individuals caring for older relatives. The typical support group is composed predominantly of middle-class women, mostly the wives and daughters of individuals with some form of cognitive impairment (Bourgeois, Burgio, & Schultz, 1996; Toseland & Rossiter, 1989). In some communities, support groups are ongoing; in others they are time limited (e.g., six to eight sessions). Support groups typically provide both education and support and are built around seven major themes: information about the care receiver's situation, the group and its members as a mutual support system, the emotional impact of caregiving, self-care, problematic interpersonal relationships, the development and use of support systems outside the group, and home-care skills. The majority of leaders report positive outcomes for regular attendees, and the participants report high satisfaction with the group. Although the personal and emotional benefits resulting from group participation are often significant to the individual participants, they appear highly contextual and difficult to capture with traditional evaluation methods. Thus, outcomes often are not substantiated by formal evaluation data obtained either through the use of standardized measures in case specific evaluations or by more rigorously designed evaluation studies (Bourgeois, Burgio, & Schultz, 1996; Kaasalainen, Craig, & Wells, 2000; Lavoie, 1995).

Although clinicians and counselors use a variety of approaches when working with individual caregivers experiencing periodic or prolonged periods of personal stress and depression, their success stories are similar. Caregivers who seek individual counseling frequently report positive personal outcomes as well as enhanced abilities to provide care. For example, spouses of persons with Alzheimer's disease reported less depression after participating in brief psychodynamic psychotherapy that provided them the opportunity to understand how past conflicts influenced their reactions and responses to their current situation (Rose & DelMaestro, 1990). Daughters and daughters-in-law serving as primary caregivers for physically frail elders demonstrated more effective coping skills, improved psychological well-being, and improved relationships with their care receivers after participating in individual counseling sessions than did a comparative group of caregivers who did not receive counseling (Toseland & Smith, 1990). Behavioral therapy and cognitive-behavioral approaches have been shown to be effective in teaching management and problem-solving skills to family caregivers of persons with dementia and reducing the stressfulness of the situation for the caregivers (Corbeil, Quayhagen, & Quayhagen, 1999; Gallagher-Thompson, 1994; Roberts et al., 1999).

As Knight and McCallum (1998) point out, it is somewhat paradoxical that interventions addressing a prototypical family systems issue, such as caring for an older dependent family member, are generally targeted toward the primary caregiver. With a few notable exceptions (Mitrani & Czaja, 2000; Mittelman et al., 1995), there is a paucity of empirical literature addressing interventions that include multiple family members. One such example is an ongoing clinical trial with white and Cuban-American caregivers of persons with dementia that focuses on family interaction patterns along four lines of family functioning: family roles, developmental stages, interpersonal boundaries, and conflict resolution. The results of this project will provide valuable insight into the role of family support in caregiver outcomes (Mitrani & Czaja, 2000).

Overall, interventions with family members caring for older relatives produce modest, positive, short-term changes that intuitively should have enduring benefits throughout the course of the caregivers' career. With few exceptions (e.g., Haley, 1989; Whitlatch, Zarit, Goodwin, & von Eye, 1995), however, there is a lack of empirical evidence to support the long-term effectiveness of caregiver interventions. In addition, methodological shortcomings, including limited theoretical guidance, the lack of control variables, the absence of control groups, selective participation and insufficient sample sizes, and the insensitivity and lack of appropriate analyses of outcome measures, are evident in the caregiving intervention literature and may cause the effects of interventions to be underestimated (Bourgeois et al., 1996; Knight et al., 1993).

Respite Programs

Respite programs provide temporary, short-term supervisory, personal, and nursing care for older adults with physical and cognitive impairments. Although older adults are the recipients of care, these dual-purpose programs provide relief for family caregivers from the constant responsibilities of caring for dependent older adults. Programs provide respite services in the home or at specific sites in the community such as adult day centers, nursing homes, or hospitals. A variety of factors, including awareness, accessibility, cost, perceived need, and normative beliefs, contribute to the likelihood of caregivers using respite services.

In-home respite is the type most acceptable to family caregivers because they do not have to take the older adults out of the environment in which they are most comfortable (Lawton, Brody, & Saperstein, 1991). Depending on the needs of the caregiver, in-home respite can occur on a regular or occasional basis and can take place during the day or the evening. Some programs provide personal and instrumental care for the older person, whereas others provide only companionship or supervisory services (Lawton et al., 1991). Caregivers of older adults using in-home respite services report a higher degree of burden and provide more intense care compared with caregivers using other types of respite.

Adult day care is a structured, community-based, comprehensive program that provides a variety of health, social, and related support services in a protective setting during any part of a day but less than 24-hour care (National Institute on Adult Day Care, 2000–2001). The characteristics of caregivers who rely on adult day care services vary. For example, a comparative study of female caregivers of persons with Alzheimer's disease found that caregivers using adult day care were younger, had higher education and income levels, were more likely to have children living in the household, and reported more symptoms of stress and depression than those caregivers who are not using respite services (Guttman, 1991). In contrast, caregivers using a dementia-specific day program were more likely to be older, spousal caregivers, most of whom have served as the primary caregiver for less than two years (Monahan, 1993).

Evaluations of respite programs are mixed. Although most caregivers who use respite services report enhanced levels of well-being and reduced feelings of burden and stress (Cox, 1997; Kosloski & Montgomery, 1995), there is little evidence that respite interventions have either a consistent or enduring beneficial effect on caregivers' well-being (McNally, Ben-Shlomo, & Newman, 1999). Perhaps this is because caregivers often view respite programs as a last resort or end-of-the-road solution, rather than a preventive service. They seek respite services at a time of crisis; their situation has escalated to a point where they cannot continue providing care without some assistance. As with other types of caregiver interventions, methodological issues (e.g., lack of comparison groups, variability in the use of respite, sample size, and sensitivity of outcome measures) may bias the outcomes of participating in formal respite programs for family caregivers (McNally et al., 1999).

TRANSFORMING INTERVENTIONS FOR GRANDPARENTS RAISING GRANDCHILDREN

With adaptation, many of the lessons learned from interventions for caregivers to older adults can be adapted to grandparents caring for their grandchildren. Empirical efforts to demonstrate their efficacy are needed and ultimately will shape the programs to more closely meet needs. As this field emerges, it makes sense to look to these closely allied efforts in order to draw ideas and recommendations for potentially useful strategies.

Community Education

Community education, a strategy that has been highly successful with adult caregiver programs, is also likely to benefit grandparent caregivers. Many grandparents entered this role because it was necessary to fill in a gap left by absent or underfunctioning parents. Our culture certainly offers no formal parameters or support for this role, and thus, many grandparents find themselves facing the challenges alone, "off time" for their stage of the family life cycle, and somewhat stigmatized because of the perception that they and the missing parents have failed in some way. The purpose of community education is to prepare society to recognize and talk about the challenges of a public health problem, to more effectively seek assistance, and to more effectively support persons struggling with the problem. In other words, community education is a powerful component of primary and secondary prevention of a public health problem, particularly when mental health and social problems arise for these challenged grandparents and children.

Public health education programs help the larger community recognize the nature and scope of challenges faced by caregivers. Caregivers to older adults were hesitant to ask for support from family, friends, or professionals until public health campaigns, especially those related to Alzheimer's disease, brought attention to the scope and gravity of the challenges faced by these families. Similar efforts to educate the public about the challenges faced by grandparents rearing their grandchildren would raise awareness of these challenges and would likely mobilize support from numerous resources (e.g., media, social services, schools, and personal networks).

Although grandparents certainly have experience with childrearing, additional education about the developmental needs of their grandchildren would appear to be beneficial. Caregivers of adults with dementia report great relief from learning what to expect and how to adapt their care to meet the needs of each stage. Similarly, education about developmental needs of children should assist grandparents in providing more effective care. Childrearing strategies used previously when rearing their own children may have been inadequate, even for that time. However, given the changes in social context between the generations, even the most skilled grandparents can benefit from learning about current understanding of developmental processes, especially as evidenced by the current cohort of children.

For grandparents rearing children defined as "at risk" by virtue of physical, cognitive, or emotional disability (e.g., fetal alcohol syndrome, developmental disability) or early childhood neglect or abuse, special training would likely be helpful. These children demonstrate behaviors that are sometimes confusing because they do not respond predictably to familiar verbal or behavioral interventions. Furthermore, the contexts in which they live, play, and learn are often inadequately matched to their abilities and needs. Grandparents need to understand the causes and mechanisms of the difficulties, as well as the functional difficulties that arise in daily life.

Information about family systems and how they operate would also be useful. Grandparent caregivers can be presumed to have complications in their family structure that caused and resulted from the absence of the child's parents in their typical parental role. The circumstances that provoked the transition from parent to grandparent as primary care provider are relevant to determining the kinds of information needed by grandparent caregivers. If the parent becomes suddenly unavailable due to death, illness, or incarceration, for example, the child is likely to experience significant grief and perhaps even trauma reactions to the parent's exit from the parenting role. Conversely, many grandparents step in to rear their grandchildren only when the parents' ability to care appropriately has been demonstrated to be blatantly inadequate, following years of abuse or neglect. If the parent continues to be part of the child's life, role confusion across the generations may well require more intensive intervention as well as education. Parents intruding into the life or parenting processes of the grandparents are likely to introduce problematic role ambiguity, at least in the eyes of the child. Grandparents may benefit from education about how to help children adjust to the new arrangement and handle the complexities of their family's structure and history. Of special note are concerns about a biological parent's role in the new grandparent–grandchild parenting structure. For example, grandparents could benefit from information about how to maintain psychological safety and well-being in the child if a low-functioning parent continues to visit. Finally, the separation of siblings can create complicated relationship experiences for the children (and other family members) that are new to the grandparents' experience with parenting.

Support Groups

As with any population, grandparent caregivers sometimes feel as if they are the only ones struggling with the problem that looms so large in their own lives. Support groups for grandparents serve many functions that provide comfort and build skill. Learning that they are not alone is a key benefit to caregivers of any special needs population because it reduces their sense of victimization. Bonding with other grandparent caregivers enhances support, demythologizes the challenges of caregiving, and offers a source of practical advice. Several national organizations sponsor support groups for grandparents raising grandchildren or provide information for communities wanting to develop such a group. For example, AARP maintains a web-based national database of support groups of grandparents who are raising grandchildren, and the American Association of Retired Persons (AARP) Grandparent Information Center (GIC) provides guidelines for communities wishing to develop support groups and other services that can help improve the lives of grandparent households (see http://www.aarp.org/confacts/health/grandsupport.html).

Two types of support groups have been found useful: educational and process-oriented groups. Educational groups usually offer a lecture by a professional expert, addressing key aspects of the needs of the population. Topics could include telling children the truth about their family circumstances, accessing services, advocacy with schools, health problems and well-being, legal issues and services, and coordinating with community and government agencies.

Process-oriented groups offer members the opportunity to check in about immediate concerns and offer each other support and ideas for handling specific challenges. As opportunities for socialization often decline, support groups can be an important vehicle in preserving a social life and validating each other's concerns and strategies for fostering the well-being of all family members. Typically, a facilitator who is either a professional (e.g., social worker), or a mature family member with experience as a caregiver will monitor the process and guide as needed.

Key concerns for grandparent caregivers about attending groups is how to create time to attend a meeting, how to arrange childcare, cost, and independence of the support group from their service delivery network. The demands of childrearing may be sufficiently great that support group meetings are experienced as a burden or simply another demand on time, energy, or money. Furthermore, the group may not be perceived as a safe place to express concerns or explore one's own weaknesses as a caregiver if the facilitator is linked to an agency that funds or provides oversight of supportive services. Offering childcare is likely to be a necessary adjunct to support groups if the grandparents of small children are to be included.

Another major concern is outreach to underserved populations. Support groups for caregivers of older adults have tended to appeal to middle-class, educated groups, and have not served well the lower income, less educated, or culturally diverse segments of the population. Most people respond best when support groups are offered within their own communities by persons indigenous to their groups, thus providing a language and framework appropriate to their cultures. In the case of racial and ethnic subgroups, structures such as community centers or churches may be more valuable sites for outreach education than government organizations or health care settings. Suggestions for framing interventions to support caregivers of older adults are likely to be applicable to other caregiver populations as well (Gallagher-Thompson et al., 2000). In essence, the cultural taboos against seeking assistance from formal providers who are outside the subculture group will preclude some underserved populations from accessing the support unless the program is packaged in a way that is culturally acceptable.

Psychotherapy—Individual and Family

Psychotherapeutic approaches to help grandparent caregivers could beneficially focus on many of the same themes that are addressed in therapy with caregivers of older adults. Special attention needs to be paid to reducing adverse reactions to stress (e.g., depression, anxiety) that are common among caregivers. In particular, therapy would focus on enhancing skills for coping with common stressors, building social support, balancing caregiving demands with self-care, processing grief, and reducing interpersonal conflict. In addition, grandparent caregivers who have experienced a traumatic loss of the middle generation may need treatment of longer-term effects of trauma (e.g., posttraumatic stress disorder).

Family therapy could beneficially focus on two primary goals: establishing healthy family structures that support development in all members, and creating effective strategies for managing common as well as unusual behavior problems (Qualls, 1999; Shields, King, & Wynne, 1995). Family structures need to ensure that all members have access to warm, supportive attachment relationships, effective conflict-resolution strategies, and conditions that foster individual development (e.g., safety, appropriate freedoms, resources, and interpersonal support). The circumstances that removed the middle generation from the parenting role may well challenge the family to construct a stable structure that meets these criteria. Family therapy assists families with creating appropriate boundaries around the parent role so that all are clear about how child rearing decisions will be made, who is responsible to provide attachment functions, and how various family members' needs will be negotiated. Work on family structure needs to be particularly sensitive to cultural beliefs and rules about appropriate family roles for members of different generations.

A second focus for family work would be to address specific problem behaviors that may arise in the children being reared by their grandparents. Given their often complicated histories, these children are likely to pose particular challenges to their caregivers, especially during difficult developmental transitions such as adolescence. Family therapists are skilled at designing interventions that empower parents to gain control of problem behaviors.

Respite Programs

Day care programs and in-home respite care provide a much-needed break to caregivers of all populations. Although parents of any type often access respite care through babysitting, formal day care programs, or more formal respite programs (e.g., Mother's Morning Out), grandparents are particularly likely to need respite. In contrast to adult day care, day care for children is a culturally sanctioned way of obtaining respite that harbors little negative stigma. However, barriers to access include mistrust of unknown formal provider programs, cost, transportation, and usefulness of available times (e.g., little evening care is available). In-home respite brings distinct challenges, such as integrating the personality and lifestyle of another person into an already complex social environment, being left without help if the formal provider is ill or quits, and fear of vulnerability to stealing or abuse.

As with respite programs for older adults and their caregivers, programs designed specifically for children can serve dual functions. For example, after-school centers, church programs, and summer camps designed to enhance learning and social interactions for children also provide grandparents with time to attend to their personal needs and responsibilities. Although these are not considered formal respite, practitioners need to ensure that grandparents are informed about the availability of such programs and encourage their use as a means of promoting the health and well-being of all members of the family.

CONCLUSIONS AND RECOMMENDATIONS

The experiences of families caring for their older relatives and their responses to individual and community level interventions provide insight and guidance for professionals developing programs to meet the needs of a growing group of caregivers facing similar or corresponding challenges—grandparents raising grandchildren. With relatively small adaptations, many of the interventions and community programs designed to support caregivers of older adults appear applicable to older adults who are the primary caregivers for the grandchildren.

Critiques of the caregiving intervention literature suggest that although caregivers' informal accounts of the benefits of most interventions are quite positive, data from psychometrically sound outcome measures are more variable in showing effectiveness of the intervention (Kennet, Burgio, & Schulz, 2000). That is, caregivers of older adults appear to garner information and learn strategies relevant to managing their situation, but the long-term impact of these programs is often not assessed or empirically substantiated. Lessons learned from past intervention studies can provide researchers with insight and direction for developing more effective programs and evaluations of interventions to support grandparents rearing grandchildren (Czaja et al., 2000; Kennet, Burgio, & Schulz, 2000; Switzer et al., 2000). These key pieces of advice from this literature include the importance of: (1) clarifying the target of the intervention (caregiver, care recipient, environment); (2) specifying the targeted domain and measuring the distal as well as proximal effects on that specific domain; (3) ensuring the validity and reliability of measures for use with the targeted population because they often vary by race, ethnicity, gender, or education; (4) developing carefully controlled clinical trials (including random assignment to treatment groups for whom a clearly specified intervention protocol is assigned) to test efficacy of the interventions; and, (5) providing treatments that incorporate multiple interventions in multiple domains to obtain the strongest impact and outcomes.

In conclusion, when designing, implementing, and evaluating programs for grandparents parenting grandchildren, researchers and community professionals need to partner and study carefully the recommendations made in the older adult caregiving intervention literature in order to benefit from the more sophisticated methodological standards available in that field. Quality program evaluations and therapy outcome studies require the use of systematic methods and principles of social and behavioral science research, which, when applied correctly, provide a standardized framework and tools for reducing error in problem formation, design, sampling, data collection, data analysis, and interpretation of outcomes (Smith, 1990). The implementation of these principles will help ensure that intervention programs designed for grandparents raising grandchildren are achieving their expected outcomes of improving the quality of life for these families.

REFERENCES

Bourgeois, M. S., Schulz, R., & Burgio, L. (1996). Interventions for caregivers of patients with Alzheimer's disease: A review and analysis of content, process, and outcomes. *International Journal of Aging and Human Development, 43,* 35–92.

Brubaker, T., & Roberto, K. A. (1993). Family life education for the later years. *Family Relations, 42,* 212–221.

Corbeil, R. R., Quayhagen, M. P., & Quayhagen, M. (1999). Intervention effects on dementia caregiving interaction: A stress-adaptation modeling approach. *Journal of Aging and Health, 11,* 79–95.

Cox, C. (1997). Findings from a statewide program of respite care: A comparison of service users, stoppers, and nonusers. *The Gerontologist, 37,* 511–517.

Czaja, S. J., Eisdorfer, C., & Schulz, R. (2000). Future directions in caregiving: Implications for intervention research. In R. Schulz (Ed.), *Handbook of dementia caregiving* (pp. 283–319). New York: Springer.

Farran, C. J. (2000). Family caregiver intervention research: Where have we been? Where are we going? *Journal of Gerontological Nursing, 27,* 38–45.

Gallagher-Thompson, D. (1994). Direct services and intervention programs for caregivers: A review of extant programs and a look to the future. In M. H. Cantor (Ed.), *Family caregiving: Agenda for the future* (pp. 102–122). San Francisco: American Society on Aging.

Gallagher-Thompson, D., Arean, P., Coon, D., Menedez, A., Takagi, K., Haley, W. E., Arguelle, T., Rubert, M., Loewenstein, D., & Szapocznik, J. (2000). Development and implementation of intervention strategies for culturally diverse caregiving populations. In R. Schulz (Ed.), *Handbook on dementia caregiving* (pp. 151–185). New York: Springer.

Guttman, R. (1991). *Adult day care for Alzheimer's patients: Impact on family caregivers.* New York: Garland.

Haley, W. E. (1989). Group intervention for dementia family caregivers: A longitudinal perspective. *The Gerontologist, 29,* 481–483.

Hirshorn, B. (1998). Grandparents as caregivers. In M. Szinovacz (Ed.), *Handbook on grandparenthood* (pp. 200–214). Westport, CT: Greenwood.

Institute for Health & Aging. (1996). *Chronic care in America: A 21st century challenge.* Princeton, NJ: Robert Wood Johnson Foundation.

Kaasalainen, S., Craig, D., & Wells, D. (2000). Impact of the caring for the aging relatives group program: An evaluation. *Public Health Nursing, 17,* 169–177.

Kennet, J., Burgio, L., & Schulz, R. (2000). Interventions for in-home caregivers: A review of research 1990 to present. In R. Schulz (Ed.), *Handbook of dementia caregiving* (pp. 61–125). New York: Springer.

Knight, B. G., Lutzky, S. M., & Macofsky-Urban, F. (1993). A meta-analytic review of interventions for caregiver distress: Recommendations for future research. *The Gerontologist, 33,* 240–248.

Knight, B. G., & McCallum, T. J. (1998). Psychotherapy with older adult families: The contextual, cohort-based maturity/specific challenge model. In I. H. Nordhus, G. R. VandenBos, S. Berg, & P. Fromholt (Eds.), *Clinical geropsychology* (pp. 35–49). Washington, DC: American Psychological Association.

Kosloski, K., & Montgomery, R. J. V. (1995). The impact of respite use on nursing home placement. *The Gerontologist, 35,* 67–74.

Lavoie, J. P. (1995). Support groups for informal caregivers don't work! Refocus the groups or evaluations. *Canadian Journal of Aging, 14,* 580–603.

Lawton, M. P., Brody, E., & Saperstein, A. (1991). *Respite for caregivers of Alzheimer's patients: Research and practice.* New York: Springer.

McNally, S., Ben-Shlomo, Y., & Newman, S. (1999). The effects of respite care on informal carers' well-being: A systematic review. *Disability and Rehabilitation, 21,* 1–14.

Mitrani, V., & Czaja, S. (2000). Family-based therapy for dementia caregivers: Clinical observations. *Aging and Mental Health, 4,* 200–209.

Mittelman, M. S., Ferris, S. H., Shulman, E., Steinberg, G., Ambinder, A., Mackell, J. A., & Cohen, J. (1995). A comprehensive support program: Effect on depression in spouse-caregivers of AD patients. *The Gerontologist, 35,* 792–802.

Monahan, D. (1993). Utilization of dementia-specific respite day care for clients and their caregivers in a social model program. *Journal of Gerontological Social Work, 20,* 57–70.

National Institute on Adult Day Care. (2000–2001). *Facts about adult day services* [On-line]. Available: http://www.ncoa.org/nadsa/ADS_factsheet.htm

Poe, L. M. (2001). The changing family: Social and emotional needs of grandparents parenting a second shift. *Grandparent Information Center Newsletter* [On-line]. Available: http://www.aarp.org/grandparents/gpsocialemo.html

Qualls, S. H. (1999). Family therapy with older adult clients. *In Session: Psychotherapy in Practice, 55*(8), 1–14.

Roberto, K. A. (1990, April). *Education and training of family caregivers in rural areas.* Paper presented at the meeting of the National Council on Aging, Washington, DC.

Roberts, J., Browne, G., Milne, C., Spooner, L., Gafni, A., Drummond-Young, M., LeGris, J., Watt, S., LeClair, K., Beaumont, L., & Roberts, J. (1999). Problem-solving counseling for caregivers of the cognitively impaired: Effective for whom? *Nursing Research, 48,* 162–172.

Rose, J., & DelMaestro, S. G. (1990). Separation-individuation conflict as a model for understanding distressed caregivers: Psychodynamic and cognitive case studies. *The Gerontologist, 30,* 703–705.

Shields, C. G., King, D. A., & Wynne, L. C. (1995). In R. H. Mikesell, D. D. Lusterman, & S. H. McDaniel (Eds.), *Integrating family therapy* (pp. 141–158). Washington, DC: American Psychological Association.

Smith, G., Smith, M., & Toseland, R. (1991). Problems identified by family caregivers in counseling. *The Gerontologist, 31,* 15–22.

Smith, M. (1990). *Program evaluation in the human services*. New York: Springer.

Stone, R., Cafferata, G., & Sangl, J. (1987). Caregivers of the frail elderly: A national profile. *The Gerontologist, 27*, 616–626.

Switzer, G. E., Wisniewski, S. R., Belle, S. H., Burns, R., Winter, L., Thompson, L., & Schulz, R. (2000). Measurement issues in intervention research. In R. Schulz (Ed.), *Handbook of dementia caregiving* (pp. 187–224). New York: Springer.

Toseland, R. W., & Rossiter, C. M. (1989). Group interventions to support family caregivers: A review and analysis. *The Gerontologist, 29*, 438–448.

Toseland, R. W., & Smith, G. C. (1990). Effectiveness of individual counseling by professional and peer helpers for family caregivers of the elderly. *Psychology & Aging, 5*, 256–263.

United States Census Bureau. (2001). Census 2000 Supplementary Survey: Profile of selected social characteristics. Available: http://www.census.gov/c2ss/www/Products...les/2000/Tabular/C2ssTable2/01000Us. htm.

Whitlach, C., Zarit, S., Goodwin, P., & von Eye, A. (1995). Influence of the success of psychoeducational interventions on the course of family care. *Clinical Gerontologist, 16*, 17–30.

CHAPTER 3

Links Between Custodial Grandparents and the Psychological Adaptation of Grandchildren

Sally Keller and George Stricker

This chapter examines the impact of grandparent-grandchild relationships with regard to the psychological adjustment of custodial grandchildren. Grandparents who raise grandchildren routinely assume the care of a child or children who have experienced a disruption in primary parenting. Based on the view of attachment theorists that early relationship experiences greatly influence a child's interpersonal, cognitive, and affective development, attachment research has focused on the sequelae of adverse early caregiving. Among children who have experienced parental loss or maltreatment, studies have documented a high incidence of depression, low self-esteem, poor social functioning, and low perceived competence (Armsden, McCauley, Greenberg, Burke, & Mitchell, 1990; Cicchetti, Toth, & Lynch, 1995; Papini & Roggman, 1992). However, the literature of resilience is replete with studies of at-risk children who demonstrate adaptive functioning. The presence of a good relationship with one caregiving figure has been recognized to be a protective factor (Farber & Egeland, 1987; Masten, Best, & Garmezy, 1990; Radke-Yarrow & Brown, 1993). This chapter explores the possibility that the relationship between custodial grandparent and grandchild may compensate for early adversity and help to interrupt the link between deprivation and psychological ill health.

In the context of attachment theory, resilience implicates the quality of the caregiving relationship. Time and again, research has documented a link between secure attachment and positive outcomes for children with adverse early experiences (e.g., Armsden & Greenberg, 1987; Fonagy, Steele, Steele, Higgitt, & Target, 1992; Sroufe, 1989; Stocker, 1994; Vivona, 2000). For custodial grandparents, several questions arise. First, does the custodial relationship constitute an attachment relationship? If so, how does that relationship impact children's development? Finally, is there an association between the grandparent-grandchild relationship and specific areas of children's psychological functioning?

BACKGROUND

Attachment theory originated with the observations of John Bowlby (1973, 1988) concerning the adverse effects on personality development of institutional care and loss or separation from the primary caregiver during early childhood. Bowlby believed that the early family relationship was of paramount importance. He posited the consolidation of early attachment experiences into an "internal working model" that served as a template for interpersonal interactions and their accompanying cognitions, affects, and behaviors.

The internal model, which governed perceptions and actions with respect to the availability and responsiveness of caregiving others, influenced the behaviors and expectations of children in the development of future relationships. That is, the internal working model was the mechanism by which individuals came to repeat early, maladaptive relationships in later life. According to Crittenden (1990), working models built upon secure caregiving relationships reflect a flexible inner organization open to new interpretations of interactional experience. By contrast, a history of disturbed relationships is likely to lead to a closed or nonworking model in which new information is processed in accordance with existing cognitions. This creates a risk that early negative experiences will generate negative expectations of self and others in the context of future relationships. For example, a child might misperceive a friend's behavior as rejecting and might distance him- or herself from that person, who might in turn view the child as unfriendly.

The degree to which early attachment experiences generalize to future relationships raises questions about adaptation and psychological adjustment across the life span. The field of developmental psychopathology has begun to explore connections between attachment and emotional disturbance. Several studies have documented an association between the quality of attachment and depression (as reviewed, for example, by

Blatt & Homann, 1992; Cicchetti et al., 1995; Gerlsma, Emmelkamp, & Arrindell, 1990). Cicchetti et al. (1995) argued that children with insecure early attachment experiences might be vulnerable to depression because they have low internalized feelings of security. These children are ill equipped to face stressful life events, and therefore might react to adversity with increased insecurity, sadness, and low self-esteem. Other studies have demonstrated a positive correlation between the quality of parental attachment and adaptive psychological functioning, including self-worth, perceived competence, and security of attachment (e.g., Armsden & Greenberg, 1987).

Attachment literature thus raises two separate but related issues. With regard to continuity, why is it that early relationship experiences generalize to future relationships in some children but not in others? With regard to development, under what circumstances do attachment relationships contribute to psychological adaptation versus maladaptation? The developmental impact of adverse early caregiving is of particular concern with regard to custodial grandchildren, many of whom have experienced the failure or loss of a primary parent. Attachment theory raises the possibility that the relationship experience provided by the grandparent may alter or modify preexisting expectations, attitudes, or behaviors in ways that affect future relationships and the sense of self.

GRANDPARENTS AS ATTACHMENT FIGURES

Although early attachment research focused largely on mother-infant interactions, Bowlby (1969) and Ainsworth, Blehar, Waters, and Wall (1978) posited a role for other attachment figures. Howes (1999) reviewed attachment literature regarding multiple caregiving relationships. She noted that the establishment of alternative attachment relationships in later childhood injects a developmental perspective. This is certainly true for alternative caregivers who assume custody of latency-aged or even adolescent children. Developmental factors require reconsideration of the theoretical underpinnings of attachment theory concerning the formation of attachment relationships and the impact of such relationships on psychological adaptation.

Howes defined an attachment figure as one who provides physical and emotional care, is a continuous or consistent presence in a child's life, and demonstrates emotional investment in the child. Because the needs of children for security and support change markedly between infancy and later childhood, the role of alternative attachment figures may also change in later childhood.

Howes also questioned whether alternative attachment relationships differentially impact developmental outcomes. The research of Main, Kaplan, and Cassidy (1985) supported the primacy of the mother-child attachment in predicting psychological adjustment. Other studies, however, have found that relationships with fathers and with child care providers were more closely associated than the mother-child relationship with certain realms of psychological functioning, such as social competence with peers (e.g., Howes, Matheson, & Hamilton, 1997). Howes drew a distinction between a "hierarchical model," in which alternative attachment relationships are subordinate to that of the mother-child relationship, and an "independent model," in which alternative relationships contribute uniquely to developmental outcomes (Howes, 1999, p. 682). To the extent that the independent model governs attachment experience, this model strengthens the hypothesis that the custodial grandparent-grandchild relationship may compensate for negative early experiences and positively impact personality development.

KINSHIP CAREGIVER STUDY

The aim of this study was to explore the role of relationship experiences in the psychological adaptation of preadolescent and adolescent children in kinship care. In accord with attachment research, it was hypothesized that reports of adverse early relationships would generalize to subsequent childhood relationships and would predict poor psychological adjustment. On the other hand, in view of previous findings on the positive impact of alternative caregivers, it was hypothesized that reports of a supportive relationship with the kinship caregiver would have a compensatory effect, and would predict better psychological adjustment than would occur in the absence of a positive relationship.

Method

Sixty children participated in this study, including 28 girls and 32 boys, ranging in age from 11 to 15 years. The children in this study had been in kinship care since at least age 7, with an average length of custody 9.8 years and a range from 4 to 15 years. For 25% of the children, the biological mother was deceased, and another 33% had either no contact or less than monthly contact with their mother. Grandparents were custodial caregivers for 52 of the 60 participants, and the remaining eight were in the custody of maternal and paternal aunts. Of the custodial grandparents, approximately two thirds were grandmothers living alone. Ninety percent of all families belonged to a minority group, including 80% black and 10% Latino. Although families were recruited without regard to socioeconomic status, roughly one third reported annual incomes of less than $10,000, and 91% reported annual incomes below $30,000. Substance abuse of the biological parent accounted for 50% of kinship care placements, with abuse or neglect and substance abuse accounting for another 25% of placements.

All children were interviewed individually in their homes. Informed consent was given by kinship caregivers of all children, and the children also agreed to be interviewed and were paid $15.00. The caregiver was interviewed to obtain sociodemographic information and to corroborate certain self-report items asked of the children.

Measures

The following measures were administered individually to all children:

Relatedness Questionnaire

Feelings of relatedness to mother, kinship caregiver, siblings, and peers were assessed using the 17-item Relatedness Questionnaire taken from the Rochester Assessment Package for Schools developed by Wellborn and Connell (1987). Two factor analytically derived scales (emotional quality and psychological proximity seeking) were used. The subscales have been used to assess children's perceptions of the emotional quality of a relationship and of how close the child feels to the relationship figure. The emotional quality subscale contains eleven items, each of which identifies a positive or negative emotion regarding the relationship figure, such as "when I'm with ________ I feel happy." The Cronbach's alpha for this scale ranges from .67 to .83 (Lynch, 1992). The psychological proximity subscale contains six items that assess the degree to which the child wishes he or she were psychologically closer to the relationship figure, such as "I wish ________ knew me better." The Cronbach's alpha for this scale ranges from .83 to .93 (Lynch, 1992). Children were asked to rate each item on a four-point Likert scale ranging from "not at all true" to "very true." The subscales were examined as separate constructs, and data also were categorized in accordance with the norms established by Lynch and Cicchetti (1991) as having either optimal-adequate or nonoptimal feelings of relatedness.[1]

Adolescent Depressive Experiences Questionnaire

The Adolescent Depressive Experiences Questionnaire (DEQ-A: Blatt, Schaffer, Bers, & Quinlan, 1990) was used to assess interpersonal and self-critical dysphoric

---

[1]For a detailed discussion of the reliability and validity of the Relatedness Scales and of other measures used in this study, see Keller (2001).

experiences. The DEQ-A contains 43 items that assess areas including a negative sense of self, feelings of dependency and helplessness, loss of autonomy, and disturbances in family relations. Examples of these items include the following statements: (1) "Without support from others who are close to me, I would be helpless"; and (2) "I often find that I fall short of what I expect of myself." Children are asked to rate each item on a 7-point Likert scale, from "strongly disagree" to "strongly agree."

Factor analysis of the DEQ-A yields two orthogonal factors. The interpersonal factor (labeled "dependency") addresses concerns about abandonment, loneliness, desires for closeness, and dependency on others. The self-critical factor (labeled "self-criticism") refers to feelings of guilt, emptiness, hopelessness, dissatisfaction, failing to meet expectations, and being burdened by responsibility (Blatt, Hart, Quinlan, Leadbeater, & Auerbach, 1993).

Children's Depression Inventory

The Children's Depression Inventory (CDI) is a self-report measure developed by Kovacs (1983) to assess depressive symptomatology. The inventory contains 27 items that address the affective, cognitive, and behavioral signs of depression. For each item, children are asked to choose among three responses that best characterized them during the previous two weeks. For example, one item asks children to choose among the following three statements: (1) I am sad once in a while, (2) I am sad many times, and (3) I am sad all the time.

The CDI has five factors. They are: negative mood (factor "A"), interpersonal problems (factor "B"), ineffectiveness (factor "C"), anhedonia (factor "D"), and negative self-esteem (factor "E"). A "CDI total score" is a composite of the five factor scores. In this study, CDI total scores and factor scores were calculated. Also, items from the CDI that addressed overt behaviors ("objective outcome variables") were assessed separately, in addition to being included in CDI total and relevant factor scores. Objective outcome variables included difficulty sleeping, feelings of fatigue, appetite disturbances, poor scholastic performance, fighting behavior, and disobedience. The caregivers also were asked to answer questions for objective outcome variables. The purpose of separating out observable behavioral symptoms was to address the possibility that psychological defenses might lead to underreporting of depressive symptomatology.

Self-Perception Profile for Children

Children's perceived competence was measured using the Self-Perception Profile for Children (SPPC), developed by Harter (1985). The SPPC assesses children's judgments of their global self-worth, and of their perceived competence in specific domains. In addition to perceptions of global self-worth, this study measured scholastic competence, social acceptance, and behavioral conduct. There are six items for each domain (or subscale). Separate scores were assigned for each of the four domains.

Results

Preliminary Analyses

Scores on the Relatedness Scales were examined in two different ways. First, relatedness scores were quantified according to the original subscales, "emotional quality" and "psychological proximity." Next, scores were used to divide participants into two categories, "optimal-adequate" and "nonoptimal" for each reported relationship. These categories were obtained by first assigning each participant to one of five patterns of relatedness. "Optimal" and "adequate" patterns were then combined to form the category "optimal-adequate." "Deprived," "disengaged," and "confused" patterns were combined to form the category "nonoptimal." More than 75% of all children reported nonoptimal relationships with their mother, and a total of 61% were categorized as confused, meaning that they reported a desire for greater psychological proximity but high emotional quality. For kinship caregivers, optimal-adequate and nonoptimal relatedness were evenly split, 50% and 50%. Thirty-eight percent of all children were categorized as confused with respect to the kinship caregiver.

With respect to generalizability of relationship quality, desire for psychological proximity was highly correlated across all six relationship figures: mother-kin, $r = .55$, $p < .001$; mother-sibling, $r = .49$, $p < .001$; mother-peer, $r = .43$, $p = .001$; kin-sibling, $r = .66$, $p < .001$; kin-peer, $r = .72$, $p < .001$; sibling-peer, $r = .55$, $p < .001$. By contrast, the correlations across relationship figures for emotional quality were significant only for the dyads mother-kin, $r = .40$, $p < .01$, and sibling-peer, $r = .28$, $p < .05$. These results suggested that desire for psychological proximity more closely approximates a trait, whereas emotional quality is more relationship specific. This finding is consistent with the observations of Bowlby and others that institutionalized or adopted children often demonstrate high proximity-seeking behaviors (Greenberg, 1999). The results suggest that the children in this study, having experienced the loss of a primary caretaker, have attempted to minimize emotional distance with their kinship caregiver and other important relationship figures.

A Pearson chi-square analysis was used to compare the frequency with which the children reported relatedness concordance (defined to mean that a participant reported the same category of relationship, either optimal-adequate or nonoptimal, for different relationship figures). Relatedness concordance was demonstrated for the mother and kinship caregiver, chi-square (1,N = 55) = 4.61, $p = .03$, and for all other relationship pairs. Thirteen percent of children who reported a nonoptimal relationship with their mother also reported a nonoptimal relationship with the kinship caregiver, siblings, and peers, demonstrating full concordance. These results demonstrated that children who report a nonoptimal relationship with their mother are more likely to have a nonoptimal relationship with their kinship caregiver than are children who report an optimal-adequate relationship with their mother. The findings highlight the importance for custodial grandparents to provide supportive and sensitive caregiving to their grandchildren in order to foster the establishment of new relationship patterns.[2]

Mother and Caregiver Relatedness as Predictors of Adaptation

To determine whether the children's psychological adjustment differed as a function of their reported relationships with mother and kinship caregiver, one-way analyses of variance (ANOVAs) were conducted, with relatedness to mother or to kinship caregiver as the independent variable, and outcome measures (the CDI, SPPC, and DEQ-A) as dependent variables. Summaries of means and standard deviations for these analyses are set forth in Tables 3.1, 3.2, and 3.3.

Relatedness to mother (optimal-adequate versus nonoptimal) was significant in the expected direction only for the CDI objective outcome variables and for the CDI factor "ineffectiveness." ANOVAs also revealed effects in the expected direction for the SPPC factors "scholastic competence" and "behavioral conduct," and for the DEQ-A variable "dependency." There was no significant relationship between relatedness to mother and the DEQ-A variable "self-criticism."

For relatedness to kinship caregiver, ANOVAs revealed a main effect for total CDI score, for the factors "ineffectiveness," "anhedonia," and "negative self-esteem." On the SPPC, significance was demonstrated for factors "social acceptance" and "global self-worth." On the DEQ-A, significance was demonstrated for "self-criticism" but not for dependency. For both relatedness to mother and relatedness to kinship caregiver, significant results were in the expected direction, suggesting that children who reported optimal-adequate relationships were less likely to report emotional or behavioral difficulties than were children who reported nonoptimal relationships.

Further analyses examined the relative contributions of relatedness to mother and relatedness to kinship caregiver with respect to outcome variables. Regression analyses

---

[2]For a more complete discussion of relatedness concordance, see Keller (2001).

TABLE 3.1a. Relatedness to Mother as Predictor of CDI Total Scores, CDI Objective Outcome Variables, and CDI Factor Scores: Summary of Means and Standard Deviations (in parentheses)

Group	CDI Total	Objective Outcome	Factor A	Factor B	Factor C	Factor D	Factor E
Optimal-	6.54	1.15*	1.54	.38	1.08*	2.62	.92
Adequate	(5.35)	(1.21)	(1.13)	(.65)	(1.38)	(2.29)	(1.89)
Nonoptimal	9.93	2.81*	2.40	1.21	2.31*	3.05	.95
	(6.14)	(2.20)	(1.74)	(1.49)	(1.65)	(2.39)	(1.08)

*$p < .05$, N = 55

b. Relatedness to Kin as Predictor of CDI Total Scores, CDI Objective Outcome Variables, CDI Factor Scores: Summary of Means and Standard Deviations (in parentheses)

Group	CDI Total	Objective Outcome	Factor A	Factor B	Factor C	Factor D	Factor E
Optimal-	6.83**	1.83	1.87	.73	1.57*	2.17*	.50**
Adequate	(4.86)	(1.86)	(1.55)	(1.11)	(1.50)	(2.04)	(.78)
Nonoptimal	11.10**	2.80	2.33	1.33	2.53*	3.53*	1.37**
	(6.43)	(2.19)	(1.75)	(1.54)	(1.78)	(2.45)	(1.50)

*$p < .05$; **$p = .01$, N = 60

TABLE 3.2a. Relatedness to Mother as Predictor of SPPC Factors Scholastic Performance, Social Acceptance, Behavioral Conduct, and Global Self-Worth: Summary of Means and Standard Deviations (in parentheses)

Group	Scholastic Competence	Social Acceptance	Behavioral Conduct	Global Self-Worth
Optimal-	20.00*	19.38	20.92***	21.15
Adequate	(3.34)	(4.15)	(2.56)	(4.51)
Nonoptimal	17.60*	19.38	16.38***	19.29
	(3.61)	(3.55)	(4.53)	(3.92)

*$p < .05$; ***$p = .001$, N = 55

b. Relatedness to Kin as Predictor of SPPC Factors Scholastic Performance, Social Acceptance, Behavioral Conduct, and Global Self-Worth: Summary of Means and Standard Deviations (in parentheses)

Group	Scholastic Competence	Social Acceptance	Behavioral Conduct	Global Self-Worth
Optimal-	18.73	20.77**	18.43	21.83***
Adequate	(4.10)	(3.24)	(4.08)	(2.68)
Nonoptimal	17.27	17.93**	16.50	17.87***
	(3.80)	(3.79)	(4.72)	(4.14)

**$p < .01$; ***$p < .001$, N = 60

were conducted with respect to all outcome measures where only one of the predictor variables—relatedness to mother or relatedness to kin—was a significant predictor. These analyses demonstrated a unique contribution of one of the two predictor variables to individual outcome measures. For the CDI, relatedness to mother was significant for CDI objective outcome variables, Beta = .28, $p < .05$. For kin, results were significant for CDI total, Beta = .34, $p < .05$, and for the factors anhedonia, Beta = .31, $p < .05$, and negative self-esteem, Beta = .41, $p < .01$. With respect to the SPPC, relatedness to mother significantly predicted behavioral conduct, Beta = −.38, $p < .01$. Relatedness to kin predicted SPPC factors social acceptance, Beta = −.37, $p = .01$, and global self-worth, Beta = −.51, $p < .001$.

Although ANOVAs demonstrated a statistically significant impact of relatedness to mother on the SPPC factor scholastic performance, regression analyses revealed no significant contribution over and above that of relatedness to kin. With respect to the DEQ-A, relatedness to mother uniquely predicted dependency, Beta = .35,

TABLE 3.3a. Relatedness to Mother as Predictor of DEQ-A Variables Dependency and Self-Criticism: Summary of Means and Standard Deviations (in parentheses)

Group	DEQ-A Variable Dependency	DEQ-A Variable Self-Criticism
Optimal Adequate	−.03**	−.81
	(.99)	(.85)
Nonoptimal	.53**	−.49
	(.70)	(.99)

**p < .01, N = 55

b. Relatedness to Kin as Predictor of DEQ-A Variables Dependency and Self-Criticism: Summary of Means and Standard Deviations (in parentheses)

Group	DEQ-A Variable Dependency	DEQ-A Variable Self-Criticism
Optimal Adequate	−.08	−1.08***
	(1.02)	(.77)
Nonoptimal	.09	−.40***
	(.95)	(.82)

***p < .001, N = 60

$p < .05$, whereas relatedness to kin demonstrated significance for self-criticism, Beta = .37, $p < .01$. With the exception of the SPPC factor scholastic competence, these results demonstrated that relatedness to one caregiving figure (mother or kin) significantly predicted psychological adjustment even after controlling for the independent contribution of relatedness to a second caregiving figure (kin or mother).

The Cumulative Impact of Nonoptimal Relatedness

Correlations were calculated to determine whether psychological adjustment differed as a function of the number of nonoptimal relationships reported by each participant. For CDI total, this analysis revealed significance in the expected direction, $r = .39$, $p < .01$. On every other CDI factor except anhedonia, there was significance at the .05 level. For the SPPC, significant correlations were demonstrated for "social acceptance," $r = -.28$, $p = .03$; for "behavioral conduct," $r = -.28$, $p = .03$; and for "global self-worth," $r = -.45$, $p < .001$. For the DEQ-A, there was significance for dependency, $r = .33$, $p = .01$, and self-criticism, $r = .34$, $p < .01$. The direction of all correlations was consistent with the hypothesis that the greater the number of nonoptimal relationships, the more likely a child is to report emotional or behavioral difficulties.

DISCUSSION

This study examined the role of relationships in predicting psychological adjustment. The findings demonstrated that relationship experiences with the mother and the kinship caregiver both predicted psychological functioning, but that each relationship uniquely predicted adjustment in different realms of development. The relationship with the kinship caregiver predicted depressive symptomatology and certain self-constructs, whereas the relationship with the mother predicted more observable symptomatology such as behavioral conduct and scholastic performance. The data lend support to an independent model of attachment organization in which alternative attachment figures influence development and adaptation independent of the maternal attachment.

Consistent differences between the findings with respect to mother and kinship caregiver suggested a differentiated internal working model for these two relationships. For the mother, the working model appeared to be more rigid and stereotyped, with nonoptimal relatedness manifesting itself in externalizing behaviors (conduct and school performance) and in a need for proximity (dependence). For the kinship caregiver, the internal working model appeared to implicate self-constructs, including self in relation to others. These differences between mother and kin make sense in the context of this study, where there was an early failure in parenting, and where the kinship caregiver had primary caregiving responsibilities for a minimum of four years.

The data also demonstrated that cumulative negative relationships contributed to psychological ill health. The findings highlight the importance of interventions that interrupt negative relationship patterns. One such intervention is the presence of a stable and secure relationship.

THE ROLE OF CUSTODIAL GRANDPARENTS

This study suggests that custodial grandparents have a defining role in the development and psychological well-being of their grandchildren. The grandparent-grandchild relationship may compensate for early adverse experiences with respect to critical aspects of psychological functioning. The data demonstrated that a positive relationship with a kinship caregiver might serve as a buffer against depression, low social acceptance, and low self-worth. Thus there is the possibility that the custodial relationship serves as a protective factor with respect to core aspects of personality development and potentially crippling pathology.

Luthar, Cicchetti, and Becker (2000), in their discussion of resilience, addressed the "multidimensional nature of resilience," noting that at-risk children may demonstrate varying levels of competence across different adjustment domains. They raised the question of whether certain domains should be accorded more importance than others with respect to resilience. For example, a focus on internalizing behaviors would be more effective than a focus on school performance in order to combat a mood disorder. At least for children who tend to internalize feelings, a supportive relationship might offer greater protection against disturbances in development than would an intervention focused on behavioral conduct or scholastic performance.

Grandparenting research documents a higher than average incidence of both emotional and behavioral problems among custodial grandchildren (e.g., Silverthorn & Durrant, 2000; Thomas, Sperry, & Yarbrough, 2000). One reason for this is that many kinship care placements result from substance abuse by the primary parent (as evidenced in this study), and that children born to substance-abusing parents are at risk for developmental disturbance (Silverthorn & Durrant). A second reason is that children who have experienced early parental loss or deprivation are vulnerable to psychopathology (Harris & Bifulco, 1991). Research on institutionalized children has found that the children's predominant attachment classification is likely to be either ambivalent or disorganized, and to be characterized by high proximity-seeking behaviors. (Greenberg, 1999). This research suggests that custodial grandchildren are likely to have a greater than average need for stability and security in their attachment relationships, and underscores the pivotal role of the caregiving grandparent in providing emotional support.

Finally, the literature on loss and bereavement similarly points to the centrality of the caregiving relationship. Bowlby (1980) distinguished between healthy mourning, in which a child emerges "undamaged" from the experience of loss, and disordered mourning, in which the child fails to successfully negotiate the three stages labeled "protest," "despair," and "detachment." The stage of detachment also was characterized by Bowlby as one of "reorganization." Bowlby (1980) identified three variables that contributed to the course of childhood mourning: (1) the circumstances of loss and opportunities for inquiry provided to the child; (2) the patterns of relationships within the family prior to the loss, specifically the relationships of the parents to each other and of each parent to the child; and (3) the relationship with the surviving parent or other caregiver following the loss. In their exploration of resilience, Egeland, Carlson, and Sroufe (1993) found that children who recovered following stress or trauma were more likely to have had early secure attachments or to have had increased support during the time of recovery from trauma. This research suggests that a consistent and supportive relationship between the custodial grandparent and the grandchild helps to facilitate the reorganization of internal representations of the self and others and to allow for the cognitive and affective processing of loss.

Fraley and Shaver (1999) reviewed a body of research demonstrating a link between unresolved or chronic mourning and a preoccupied attachment organization (equivalent on the relatedness scales to high proximity seeking and low emotional quality). Chronic mourning was associated with low self-esteem and with depression (Stroebe & Stroebe, 1993). Fraley and Shaver noted that the research was consistent with Bowlby's view that chronic mourning signaled a heightened sensitivity to signs of separation, rejection, and loss. Associations among chronic mourning, low self-esteem, and depression have particular significance in light of the findings described above concerning the links between kinship caregiving, depression, and self-constructs. Taken together, the data reinforce the potential significance of the kinship caregiver relationship in facilitating adaptation and in buffering against developmental disturbance.

CONCLUSION

What do these findings mean for grandparents? They tell us that custodial grandparents should be strongly encouraged to play a significant role as caregivers to their grandchildren. Past research has demonstrated that children have a lot to gain from both custodial and noncustodial grandparents, in areas ranging from identity formation to life beliefs (e.g., Kopera-Frye & Wiscott, 2000). The current study suggests that custodial grandparents can help their grandchildren to move beyond experiences of rejection and loss. Even damaged children can get a fresh start if the grandparent is able to offer a secure, stable, and caring home. Grandparents facing the daunting task of raising custodial grandchildren should be buoyed by the prospect that their caregiving may become a lifeline of transformation and renewal.

REFERENCES

Ainsworth, M. D., Blehar, M. C., Waters, E., & Wall, S. (1978). *Patterns of attachment*. Hillsdale, NJ: Erlbaum.

Armsden, G. C., & Greenberg, M. T. (1987). The inventory of parent and peer attachment: Individual differences and their relationship to psychological well-being in adolescence. *Journal of Youth and Adolescence, 16,* 427–454.

Armsden, G. C., McCauley, E., Greenberg, M. T., Burke, P. M., & Mitchell, J. R. (1990). Parent and peer attachment in early adolescent depression. *Journal of Abnormal Child Psychology, 18,* 683–697.

Blatt, S. J., Hart, B., Quinlan, D. M., Leadbeater, B., & Auerbach, J. (1993). Interpersonal and self-critical dysphoria and behavioral problems in adolescents. *Journal of Youth and Adolescence, 22,* 253–269.

Blatt, S. J., & Homann, E. (1992). Parent–child interaction in the etiology of dependent and self-critical depression. *Clinical Psychology Review, 12,* 47–91.

Blatt, S. J., Schaffer, C. E., Bers, S. A., & Quinlan, D. M. (1990). *Adolescent Depressive Experiences Questionnaire.* Unpublished research manual, Yale University, New Haven, CT.

Bowlby, J. (1969). *Attachment and loss: Vol. 1: Attachment.* New York: Basic Books.

Bowlby, J. (1973). *Attachment and loss: Vol. 2: Separation: Anxiety and anger.* New York: Basic Books.

Bowlby, J. (1980). *Attachment and loss: Vol. 3: Loss: Sadness and depression.* New York: Basic Books.

Bowlby, J. (1988). *A secure base: Parent–child attachment and healthy human development.* New York: Basic Books.

Cicchetti, D., Toth, S. L., & Lynch, M. (1995). Bowlby's dream comes full circle: The application of attachment theory to risk and psychopathology. *Advances in clinical child psychology* (Vol. 17, pp. 1–75). New York: Plenum.

Crittenden, P. M. (1990). Internal representational models of attachment relationships. *Infant Mental Health Journal, 11,* 259–277.

Egeland, B., Carlson, E., & Sroufe, L. A. (1993). Resilience as process. *Development and Psychopathology, 7,* 517–528.

Farber, E. A., & Egeland, B. (1987). Invulnerability among abused and neglected children. In E. J. Anthony & B. J. Cohler (Eds.), *The invulnerable child* (pp. 253–288). New York: Guilford.

Fonagy, P., Steele M., Steele, H., Higgitt, A., & Target, M. (1992). The Emanuel Miller Memorial Lecture 1992: The theory and practice of resilience. *Journal of Child Psychology and Psychiatry, 35,* 231–257.

Fraley, R. C., & Shaver, P. R. (1999). Loss and bereavement: Attachment theory and recent controversies concerning "grief work" and the nature of detachment. In J. Cassidy & P. R. Shaver (Eds.), *Handbook of attachment: Theory, research, and clinical applications* (pp. 735–759). New York: Guilford.

Gerlsma, C., Emmelkamp, P. M. G., & Arrindell, W. A. (1990). Anxiety, depression, and perception of early parenting: A meta-analysis. *Clinical Psychology Review, 10,* 251–277.

Greenberg, M. T. (1999). Attachment and psychopathology in childhood. In J. Cassidy & P. R. Shaver (Eds.), *Handbook of attachment: Theory, research, and clinical applications* (pp. 469–496). New York: Guilford.

Harris, T. O., & Bifulco, A. T. (1991). Loss of parent in childhood, attachment style, and depression in adulthood. In C. M. Parkes, J. Stevenson-Hinde, & P. Marris (Eds.), *Attachment across the life cycle* (pp. 234–267). New York and London: Routledge.

Harter, S. (1985). *The Social Support Scale for Children: Manual.* Denver, CO: University of Denver.

Howes, C. (1999). Attachment relationships in the context of multiple caregivers. In J. Cassidy & P. R. Shaver (Eds.), *Handbook of attachment: Theory, research, and clinical applications* (pp. 671–687). New York: Guilford.

Howes, C., Matheson, C. C., & Hamilton, C. E. (1997). Maternal, teacher and child care history correlates of children's relationships with peers. *Child Development, 55,* 257–273.

Keller, S. (2001). *Links between relationship patterns, psychological adjustment and depressotypic cognition of children in kinship care.* Unpublished doctoral dissertation, Adelphi University, Garden City, NY.

Kenny, M. E., Moilanen, D. L., Lomax, R., & Brabeck, M. M. (1993). Contributions of parental attachments to view of self and depressive symptoms among early adolescents. *Journal of Early Adolescence, 13,* 408–430.

Kopera-Frye, K., & Wiscott, R. (2000). Intergenerational continuity: Transmission of beliefs and culture. In B. Hayslip, Jr. & R. Goldberg-Glen (Eds.), *Grandparents raising grandchildren: Theoretical, empirical, and clinical perspectives* (pp. 65–84). New York: Springer.

Kovacs, M. (1983). *The children's depression inventory: A self-rated depression scale for school-aged youngsters.* Unpublished manuscript, University of Pittsburgh School of Medicine.

Luthar, S., Cicchetti, D., & Becker, B. (2000). The construct of resilience: A critical evaluation and guidelines for future work. *Child Development, 71,* 543–562.

Lynch, M. (1992). *Modes of linkage between relationship disturbances and maladaptation: Issues in the area of child maltreatment.* Unpublished doctoral dissertation, University of Rochester, Rochester, NY.

Lynch, M., & Cicchetti, D. (1991). Patterns of relatedness in maltreated and nonmaltreated children: Connections among multiple representational models. *Development and Psychopathology, 3,* 207–226.

Main, M., Kaplan, N., & Cassidy, J. (1985). Security in infancy, childhood, and adulthood: A move to the level of representation. In I. Bretherton & E. Waters (Eds.), Growing points of attachment theory and research. *Monographs of the Society for Research in Child Development, 50*(1–2, Serial No. 209), pp. 66–104. Chicago: University of Chicago Press.

Masten, A. S., Best, K. M., & Garmezy, N. (1990). Resilience and development: Contributions from the study of children who overcome adversity. *Development and Psychopathology, 2,* 425–444.

Papini, D. R., & Roggman, L. A. (1992). Adolescent perceived attachment to parents in relation to competence, depression, and anxiety: A longitudinal study. *Journal of Early Adolescence, 12,* 420–440.

Radke-Yarrow, M., & Brown, E. (1993). Resilience and vulnerability in children of multiple-risk families. *Development and Psychopathology, 5,* 581–592.

Silverthorn, P., & Durant, S. L. (2000). Custodial grandparenting of the difficult child: Learning from the parenting literature. In B. Hayslip, Jr., & R. Goldberg-Glen (Eds.), *Grandparents raising grandchildren: Theoretical, empirical, and clinical perspectives* (pp. 47–63). New York: Springer.

Sroufe, L. A. (1989). Relationships, self and individual adaptation. In A. Sameroff & R. Emde (Eds.), *Relationship disturbance in early childhood* (pp. 70–94). New York: Basic Books.

Stocker, C. M. (1994). Children's perceptions of relationships with siblings, friends, and mothers: Compensatory processes and links with adjustment. *Journal of Child Psychology and Psychiatry, 35,* 1447–1459.

Stroebe, M., & Stroebe, W. (1993). The mortality of bereavement: A review. In M. S. Stroebe, W. Stroebe, & R. O. Hansson (Eds.), *Handbook of bereavement: Theory, research, and intervention* (pp. 175–195). New York: Cambridge University Press.

Thomas, J. L., Sperry, L., & Yarbrough, M. S. (2000). Grandparents as parents: Research findings and policy recommendations. *Child Psychiatry and Human Development, 31,* 3–22.

Vivona, J. (2000). Parental attachment styles of late adolescents: Qualities of attachment relationships and consequences for adjustment. *Journal of Counseling Psychology, 3,* 316–329.

Wellborn, J. G., & Connell, J. P. (1987). *Manual for the Rochester Assessment Package for Schools*. University of Rochester, Rochester, NY.

CHAPTER 4

An Integrative Assessment Model as a Means of Intervention With the Grandparent Caregiver

Francine Conway and George Stricker

INTRODUCTION

Most of us will readily agree that part of what makes us human is our ability to adapt to change. Therefore, it is reasonable to expect that grandparent caregivers will adapt to the role of parenting their grandchildren. There is less agreement, however, about whether the grandparent caregiving situation facilitates the adjustment and enjoyment of the caregiver. In fact, a problem-focused view of the grandparent caregiving situation has evolved because the reasons underlying the grandparents' assumption of caregiving for their grandchild often stem from problems or deficits in the birth parents' relationship with the child. Jendrek (1993) found that grandparenting adversely impacted four areas of the grandparent's life: changes in lifestyle, relationships with friends, relationships with family, and relationships with spouse. Similarly, Bongaarts, Menken, and Watkins (1984) found that parental responsibilities adversely affected developmental milestones such as retirement and leisure. Even in situations where grandmothers are married, Minkler, Roe, and Price (1994) found that their marital relationships were negatively affected by the assumption of the caregiver role. Furthermore, guilt, feelings of self-blame, obligations, and a sense of betrayal characterized most grandparents' experience of caregiving, particularly where their role stemmed from their birth child's drug use (Poe, 1992). Grandparent caregivers reported poorer health, increases in physical illness, alcoholism, smoking, depression, and anxiety (Burton, 1992; Force, Botsford, Pisano, & Hobert, 2000; Roe, Minkler, Saunders, & Thompson 1996). Kelly (1993) found that 56% of grandparents reported financial difficulty associated with caregiving. In addition, grandchildren who are being parented by their grandparents have the task of adapting to the loss of their parents, and frequently to changes in their living environment.

Factors precipitating the child's placement often can lead the child to exhibit disruptive behaviors manifested as inattention and conduct problems resulting in difficulties in caregiver, teacher, and peer interaction (Silverthorn & Frick, 1999). The consequences of the child's behavior are debilitating, as they often impinge on his or her concentration and compromise the ability to attend to studies and learning. For example, disruptive behavior often leads to the child's removal from the classroom for part or all of the day, suspension, and at times expulsion. The child's emotional development is marked by feelings of loss, anger, and rejection, leading to difficulty in forming trusting relationships, as evidenced in the overall increase in the grandparent caregiver's request for psychological help for these children (Emick & Hayslip, 1996; Kennedy & Keeney, 1988). The events precipitating the child's placement with a grandparent tend to have an adverse impact on the child's social and emotional development, often resulting in delays in language and cognitive functioning, and lowered self-esteem, important factors influencing the child's ability to perform academically (Bowlby, 1988).

Given the array of problems found in the grandparent caregiver situation, an assessment of the caregiver and the child's adaptation to the unexpected and sometimes unusual caregiving situation is often difficult. Deciding on where to intervene may be a challenging and daunting task. This chapter does not allow for a complete discussion of all the variables contributing to the grandparent and child's adaptation to this unique parenting arrangement, or to the literature suggesting some positive effects of the caregiving situation. It does, however, offer an alternative way of assessing the grandparent caregiver situation and it identifies points of intervention. Before discussing how to competently assess and intervene with grandparent caregivers, it is necessary to address three of the main theoretical constructs on which the assessment model is based: Erikson's psychosocial model of development, attachment theory, and Bronfenbrenner's ecological systems theory.

Although various theories provide evidence and support for the progression of human growth and development, Erikson's (1963) psychosocial model of development offers a useful framework for understanding the grandparent caregiver situation.

For Erikson, development of personality includes the sequential reorganization of ego and character structures as progression is made through the eight stages of life. For purposes of this discussion, we will use Freud's (1983) view of the ego as the rational, conscious, problem-solving part of the personality. As such, mastery of the challenges posed by each psychosocial developmental stage and the ego's resolution of the conflict allows for progression to the next developmental level. Not only is Erikson's theory relevant to a psychodynamic perspective of emotional development, but it is also concerned with three main aspects of human development: "the individual's biological and physical strengths and limitations; the person's unique life circumstances and developmental history, including early family experiences and degree of success in resolving earlier developmental crises; and the particular social, cultural, and historical forces at work" (Seifert, Hoffnung, & Hoffnung, 1997, p. 38).

A discussion of any aspect of human development would be incomplete without attention paid to attachment, a central aspect of humanity. Therefore, we propose that successful progression through Erikson's eight developmental stages[1] and resolution of their corresponding conflicts[2] is predicated on the extent to which the individual's physical, emotional, and social needs are met. The attainment of these needs hinges on the individual's capacity for attachment and, by extension, for relationships. Emotional development and attachment are viewed by some theorists as being inextricably linked to the survival of humanity. Fromm (1970) believed that, over the course of development, attachment pathways are redirected either to accommodate or to deny the reality of one's separateness from the mother. Furthermore, it is this process of overcoming aloneness, from birth throughout the life span, that is the driving force behind actions in human society and culture (Greenberg & Mitchell, 1983). Other theorists, such as Bowlby (1988), speak more directly to the importance of the emotional life, particularly the attachment to mother, for one's survival. The child's attachment to the mother is the primary relationship that is of greatest importance from the start of the child's life. Confidence in the attachment underlies emotional stability, whereas disturbances in attachment underlie emotional struggles (Bowlby, 1973). In like manner, Mahler's theory of the existence of a symbiotic relationship between the child and mother, their impending separation, and eventual individuation, supports the child's instinctual need of the mother for survival (Mahler, Pine, & Bergman, 1975). For this reason, disruptions in the maternal attachment to the child have the potential for problems in attachment to future attachment figures. Without the security and provision of concrete and emotional nurturing, the physical

---

[1]Oral-sensory, muscular-anal, locomotor, latency, adolescence, young adulthood, middle adulthood, and maturity

[2]Trust vs. Mistrust, Autonomy v. Shame/Doubt, Initiative vs. Guilt, Industry vs. Inferiority, Identity vs. Role Confusion, Intimacy vs. Isolation, Generativity vs. Stagnation, Ego Integrity vs. Despair

integrity of the child is threatened. This disruption in attachment to a primary caregiving figure is a common experience in the lives of children being parented by their grandparents and underlies the child's resulting struggles in developing new positive attachments to their grandparent caregivers, to other adults such as teachers, and to peers.

In thinking about the practical implications of the developmental process for the grandparent caregiver, it is also useful to examine the three developmental planes (emotional, physical, and social) in the context of an ecological systems framework. Bronfenbrenner's (1989) ecological system for developmental change described the developmental context as "sets of people, settings, and recurring events [that are] related to one another, have stability, and influence the person over time" (Seifert et al., 1997, p. 7). For the purposes of this chapter, the focus will be on three of Bronfenbrenner's four systems: Microsystems, Mesosystems, and Exosystems. Specifically, the individual's physical, emotional, and social development will be considered in the context of his or her Microsystems (individuals with whom they have face-to-face contact, e.g., immediate family, teachers, peers, church, workplace), Mesosystems (connections and relationships that exist between two or more microsystems, e.g., home-school, workplace-family, school-neighborhood), and Exosystems (e.g., extended family, friends of family, mass media, social welfare services, legal services, neighbors).

In Bronfenbrenner's model, the individual is central and all other relational influences are considered with respect to the individual. Although this approach is a valid and worthwhile one, it misses the mark when it comes to working with grandparent caregivers. It is not unusual for those wishing to intervene to view the grandparent as the identified client and intervene in ways that make sense for the grandparent. Grandparents, however, rarely view themselves as individuals, but as part of a unit consisting of themselves and their grandchild. For example, several grandmothers have repeatedly said, "we're a package deal," referring to themselves and the child. It behooves us, therefore, as helping professionals, to adopt the client's view and work from a perspective where there is not only one recipient of intervention (the grandparent) but also additional stakeholders (the child and the birth parent).

Although the grandparent-grandchild relationship is the typical dyad, we propose that the birth parent greatly impacts the duo. The birth parent must be included as central to the system even though, for most grandparent caregivers, the birth parent is not present in the home and the grandparent has sole caregiving responsibilities. We submit that the parent is always emotionally present, even if his or her physical presence is erratic or absent. The birth parent may, in fact, be a phantom parent, but his or her contribution to this triad is a powerful one. The birth parent's very absence from the relationship impacts the child's attachment profile and the grandparent's own relationship with the child comes into focus. Ignoring the role the parent plays can be a crucial error.

It would not be prudent to consider any one individual in the triad independently from the others. Each member of this triad has overlapping systems that are shaped by and dependent on the triadic relationship. Each individual in this triadic relationship holds a deterministic role creating a united bond, for better or for worse. Unfortunately for all parties involved, the bond between them is so precariously held together that attempts to differentiate threaten the continuity of the relationship. It is the tenuousness of the triadic relationship that often keeps grandparents from pursuing formal custodial care of their grandchild, although doing so would secure their caregiving arrangements financially, help them to procure benefits for the child, and alleviate their fears of losing the child to a poorly functioning parent or the social welfare system. Clinicians working with grandparent caregivers need to understand that the triadic relationship is an important one and a necessary one. Attempts to encourage the grandparent to think and make decisions as an independent individual are misguided and can result in the grandparent experiencing the clinician as unempathic.

For the child, the parental relationship is paramount. The child struggles with a range of feelings, from anger and sadness to hope toward their birth parent. Children may experience confusion about how they should feel toward their parent and grandparent as their feelings alternate between a sense of loyalty and betrayal. Their attachment to their parent becomes a point of conflict in the triad, particularly when the parent visits. One grandparent reports, "when their mother is around, they forget all the rules and act up." Other grandparents have talked about their feelings of pain and hurt because of their wish to protect the child from future disappointment when the child is disappointed by the parent, and by the child's subsequent perception that the grandparent wants to keep the child from seeing the parent.

Conventional knowledge among most psychodynamic theorists suggests that the parent-child relationship sets the template for other relationships. If we accept the premise that the parent–child dyad is an important one, what the grandparent caregiving situation calls for is a reorganization of the importance of dyadic relationships to include multiple parent–child dyads. A total of three parent–child dyads is evident in the grandparent caregiving situation: birth parent and child, grandparent and birth parent, and grandparent and child. In fact, this last dyad constitutes a new relationship between grandparent and child that is superimposed on their previous caregiving relationship. More important, the extent to which each (grandparent, birth parent, and child) embraces or opposes a relationship with the others has direct implications for the quality of their relationship with others in their Microsystems. For example, a child who perceives his or her relationship with mother as abandoning and rejecting may have difficulty coming to trust other adults such as teachers, and may act out anger toward peers; the subsequent relational problems can be extensive. Reliance on the resulting relationship paradigm in the triad as a model for other relationships may well lead to conflict in the Microsystems, as well as in the Mesosystems.

Based on the discussion of Erikson's theoretical constructs of development, the importance of maternal attachment, and Bronfenbrenner's Ecological Systems Theory, several important elements of the assessment model for grandparent caregivers emerge. First, we need to view development from a systems perspective, which examines the individual relative to the world. Second, the individual is part of a triadic unit consisting of the grandparent, child, and birth parent. Third, at the core of the triad is their attachment (relationship quality), which consequently impacts their relationship to each other and others in their world.

CASE ASSESSMENT/FORMULATION

Although there are predictable stressors in the grandparent caregiving relationship, each experience is uniquely shaped by biological, social, and psychological tasks that impact the life course of grandparents. Not only are there identifiable stressors associated with caregiving, but grandparents also acknowledge positive aspects of the caregiving experience. The assessment process should help the clinician to understand the complexity of the grandparent caregiver situation as well as to consider the strengths of caregiving. The grandparent should be viewed as a whole person who has been molded in part by his or her culture and has a societal cohort. The proposed assessment approach should be used in the context of a developing therapeutic relationship meant to provide a guide for exploration. Therefore, questions should be adapted linguistically to match the grandparent's level of education and cultural disposition. This said, through a process of weaving together the grandparent caregiver's history of the assumption of the caregiver role and the constellation of emotional responses to the caregiving situation, the clinician will have a better and more complete understanding of the difficulties caregivers encounter. A well-formulated case helps to guide or direct the work done in each session (Persons, Curtis, & Silberschatz, 1991). The essential components of a grandparent caregiver case formulation are as follows:

1. Relevant background data
2. Current life problems and life changes
3. Emotional, social, and physical development
4. Attachment in the dyadic and triadic relationships
5. Individual Microsystems and shared Microsystems
6. Mesosystem
7. Exosystem
8. Integration of the above data

In the following discussion, case scenarios and quotations presented are based on intensive interviews with grandmothers parenting their grandchildren.

Relevant Background Information

Relevant background information consists of those experiences that contributed or led up to the grandparent's assumption of the caregiver role. The goal is to identify precipitants of the caregiver relationship, the child's previous caregiving experience, and the birth parent's level of functioning. For example, when one grandmother was asked "What are some of the reasons that led you to assume care for your grandchild?" she responded, "His mother is schizophrenic and on drugs. She threatened him with a razor to his neck so I moved him out." Responses to questions in this area provide added pertinent information about the birth parent's level of functioning and ability to care for the child. Usually, grandparent caregiving stems from an adverse event such that the grandmother's biological child (usually the mother) is unable to continue caring adequately for her children. However, grandparents' response to this adversity generally originates from a position of strength and a desire to help the vulnerable grandchild.

Current Life Problems/Life Changes

Current Life Problems/Life Changes comprises the full spectrum of difficulties and resources resulting from caregiving. The goal of this exploration is to determine short-term and long-term goals and strengths, and to ascertain whether problems require crisis intervention. These problems commonly include financial stresses or resources; deterioration of physical health; positive or negative impact on psychological health; needed assistance or available resources in negotiating the various systems, such as legal services, educational, and welfare systems; knowledge of the educational system; and respite from caregiving. For example, when one grandmother was asked, "What problems arise from taking care of your grandchild?" she responded, "The thing I wanted was a Medicare card. Life is getting harder so I had to get custody. I got tired of people looking at me like I was crazy because I have no legal custody . . . I'm pushed to get benefits for her but I can't keep up the meetings required by the system." However, when asked about the benefits of caring for her grandchild, the grandmother responded, "I learn so much from her. She comes home and shares with me what she learned at school. It is so much more than I did." It is equally important to explore further whether the grandparents experienced the problem prior to the caregiving relationship or as a result of caregiving. If able to, grandparents should order their problems according to severity and immediacy of needs.

Developmental Expectations and Tasks

Caregiver

Consider the age of the grandparents and their developmental stage according to Erikson's psychosocial developmental stages. Inquire about grandparents' roles relative to those dictated by the expected developmental stage. Do the grandparents perceive their role as out of stage or unusual? One way of arriving at responses reflecting a developmental approach or out of stage experience would be to inquire about grandparents' expectations and changes in their plans for the future. The goal of this line of inquiry is to determine the grandparents' developmental position within Erikson's psychosocial stages. For example, one grandmother reported, "I wanted to work and go to school. Every year something came up. I wanted to study counseling or become a psychotherapist so I could help people, do something meaningful. When the kids grew I was still at step one. Work and put out. In hindsight, maybe I could have done it and sacrificed but I'm not going to sit and mourn. Now I have to be a mother again. I'm in the same fix."

This grandmother's response should be differentiated from other responses where the parenting experience is more congruent with the grandparent's expectation. For example, if a grandmother was a teenage parent, she may experience her own premature grandparenthood as syntonic with previous life experiences. Role strain may not be as much a problem for this grandparent as is the need for financial assistance.

Other developmental considerations for the caregiver include assessing the impact of caregiving on his or her social functioning and physical and mental health. The following are some examples of grandmothers' responses to questions about the impact of caregiving on the above-mentioned areas of their lives: (social) "I have no social life . . . I don't go out that much anymore . . . I go to church"; (peer relationships) "None . . . I have none (friends)"; (physical health) "I'm getting slower, but I have more mind than energy. I do what I have to do. I don't give in to my illness and wonder about vacation"; and (emotional health) "[Relationship with children] Not too good. It's a blame game. She blames me for her condition. I don't think I could do more with what I had. I worked 7 days a week to take care of them. You make choices and you don't know how it'll affect your kid."

It is important to note that not all grandmothers experience difficulties in these areas. However, for the purpose of assessing problems, the examples reflect some of the problem-oriented responses grandmothers provide. Each response should be considered in the context of the grandparents' developmental stage. For example, for grandparents reporting few peer relationships, clarification should be made about whether those peer relationships may have declined due to their elderly status, the tendency to increased social isolation, or the loss of relationships due to the death of their friends. In contrast, it is likely that younger grandparents experience isolation in the caregiving role because of having to relinquish their jobs, resulting in severed social relationships. In general, custodial grandparents at any developmental stage have less opportunity for leisure than their traditional counterparts.

Child

Identify the child's developmental stage according to Erikson's psychosocial model. The child's placement on this model will provide the caregiver with needed psychoeducational information about what developmental tasks are expected and allows him or her to identify developmental lags.

The child's social relationships should also be assessed by reports from teachers on behavior at school and peer relationships. Attention should be paid to any changes in the child's school environment.

The child's physical health should be assessed for possible neurological problems as a result of in utero exposure to drugs, respiratory problems such as asthma, or physical disabilities. The child should also be assessed for the attainment of developmental milestones of motor skills, speech, and cognitive abilities.

For the child, an assessment of emotional functioning is a necessary aspect of developmental inquiry. In assessing emotional functioning it is important to consider the quality of the child's relationship with the grandparent and birth parent. Children who are parented by their grandparents have many psychological problems, and the number of grandparents requesting psychological help for their grandchildren has been increasing (Hayslip & Goldberg-Glen, 2000). Children may experience emotional problems stemming from exposure to drugs in utero and grandparents may be faced with caring for a child with depression or disruptive behavioral problems. Nonetheless, grandparents who parent a child report experiencing benefits associated with caregiving. They report psychological gains including companionship, new opportunities for learning, affection, and the like.

Birth Parent

The birth parent's development should also be assessed. The emotional state of the birth parent is important whether or not he or she has contact with the child. Although the parent may not be available for interviewing, questions about the parent can be answered according to the grandparent's and the child's perception.

Identify the birth parent's developmental stage according to Erikson's psychosocial model, and assess the parent's peer groups and other social relationships. Assess to what extent the parent is isolated from family members, friends in the neighborhood, and other social relationships. It is important to assess the health status of the parent because it may have implications for the child's and grandparent's fears and for the possibility of the child's return to the parent. Is the parent terminally ill? For example, some parents are unable to care for their child due to AIDS/HIV infection or other potentially terminal diseases.

Questions should be asked to ascertain whether the birth parent is actively using drugs, experiencing a major mental disorder, incarcerated, or attending a rehabilitation or other therapeutic facility. This information has import for both child and grandparent as it may dictate the quality of their interactions as well as impact their attitude toward the return of the child to the parent.

Attachment in Dyadic and Triadic Relationships

It is important to interview each member of the triad (grandparent, child, and birth parent) or to obtain the grandparent's best guesses about the quality of relationships. Dyadic relationships of child/birth parent, grandparent/birth parent, and child/grandparent should be examined from the perspective of each member of the triad. Any member of the triad can also speculate on the relationship between the other two members. Questions about the areas of conflict and the areas of agreement within the triad are important in determining the quality of the relationships and the presence of conflict-free spheres of interaction. An example of a conflict-free sphere may be the experience of grandparents and birth parents sharing their love for the child and the child returning love to both sets of parents. In addition, there may be ways in which they show their love toward each other that is supported by all parties. For example, grandparents may enjoy seeing the child and mother interact when the parent comes to visit. Both may talk about the child's accomplishments and take pride in the child.

Individual and Shared Microsystems

It is helpful to make a list of all the individuals with whom the child, grandparent, and birth parent interact. Particular attention should be paid to which interactions are shared. For example, grandparents and child may interact with the child's teachers, and parent, grandparent, and children may all interact with other family members. Questions about the Microsystem's shared values should focus on the quality of the interactions between members of the triad and individuals in their Microsystems. Interactions that are less characterized by conflict and more positive offer an important buffer for all parties as they negotiate the stresses associated with caregiving.

Mesosystem

Interactions between individuals in the Microsystem are often necessary to advocate for their needs and share resources. Determine who in the Microsystems of each individual interact with each other. Are these interactions done in a respectful manner? Is the best interest of the individual considered during these interactions? For example, the child's teacher, grandparent, and therapist may discuss the child's behavior management in the classroom. Social workers, medical doctors, and grandparents may discuss a plan for the child's medical care.

Exosystem

The Exosystem includes extended family, friends of family, mass media, social welfare services, legal services, neighbors, and the like. These systems may not directly interface with the members in the triad but they indirectly influence their well-being. Rules, policies, and access to the various entities in the Exosystem impact on the grandparent's experience of caregiving and may be a source of stress or strength. Determine to what extent grandparents are limited in their ability to obtain adequate legal representation. For example, during a court hearing pertaining to custody, it is not unusual for the child and the mother to each have an assigned attorney. It is rare that the grandparent is provided with legal counsel. However, for those grandparents who are able to access legal support, the stress associated with assumption of the parental role may be mitigated.

Integration of the above data gathered in the assessment helps the clinician to identify points of intervention. These interventions can be two-fold: reinforcing strengths in the system, and addressing areas of weaknesses. Points of intervention include:

Strengths:

- The presence of conflict-free spheres of interaction in the triad
- Shared Microsystems in the triad that are representative of a web of supportive and respectful interactions
- Positive nurturing relationships in the dyad

- Exosystem policies and procedures that support the grandparent caregiving situation

Weaknesses:

- The presence of conflictual interactions in the triad
- Conflictual and harmful interactions in the dyad
- Shared Microsystems in the triad that are unsupportive and negative
- Exosystem policies and procedures that impinge on the grandparent caregiver's ability to provide care for the grandchildren

In addition to the clinical interview, there are self-report measures that may provide important information. These include measures of critical constructs such as depression, anxiety, stress, and parental satisfaction.

CONCLUSION

Aging is a process, yet it is one also characterized by a unique life course that may depart from the expected. Today's grandparents are not immune from experiencing predictable departures from the expected grandparenting experience. Becoming grandparents earlier than expected and assuming caregiving responsibilities when least expected are unique aspects of some grandparents' life course progression. Having accepted the uniqueness of the grandparenting situation, it is imperative that a similar acceptance of the uniqueness of the aging process be applied to the grandparenting situation. Therefore, the grandparent caregiver situation demands an assessment of the grandparenting experience that is structured, yet flexible enough to accommodate each grandparent's unique experience. An integration of theories pertinent to the life course development of grandparents yields an assessment model that provides structure for the helping professional while accommodating grandparents' unique experiences. The reorientation of helping professionals from a problem-focused approach to one that is strengths-based decreases the possibility of stereotyping the caregiving experience, and increases the accuracy of assessment that informs the interventions with grandparent caregivers. More important, this assessment model will increase the likelihood that the grandparent will experience the helping professional as empathic and helpful, leading to increases in service utilization.

REFERENCES

Bongaarts, J., Menken, J. A., & Watkins, S. C. (1984, October). *Continuities and changes in the American family.* Paper presented at the annual meeting of Social Science History Association, Toronto, Canada.

Bowlby, J. (1973). *Attachment and Loss: Vol 2. Separation, anxiety, and anger.* New York: Basic Books.

Bowlby, J. (1988). *A secure base: Parent–child attachment and healthy development.* New York: Basic Books.

Bronfenbrenner, U. (1989). Ecological systems theory. In R. Vasta (Ed.), *Annals of child development: Six theories of formulations and current issues* (Rev. ed.). Greenwich, CT: JAI.

Burton, L. M. (1992). Black grandparents raising children of drug-addicted parents: Stressors, outcomes and the social service needs. *The Gerontologist, 32,* 744–751.

Emick, M., & Hayslip, B. (1996). Custodial grandparenting: New roles for middle aged and older adults. *International Journal of Aging and Human Development, 43,* 135–154.

Erikson, E. H. (1963). *Childhood and society* (2nd ed.). New York: Norton.

Force, L., Botsford, A., Pisano, P., & Holbert, A. (2000). Grandparents raising children with and without a developmental disability: Preliminary comparisons. *Journal of Gerontological Social Work, 33,* 5–21.

Freud, S. (1983). *A general introduction to psychoanalysis* (rev. ed.). New York: Washington Square Press.

Fromm, E. (1970). *The crisis of psychoanalysis.* Greenwich, CT: Fawcett.

Greenberg, J., & Mitchell, S. (1983). *Object relations in psychoanalytic theory.* Cambridge, MA: Harvard University Press.

Hayslip, B., & Goldberg-Glen, R. (Eds.). (2000). *Grandparents raising grandchildren: Theoretical, empirical, and clinical perspectives.* New York: Springer

Jendrek, M. (1993). Grandparents who parent their grandchildren: Effects on lifestyle. *Journal of Marriage and the Family, 55,* 609–621.

Kelly, S. (1993). Caregiver stress in grandparents raising grandchildren. *Image: Journal of Nursing Scholarship, 25,* 331–336.

Kennedy, J., & Keeney, V. (1998). The extended family revisited: Grandparents rearing grandchildren. *Child Psychiatry & Human Development, 19,* 26–35.

Mahler, M., Pine, F., & Bergman, A. (1975). *The psychological birth of the human infant: Symbiosis and individuation.* New York: Basic Books.

Minkler, M., Roe, K. M., & Price, M. (1994). Raising grandchildren from crack-cocaine households: Effects of family and friendship ties of African-American women. *American Journal of Orthopsychiatry, 64,* 20–29.

Persons, J., Curtis, J., & Silberschatz, G. (1991). Psychodynamic and cognitive-behavioral formulations of a single case. *Psychotherapy: Theory, Research, Practice, Training, 28,* 608–617.

Poe, L. M. (1992). *Black grandparents as parents.* Washington, DC: Library of Congress.

Roe, K. M., Minkler, M., Sanders, F. F., & Thompson, G. (1996). Health of grandmothers raising children of the crack cocaine epidemic. *Medical Care, 34,* 1072–1084.

Seifert, K., Hoffnung, R., & Hoffnung, M. (1997). *Lifespan development.* New York: Houghton Mifflin.

Silverthorn, P., & Frick, P. J. (1999). Developmental pathways to antisocial behavior: The delayed-onset pathways in girls. *Development and Psychopathology, 11,* 101–126.

CHAPTER 5

Through My Eyes: Service Needs of Grandparents Who Raise Their Grandchildren, From the Perspective of a Custodial Grandmother

Annabel H. Baird

Before I begin, I must say that we consider ourselves the most fortunate of custodial grandparents. We are still in our fifties, are healthy, and, while the financial strain of raising another child is apparent wherever you look in our lives, we remain capable of supporting ourselves and our newest child. And, most important, we were able to step into C.'s life when she was an infant, and although she does appear to have serious abandonment issues, she is a happy, healthy kindergartner whose joy in life is apparent in everything she does.

OUR STORY

The assumption of the parent role to our granddaughter came as no surprise, and was somewhat anticipated from the moment we were made aware that her mother was pregnant. The only unknown was the actual date and time that we would either be asked or forced to step in. Like many other custodial grandparents have experienced, difficulties with our son did not begin with the birth of his daughter, nor did they end when she came to live with us, but had been ongoing since his early teens. We were already exhausted, and although having C. with us and knowing she was safe did remove some of our stress, the knowledge that we were embarking on yet another journey of child raising brought its own anxieties.

We were fortunate indeed that C.'s parents approached us to ask if we would assume "temporary" custody for six months or so while they ended their marriage and got established apart from each other. We agreed as long as the custody was "permanent," assuring them that when either or both could demonstrate a willingness and ability to care for her physical and emotional needs we would freely relinquish custody. Therefore, we were never put in the position of testifying before a court against either our son or daughter-in-law, allowing for a much smoother transition and far less cost. On the other hand, we never came in contact with Child Protective Services or any other regulatory agency, and consequently were not made aware of any service offerings from which we could benefit.

Adjustments

Our concerns were not about our physical abilities to raise a child, although as it turns out, they should have been included. The concerns were our emotional capacity and strength to assume a job we had not enjoyed very much the last time we accomplished it, and thus, our first task was to concentrate on today and not project our experiences with C.'s father and later, his sister, to her future. The second challenge was to reposition our perspective from that of grandparent to parent, meaning if we were to raise this child, we had to see ourselves as doing so. My husband began to rethink retirement, actually to remove the word from his vocabulary, and I began reordering my priorities to form a better fit with mothering an infant. The masters degree I was seeking took an extra year to achieve, the guest bedroom became a nursery, and I began a concerted effort to spend more time with our adult daughter, in order to help her know she was still our daughter and had not been displaced.

The most disturbing reality we had to face was that our private sorrow was now public. We had actually moved to a new city just four months before assuming custody of C., one purpose of which move was to disassociate ourselves from being B.'s parents. Feeling judged by the actions of our adult son were returned as fear for him in his current situation. In addition, I became quickly aware that once one assumes custody of a grandchild, several assumptions are made. First and foremost is that we had to have been bad parents or our son would have been willing and able to raise his own daughter. That put aside, there was the concern that we were clearly too old, or at least behind the times, to effectively raise a child. Some felt sorry for us, but to most persons our age, we were their worst nightmare. I began to enter any situation in which C. and I were jointly involved in a defensive posture, whether or not it was warranted.

We suddenly found ourselves with no place to belong. Our lives had changed drastically with one stroke of a pen, a change occasioned not by our actions, but by those of our son and his wife. Our friends, alongside whom we had raised our children, didn't have a baby with which to contend and were hard pressed to understand when we had to find a babysitter in order to go to a spur of the moment movie or dinner. The parents of C.'s peers were more the age of our children, and while we enjoyed their company on a limited basis, we were at a completely different developmental level and not interested in revisiting the issues and challenges of being thirty-something again. I was affected more by the disparity in ages than my husband was, and it became more and more difficult for me to avoid isolating. Although we have each been able to remain in contact with a few long-time friends and have made several new ones, there remains a sense of not having a place where we feel totally comfortable.

Conflicts

Being a custodial grandmother is, without a doubt, the most conflicted role I have undertaken. On the one hand, C. is our child, and we cannot imagine our lives without her. She brings joy into every day, and our lives are enhanced by her presence. On the other, my anger is so great that I could easily put my fist through my living room wall. I am angry over what has happened to my life, my loss of freedom, my future. I am angry that I have to deal with the biological parents, and that even though we have a strong custody agreement, there is always the possibility that one or both of them could petition for and actually be granted custody, whether or not they have shown themselves to be willing to be responsible parents. I fear for our future, both financial and emotional, and, at this point, cannot envision what we will be looking at when she is grown and gone.

This Is Not My Job

Underlying all that I do is a sense that "this is not my job." When I have conferences with the teachers or cannot find a babysitter, it rings in my ears. When I cannot keep regular hours at a job because I am no longer able to work a forty-hour week, tend to an active preschooler, and keep a house, I think, "I should not have to be doing this now." When my husband had emergency coronary bypass surgery and I was not only concerned for him, but also had to make arrangements for the care of a four-year old, I kept wondering, "Why am I having to do this?" I have already been the room mother, a Girl Scout leader, and a Cub Scout den mother. I have stood in a school carnival booth for hours, made spaghetti by the carload for school dinners, and raised money for playground equipment. I resent having to do it again, and I find myself acting passive aggressively more often than I care to admit, effectively making my life harder than it needs to be.

Grief

The longer I am a custodial grandmother, the more certain I am that I suffer from two somewhat distinct, but at the same time intertwined, maladies. First and foremost, I am in a grieving process that seems to have no end. I grieve for my future, my hopes and aspirations for myself as well as those for my son, my loss of freedom, and my relationships with my husband and daughter. And to make it worse, I cannot give voice to my grief for fear my granddaughter will believe it is her fault and carry the guilt and shame that rightfully belongs to her parents. Posttraumatic stress tends to rear its head on a frequent basis, often at the most inappropriate of times, distracting me on a crowded freeway or causing me to begin sobbing for no apparent reason at one of C.'s class parties.

RECOMMENDATIONS FOR SERVICE PROVIDERS

In light of our experiences, we have several recommendations for those who provide services to custodial grandparents. Attitudes held by the public in general and service providers in particular must change to reflect the realities facing custodial grandparents. We must be assumed to be capable of raising our grandchildren unless proven otherwise. We must be considered to have been good parents, and thus not responsible for the parental failure of our children, unless proven otherwise. Providers must realize that although the child or children in question are indeed members of the family, those of us willing to take custody face a financial burden that must be addressed, and that we can be and are a vital component of the foster care system and deserve to be compensated as such.

Service providers *must* become our advocates, working with local, state, and national law enforcement officials as well as legislative and judicial agencies to see that the laws affecting the rights of grandparents are strengthened and enforced. The judicial system in particular must be educated as to the issues facing families in which grandparents must step in to raise their grandchildren. The current judicial bias toward the parents over grandparents or other relatives must be revisited, and the "right" of parents to be bad parents eliminated. When we can be assured that the grandchildren will not be returned on the whim of a parent, the ability of the parents to "blackmail" us will be eliminated and legitimate efforts to rebuild families can begin.

Service Offerings

Care should be taken by providers to offer services in such a way that custodial grandparents are not offended, thus limiting their involvement. Although we know the challenges facing our grandchildren are far different than those faced by their parents, "parenting classes" may imply a lack of parenting skills on our part and can easily be renamed to connote an "update" or "refresher." "New Millennium Teenagers" or "Advances in Baby Care" might better attract those in need of information. Classes addressing specific issues such as dealing with a child suffering from sexual or physical abuse or helping a child with a severe sense of abandonment would also attract those with like needs.

Every custodial grandparent I have met is desperate to find others in the same situation, and methods of bringing us together must be developed. Again, care must be taken in the presentation of these offerings: "networking" or "discussion" meetings are better received than "support groups," given their link to people with problems.

Although we are eager to seek out help for our grandchildren, little research or work is available pertaining to the needs of children affected by the shift of responsibility from their parents to their grandparents. However, much has been published regarding foster care as well as adoption of older, often difficult children, that would appear applicable to grandparent-headed families as well. Social workers and other service providers would be well advised to look to these sources when attempting to assist custodial grandparents who are seeking help with their grandchildren or for them.

Attention must be paid to the guilt that often accompanies the assumption of custody for a grandchild. Many of us believe we are to blame for the failure of our children to parent and will isolate in an attempt to escape public scrutiny. Service providers must examine their own attitudes and not hold grandparents responsible for the actions of adult children, thus contributing to an already burgeoning sense of remorse.

Services must be provided that empower custodial grandparents. Access to legal information, if not actual services, should be available. Grandparents who must face off against their own children in court or elsewhere should be accompanied whenever possible, or, at the very least, provided with support before and after the encounter. Information about local school systems, daycare providers, health clinics, and so on, should be available in a form that a grandparent can take and use for reference whenever needed. Paperwork requirements (birth certificates, court orders) and steps required to reach a desired objective (e.g., enrollment in a neighborhood school) should always be researched and provided to the grandparents in advance of any appointment.

Grief Support

Most important of all, in my opinion, service providers must consider any and all custodial grandparents to be bereaved and severely conflicted unless proven otherwise. The grief process as it applies to a grandparent forced to take on the role of parent, for whatever reason, is long and protracted. There are constant reminders of losses incurred: the retirement of a friend, watching a neighbor's grandchild come and *go*, lack of personal time with a spouse, lost contact with another friend. (It has become so difficult and painful for me to be with old friends whose children are gone that I have pretty much ceased being involved in any activities in which they would participate.) Decisions regarding "where I belong" continue, never exactly fitting in either with peers or with the parents of the friends of your grandchildren. Anger is the dominant emotion, and custodial grandparents must be given or shown safe places in which to vent, or resentments are formed that are detrimental to all involved. Conflicts arise when feelings of love for their grandchildren and those of rage over what has happened to their lives as well as those of the children in their care collide. Custodial grandparents must be made aware that the service provider understands, and, more important, accepts these feelings as normal and expected and that there are safe havens in which to discuss and work through these conflicts. Grief support groups could be tailored to meet the needs of custodial grandparents.

Finally, service providers must find a way to advise grandparents of relevant service offerings. Those grandparents who are a part of the service system, whether necessitated by their own situations or by the intervention of child protection services in the life of their grandchild, most often have access to information pertaining to educational opportunities, support groups, and so on. However, those of us who are not in the formal system are often left out of the process and are therefore not able to avail ourselves of beneficial services. Pediatricians, churches, schools, and day care centers are but a few of the outlets that can be used for the distribution of pertinent information.

CONCLUSIONS

Again, we are the most fortunate of custodial grandparents and do not pretend to say that our experiences and feelings apply to others in our situation. We do not have to deal with unsafe neighborhoods or other children still at home. We do not face the challenges that come with the acquisition of an older grandchild, often having suffered from abuse and neglect, nor do we cope with behavioral, emotional, or medical problems as do many of our cohorts. We have not had to work through the feelings of guilt over the actions of our son because we did that during his many stays in drug treatment centers, thus enabling us to concentrate on the tasks at hand. And we are not, at this time, living on a fixed income or coping with our own serious disabilities as we try to raise another child.

There are certainly those among us who would like nothing better than for their children to become capable parents and to come and take the grandchild back. There are others who have found a way to coexist with their adult children and cooperate in the raising of a grandchild. And there are still more who, like us, consider their grandchild to be their own and will fight to retain custody whatever the cost.

But no matter what the circumstances, each of us experiences serious and continuing grief and we are participating in a life that in no way resembles that which was anticipated. Through no fault of our own, we are unable to continue on our developmental path and must retrace our steps through the raising of one or more children. The greatest gift would be to hear, "I know how much *you* have lost" and to know that there are those in the service community and elsewhere who truly understand the sacrifices that have to be made when one assumes custody of a grandchild.

Part II

Empirical Studies of Helping Efforts With Grandparent Caregivers

CHAPTER 6

How Caregiving Grandparents View Support Groups: An Exploratory Study

Gregory C. Smith

Corresponding to the dramatic rise in the number of grandparents who are unexpectedly raising grandchildren due to problems encountered by the parent generation, there has been a proliferation of support groups as the dominant intervention for assisting this population. Three fourths of the community programs and services for caregiving grandparents examined nationwide in the early 1990s by the Brookdale Grandparent Information Project consisted solely or primarily of support groups (Minkler, Driver, Roe, & Bedeian, 1993). By the new millennium, more than 400 grandparent support groups across the U.S. were registered with the American Association of Retired Persons (AARP) Grandparent Information Center (Vacha-Haase, Ness, Dannison, & Smith, 2000). Support groups are clearly the most widely used source of education and support among caregiving grandparents, with many regarding them as their most valued resource (Cox, 1999; Minkler et al., 1993).

An earlier version of this chapter was presented at the 53rd Annual Scientific Meeting of The Gerontological Society of America. Washington, DC, November, 2000.
The study reported here was funded by the Graduate Research Board, University of Maryland at College Park.

Despite the increasing popularity of support groups for caregiving grandparents, there is a dearth of information about their efficacy, format, goals, and other structural characteristics (Burnette, 1998; Minkler, 1999; Vacha-Haase et al., 2000). This is largely because most grandparent support groups have inadequate external funding and institutional support, and thus minimal obligation and resources to engage in planning and self-evaluation (Roe, 1999; Strom & Strom, 1993). There is also doubt about how many caregiving grandparents actually wish to participate in support groups. A focus group study sponsored by AARP, for instance, revealed that few caregiving grandparents demonstrated enthusiasm over their own participation in support groups, even though most felt that others in their situation would have a lot to gain from attending them (Robinson & Kensinger, 1996). Emick and Hayslip (1999) found in their sample that 75% of grandparents raising normal grandchildren, and over 50% of those raising problem grandchildren had never gone to any sort of supportive intervention to help cope with their caregiving responsibilities. These findings suggest that support groups may be an underutilized resource for caregiving grandparents.

In view of the above concerns, a frequently asked question in the literature on custodial grandparents has been, How can the insights of these families be incorporated in interventions that are designed to assist them? (Cox, 1999; Emick & Hayslip, 1999; Morrow-Kondos, Weber, Cooper, & Hesser, 1997; Pinson-Millburn, Fabian, Schlossberg, & Pyle, 1996). The elicitation of these insights would not only empower grandparent-headed families (Smith, 1999), but would also help to define the issues grandparents themselves view as critical, as opposed to what issues professionals might surmise to be important for them (Morrow-Kondos et al., 1997). As stated by Roe (1999):

> The most effective programs involve grandparent caregivers in every aspect of program development. Grandparents raising grandchildren are among the best experts. They have lived the many routes to their shared point, they know the most urgent needs and the most privately held fears, and they best understand the nested challenges of parenting again and understanding these circumstances . . . grandparents' unique insight into what will work and what is most important can be a key factor in wise use of limited resources and the development of relevant and effective programs. [p. 296]

The exploratory study described in this chapter was designed to obtain qualitative information from custodial grandparents on how they view key characteristics of support groups, such as their content and activities, membership composition, and type of leadership. This study was part of a larger investigation in which the views of grandparents toward support groups designed for their grandchildren were also obtained. An underlying assumption for the entire project was that a shortcoming of many preventive interventions is failure to obtain information on how best to solicit participation by the target group. Practitioners who are developing family-focused preventive interventions must have a thorough understanding of the needs, characteristics, and values of their target populations if efforts to recruit them into supportive interventions are to be successful (Langus et al., 1992).

CONTENT AND ACTIVITIES FOR GRANDPARENT SUPPORT GROUPS

The content and activities for grandparent support groups are what the support groups do and how they spend their time (Cohen & Pyle, 1999). Although most support groups for family caregivers provide emotional support as a minimum, these groups can vary greatly in terms of whether such diverse components as education, skills development, stress reduction, and information and referral are also offered (Monahan, 1994). Some support groups for caregiving grandparents have even extended their focus to include such features as tangible assistance (e.g., emergency aid, food, housing assistance, respite care), grandchildren's support groups, empowerment training, in-depth counseling, and a focus on advocacy efforts (Cohen & Pyle).

Determining the purpose or goals of a support group is critical because it is the first step in planning which activities will be most appropriate for meeting these goals. For example, training grandparents in stress reduction techniques may be pointless if they are primarily interested in enhancing their parenting skills or discovering how to access services for their grandchildren. Although there has been much conjecture among professionals over the appropriate content for these groups, the views of grandparents themselves have been virtually ignored (see, for exception, Robinson & Kensinger, 1996). One major objective of the present study, then, was to ask caregiving grandparents what content or goals for support groups are most meaningful to them.

SUPPORT GROUP COMPOSITION

Composition refers to the number and characteristics of members who participate in a support group (Cohen & Pyle, 1999). Whether a group is homogeneous or heterogeneous in membership is an important issue because this may affect the common ground felt by participants and the degree of support and sharing among them (Monahan, 1994). Although demographic data show that custodial grandparents are a diverse target population (Fuller-Thomson & Minkler, 2000), there has been scant attention to whether this diversity should be addressed in the implementation of supportive interventions. For example, although nearly half of all custodial grandparents have been caregivers for five or more years (Fuller-Thomson, Minkler, & Driver, 1997), it is unknown whether those with greater experience in this role have different needs for support than those with lesser experience.

Other key characteristics that may influence the degree and type of support needed by custodial grandparents include: (1) *grandparents' age*, with older grandparents expressing concerns about the future in terms of passing away or becoming too infirm to continue as caregivers, as well as uncertainty over how to respond to grandchildren's concern about their health (Roe, Minkler, & Saunders, 1995; Vardi & Bucholz, 1994); (2) *grandchildren's age*, given the possibility that grandparents raising teens may become frustrated in a group composed primarily of grandparents raising younger grandchildren (Cohen & Pyle, 1999; Robinson & Kensinger, 1996); (3) *grandchildren's problems*, as the severity of behavioral problems suffered by grandchildren is related to the help-seeking behavior of grandparents (Emick & Hayslip, 1999; Hayslip, Silverthorn, Shore, & Henderson, 2000); and (4) *grandparent's educational status*, as individuals with higher levels of education are more likely to have greater personal and economic resources than their less educated counterparts. Thus, an additional objective of this study was to examine whether these characteristics are associated with grandparents' preferences for support group content and leadership.

SUPPORT GROUP LEADERSHIP

Support groups for family caregivers are commonly categorized as either "self-help" or "professionally led," but sometimes they involve various types of coleadership (Cohen & Pyle, 1999; Monahan, 1994). It has been argued that no one leadership arrangement is necessarily better than another for use in grandparent support groups, with each bringing potential challenges and benefits to the group (Cohen & Pyle). However, participants in grandparent support groups frequently believe that peers can understand them better than anyone else, which may prompt them to tolerate too much complaining and to isolate themselves from people outside the group (Strom & Strom, 1993). It has also been said that grandparent caregivers who have not yet joined a support group are more likely to make the connection if another grandparent is the contact person or group leader (Cohen & Pyle). Thus, a third major objective of this study was to explore grandparents' preferences for support group leadership.

METHOD

Recruitment

Recruitment occurred in the Baltimore/Washington metropolitan area and involved such sources as newspapers, flyers, social service agencies, and grandparent support groups. Grandparents expressing interest in the study were telephoned to determine if they met the criteria of being the full-time caregiver of a grandchild for at least eight months due to parental abuse, abandonment, or neglect; to describe the study's purpose and procedures; to obtain key background information; and to elicit convenient times for attending a focus group.

Participation was restricted to grandparents who were caring for grandchildren without the assistance of the parental generation for two reasons: first, the greatest increase has occurred in families where grandchildren live with a grandparent and no parent is present (Bryson & Casper, 1999), and second, these custodial or "skipped generation" grandparents experience higher levels of strain and family vulnerability than "co-resident" grandparents due to greater child-care responsibilities, lower levels of social support, and greater exposure to adverse lifestyle changes (Bowers & Myers, 1999; Brown-Strandridge & Floyd, 2000; Jendrek, 1993).

Participants

The sample contained 42 grandparents (mean age = 57.12 yr.; range = 46–73) who were the primary caregiver of a grandchild for at least eight months (mean duration = 6.4 yr.; range = 8 mo.–18 yr.). They were predominantly female (95.2%) and said that they were caring for their grandchild(ren) due to parental neglect, abandonment, or abuse (95.2%). Two grandmothers initially said that they were not caring for their grandchildren for these reasons, but later disclosed otherwise.

Additional background characteristics of the sample are summarized in Tables 6.1 and 6.2 which show that most participants had attended grandparent support groups (59.5%), were married (40.5%), had at least some college education (64.3%), resided in large cities (50%), were black (78.6%), and rated their health as "good" or better (78.5%). Half were caring for only one grandchild, and the majority of these grandchildren were males (56.3%), reported by grandparents to have emotional or behavioral problems (59.5%), and were of diverse ages. Most grandparents (70.9%) had been caregivers for at least four years.

The present sample is similar to the recent profile of grandparents raising grandchildren presented by Fuller-Thomson and Minkler (2000) involving nationally representative data from respondents to the 1992–1994 National Survey of Families and Households (NSFH). The average age of caregiving grandparents in that profile was 59.4 years, and the majority were female (77%), married (54%), from urban areas (74%), and had 12 or more years of education (57%). One striking difference between the two samples, however, was that the majority (62%) of the NSFH grandparents were white. Yet, the overrepresentation of blacks in the present study is justified by Fuller-Thomson and Minkler's (2000) finding that blacks were 83% more likely than whites to become caregiving grandparents. Only 11% of the NSFH grandparents were from all other races.

TABLE 6.1 Demographic Characteristics of Sample (N = 42)

Trait	N	%
Past participation in grandparent support group		
Yes	25	59.5
No	17	40.5
Marital status		
Single	4	9.5
Married	17	40.5
Separated	8	19.0
Widowed	4	9.5
Divorced	9	21.4
Education		
Some high school	6	14.3
High school graduate	9	21.4
Some college	17	40.5
College graduate	1	2.4
Graduate/professional	9	21.4
Residential area		
Large city	21	50.0
Small city	7	16.7
Suburb	11	26.2
Rural	3	7.1
Race		
White	9	21.4
Black	33	78.6
Self-rated health		
Poor	0	0.0
Fair	9	21.4
Good	14	33.3
Very good	6	14.3
Excellent	5	11.9
Missing	8	19.0

Procedure

A mixed-mode format was used in which the participants first completed a self-administered questionnaire, and then participated in focus groups where the content of the questionnaire was discussed in detail. Focus groups were used to supplement the questionnaire because they permit in-depth exploration of sensitive topics, ensure

TABLE 6.2 Demographics of Caregiving Circumstances ($N = 42$)

Characteristic	N	%
Number of grandchildren cared for		
1	21	50.0
2	9	21.4
3	7	16.7
4	5	11.9
Years in caregiving role		
≤ 3	7	16.7
4–6	18	42.8
≥ 7	16	28.1
Missing	1	2.4
Emotional problems in grandchild(ren)		
Yes	25	59.5
No	17	40.5
Grandchildren's gender		
Male	45	56.3
Female	33	41.3
Missing	2	3.0
Grandchildren's ages		
≤ 4	15	18.8
5–7	17	21.3
8–10	24	30.0
11–13	11	13.8
14–16	9	11.3
17–19	4	5.0

that respondents' own thoughts are not precluded by the established views of researchers, and are effective in providing information that is essential to developing interventions for difficult-to-access populations (Carey, 1994; Langus et al., 1992; Zeller, 1993). Focus groups are especially productive with participants who have historically had limited power and influence, such as people of color and those with restricted income (Morgan & Krueger, 1993).

All 42 grandparents were first mailed a self-administered questionnaire asking their views on a wide variety of issues pertaining to support groups for grandparents, as well as on support groups for grandchildren. Relevant to the present paper, grandparents were asked to rank order potential content areas to be covered in grandparent support groups, and indicate their preference for support group leadership. Respondents completed the questionnaire at home and returned it in a prestamped envelope. A subsample of 28 grandparents then participated in focus groups where they elaborated on the issues covered on the questionnaire. The remaining 14 grandparents were unable to attend the focus groups due to scheduling difficulties.

Five separate focus groups, each lasting about 2.5 hours, were held. Four groups were structured in a 2 × 2 design according to grandchild age (< 11 vs. 11 ≥) and grandparents' education (< high school vs. some college ≥). The fifth group contained grandparents who also were human service professionals. Consistent with recommended focus group methodology (Knodel, 1993), the composition of these five groups was based on both substantive considerations specific to the topic under investigation and on considerations concerning the facilitation of frank group discussions. More specifically, grandparents' education (a proxy for socioeconomic status) was included because focus group participants are more likely to share information and have frank discussions among others of similar prestige or status (Carey, 1994). Grandchildren's age categories were selected for substantive reasons, given that the developmental challenges of preadolescence and adolescence are likely to yield different intervention needs than those associated with earlier ages (Rose, 1998).

The fifth group, with grandparents who were also human service professionals, was unanticipated, and did not emerge until their occupations were revealed in the telephone interviews. This group contained two mental health counselors, two school counselors, a family life educator, a program consultant, and an agency director. Although not proportionately representative of the target population, it was felt that this group would offer a unique perspective, given their familiarity with the concerns of these families from both a personal and a professional standpoint. Due to the small sample sizes and lack of random selection associated with the subgroups, the data analyses described in the following section were limited to descriptive statistics.

The focus groups were held in public places. Each group was comoderated by a doctoral level social worker (black female) and the author (white male). A series of prepared questions were presented to each group in the same manner, and the moderators encouraged comments from all participants. Notes were written on flip charts so the major themes of the discussions could be reviewed and verified by participants during the meetings. The discussions were audiotaped for later review by the investigators to identify verbatim examples of the major themes and to clarify the survey responses.

The focus groups ranged in size from 4 to 7 grandparents, which is within the typical size of research-oriented focus groups (Carey, 1994; Morgan & Krueger, 1993). Grandparents who both completed the questionnaire and attended a focus group were paid $30. Participants (n = 3) unexpectedly brought other family members to four focus groups, including grandchildren and spouses.

RESULTS AND DISCUSSION

Preferences for Support Group Content

All 42 grandparents were asked on the questionnaire to rank order five potential content areas for grandparent support groups that were derived from a comprehensive review of the literature on custodial grandparents. Table 6.3 contains the label and general description for each topic as presented on the questionnaire, as well as verbatim quotes from the focus groups illustrating these topics from the grandparents' perspective. Respondents were specifically instructed to rank how important each topic was to them by placing "1" next to the most important topic, "2" next to the second most important topic, and so on until each topic had been ranked. If two or more topics were judged to be equally important, these topics received the same rank.

Do Caregiving Grandparents Who Are Human Service Professionals View Support Groups Differently Than Nonprofessional Grandparents?

Given the possibility that those grandparents who were also human service professionals might hold different views of support groups than their lay counterparts, the rankings assigned by these two types of caregiving grandparents were compared, as shown in Table 6.4. It is evident that the preferences reported by the grandparents who were also human service professionals are noticeably different from the rankings by their nonprofessional counterparts. These differences are especially noticeable when the percentages of respondents who assigned combined ranks of 1 and 2 for each content area are considered. For example, whereas over 85% of those grandparents who were human service professionals assigned ranks of 1 or 2 to the topic labeled "Taking Care of My Needs," only 58.8% of the nonprofessional grandparents gave high ranks to this topic. On the other hand, the nonprofessional grandparents were much more likely to give high ranks to "Finding My Way through the System," "How Can I Be a Better Parent to My Grandchildren?," and "What Does the Future Hold?"

It must be cautioned that the generalizability of these findings is severely threatened by the small number (n = 7) of grandparents in the study who were also human service professionals. Nevertheless, they do raise a number of intriguing questions to be addressed in future research. For example, to what extent are the views of caregiving grandparents who are human service professionals shaped by their professional status? Are their views more similar to those of other caregiving grandparents,

TABLE 6.3 Prospective Support Group Topics

Topics	Descriptions Shown on Questionnaire and Representative Quotes From Focus Groups
Finding My Way Through the System (Getting help from others)	Concerns such issues as: dealing with or getting help from family and friends, service providers/community agencies, schools; and obtaining legal/financial aid or advice. *("Just to find out where you go in the system. You look at this great big thing called Social Services and say to yourself: 'Where in the world do I go when all I want is this one little thing?' It's a bureaucracy out there!")*
What's My Place in the Family? (Dealing with family issues and conflict)	Concerns such family issues as: anger/resentment toward your son or daughter, who should have custody of your grandchild(ren), who sets the family rules, and parental visitation. *("A problem that I have with my husband is that he sometimes oversteps his role and doesn't realize that he's the grandfather and not the father. This is important because my grandchild's father isn't going to stay in jail forever.")*
Taking Care of My Needs	Venting or expressing your feelings, learning how to cope, taking care of your health, and finding time for yourself. *("We're so busy taking care of everybody else that I don't even have time to buy myself some clothes! Now I eat, and I'm addicted to food. That used to be the last thing on my mind.")*
How Can I Be a Better Parent to My Grandchildren	Learning new information on child development, developing parenting skills, managing behavioral problems, interacting with schools and teachers, helping your grandchild(ren) with school-related issues, and helping your grandchild(ren) with their friendships and social concerns. *("To be a good grandparent you have to listen to and understand your grandchild, but this is difficult because of the generation gap that exists. . . . You can't trust them like your mother trusted you.")*
What Does the Future Hold?	Who will assume care if you become sick or die, helping your son or daughter to become a parent again, and maintaining your energy and health for as long as possible. *("I fear what would happen to my grandchild if something happened to me. That's a major concern!")*

TABLE 6.4 Potential Topic Ratings in Percentages for Nonprofessional (n = 35) and Professional (n = 7) Grandparents

	Potential Topics									
	Deal With System		Family Issues		Taking Care of Self		Parenting Issues		The Future	
Rank	Nonprof	Prof	Nonprof	Prof	Nonprof	Prof	Nonprof	Prof	Nonprof	Prof
1	60.0	28.6	40.6	57.1	44.1	28.6	51.5	14.3	34.4	—
2	22.9	14.3	15.6	—	14.7	57.1	27.3	28.6	31.3	14.3
3	17.1	28.6	15.6	—	11.8	—	6.1	28.6	6.3	42.9
4	—	14.3	18.8	28.6	8.8	14.3	12.1	28.6	12.5	14.3
5	—	14.3	9.4	14.3	20.6	—	3.0	—	15.6	18.5

or to those of human service professionals in general? Do caregiving grandparents have substantially different goals for support groups than the professionals who may be sponsoring or conducting these groups?

Should Support Groups for Caregiving Grandparents Be Homogeneous or Heterogeneous in Their Composition?

Although the participants in the present study were not asked this question directly, the data shown in Table 6.5 were examined to shed initial light on this issue. This table contains the percentages of grandparents within various comparison groups who assigned ranks of either 1 or 2 to each of the five prospective areas for grandparent support groups. It was assumed that any striking differences between these comparison groups would suggest the need for heterogeneous support groups. Those grandparents who were human service professionals were dropped from these comparisons in view of the findings described above, which suggest they hold different views than the general population of caregiving grandparents.

On the whole, Table 6.5 reveals more evidence of similarity than differences between the various comparison groups. This trend is most obvious with respect to "Finding My Way Through the System," which received high rankings from over three fourths of the respondents in each of the comparison groupings. A very high percentage of respondents within each of the comparison groups similarly assigned high rankings to "How Can I Be a Better Parent to My Grandchildren?". These findings suggest that greater numbers of caregiving grandparents might be persuaded

TABLE 6.5 Grandparents' Preferences for Support Group Content by Comparison Groupings

	% Respondents Assigning Ranks of 1 or 2				
Comparison	System	Family	Self	Parenting	Future
Grandparent's Education					
College Graduate (n = 18)	88.9	70.6	64.7	77.8	83.3
< College Graduate (n = 17)	76.4	40.0	52.9	80.0	42.8
Grandchild Problems					
With problems (n = 20)	85.0	61.1	68.4	89.4	70.6
Without problems (n = 15)	80.0	50.0	46.7	64.3	60.0
Prior Support Group Attendance					
Yes (n = 20)	85.0	47.4	55.0	68.4	55.0
No (n = 15)	80.0	69.2	64.3	92.8	83.3
Grandparent's Age					
≤ 55 years (n = 16)	84.2	53.0	55.5	77.8	64.7
≥ 56 years (n = 19)	81.3	60.0	62.6	80.0	66.7
Grandchild's Age					
≥ 11 years (n = 15)	80.0	57.1	66.7	85.8	57.1
< 11 years (n = 20)	85.0	55.5	52.7	73.7	72.7
Time in Caregiver Role					
≤ 5 years (n = 18)	77.8	50.0	50.0	77.8	58.8
≥ 6 years (n = 16)	87.6	61.5	66.7	78.6	71.4

to join and remain in support groups if a focus on these two areas was emphasized in recruitment efforts and within support sessions. It also noteworthy that the three remaining content areas were ranked highly by at least half of the respondents in virtually all of the groupings included in Table 6.5. As one focus group participant remarked about the content areas included on the questionnaire, "These are all important issues. I'd come to a support group to work on any of them." Thus, there appear to be multiple goals that grandparents hope to achieve from belonging to support groups.

There was also modest evidence of some differences in preferences for support group content among the various groupings shown in Table 6.5. For example, substantially more respondents who had never attended a grandparent support group in the past assigned ranks of 1 and 2 to "What's My Place in the Family?," "How Can I Be a Better Parent to my Grandchildren?," and "What Does the Future Hold?" than their counterparts who had attended support groups. One possible explanation for these findings, as described below, is that grandparents' hopes for what may be accomplished in a support group may be lessened by their experience with these groups.

Grandparents' educational status is another differentiating characteristic with respect to preferences for support group content. Specifically, caregiving grandparents without a college education were more likely than college graduates to assign high ranks to "What's My Place in the Family?" and "What Does the Future Hold?." It may be that grandparents with less education have fewer resources available to them to deal with these issues on their own. For example, they are likely to have fewer financial means and problem-solving skills that are required to plan adequately for the future. In any event, these findings suggest that grandparents' educational status may be an important consideration in determining support group composition. In contrast, such variables as grandchild's problems, grandparent's age, grandchild's age, and time in the caregiver role were largely unrelated to the rankings assigned to the content areas on the questionnaire.

Discussions within the focus groups offered a somewhat more direct perspective on how to deal with heterogeneous or divergent goals among the members of a given support group. A consistent theme across the focus groups was that, although support group members have many shared issues to work on, issues also arise that may pertain to certain members only. The concept of a buddy system within support groups was widely mentioned in the focus groups as a way to address members' distinctive needs. The following discussion from one of the focus groups exemplifies this suggestion:

Participant: Support groups should include the opportunity to work on a more individual level among people with similar needs.

Facilitator: In another focus group someone used the term "buddy system." Does that capture what you're saying?

Participant: Yeah.

Facilitator: So, there would be a larger group and people with common goals might form a subgroup of two, three, or four people. Is that right?

In Background: Uh huh. (expressed by several participants)

Grandparents' Preferences for Support Group Leadership

Preferences for support group leadership were probed by the following item on the self-administered questionnaire: "Do you believe that support groups for grandparents raising grandchildren are most effective when they are led by (select one)

______ Professionals ______ Other Grandparents ______ Not Sure." Responses to this query by the seven grandparents who were also human service professionals were excluded from analyses, given their likely bias for professional leadership. It was found that the majority (52.9%) of the remaining 35 grandparents preferred peer leadership. Less than one quarter (23.5%) favored professional leadership, and another 11.8% said that they were not sure. Interestingly, 4 grandparents (11.8%) spontaneously jotted a preference for combined leadership, although this was not a choice on the questionnaire.

Responses to this query were also examined, as shown in Table 6.6, to see if leadership preferences were related to key characteristics of the respondents or their caregiving circumstances. Although there was a clear preference for peer leadership across the various comparison groups, this type of leadership was more favored among those grandparents who were less educated, caring for grandchildren without

TABLE 6.6 Grandparents' Preferences for Support Group Leadership by Comparison Groupings

	% Respondents Indicating Preference for Leadership Type			
Comparisons	Professional	Peer	Combined	Not Sure
Grandparent's Education				
< College Graduate (n = 18)	22.2	61.1	5.6	11.1
College Graduate (n = 16)	25.0	43.8	18.8	12.5
Grandchild Problems				
With Problems (n = 19)	26.3	47.4	10.5	15.8
Without Problems (n = 15)	20.0	60.0	13.3	6.7
Prior Support Group Attendance				
Yes (n = 20)	20.0	45.0	20.0	15.0
No (n = 14)	28.6	64.3	0.0	25.0
Grandparent's Age				
≤ 55 years (n = 19)	10.5	52.6	21.1	15.8
≥ 56 years (n = 16)	40.0	53.3	0.0	6.7
Grandchild's Age				
< 11 years (n = 20)	35.0	45.0	15.0	5.0
≤ 11 years (n = 14)	7.1	64.3	7.1	21.4
Time in Caregiver Role				
≤ 5 years (n = 18)	16.7	44.4	16.7	22.2
≥ 6 years (n = 16)	26.7	66.7	6.7	0.0

problems, had never attended a grandparent support group, were caring for older grandchildren, and had been caregivers for six or more years.

It must be noted, however, that a caveat regarding the strong preference for peer leadership found in the questionnaire data became evident during the focus group discussions where grandparents revealed that they were well aware of the advantages and disadvantages attached to both peer and professional leadership (Cohen & Pyle, 1999; Strom & Strom, 2000). Consequently, the consensus that emerged within the focus groups was that some form of combined leadership is best for grandparent support groups. For example, it was often mentioned that grandparents have a tendency to ramble, remain unfocused, and repeat the same feelings and stories in support groups that lack professional guidance. Witness the following discussion that occurred in one focus group when asked which type of leadership is best:

Participant 1: Grandparents like ourselves!

Participant 2: I think that's good, but it also needs somebody professional there.

Participant 3: Both!

Participant 1: Yes, but some people say to professionals "Who are you to tell me, you don't know!" Professionals have just read a book and have gone to school, but they don't know a damn thing.

Participant 3: In one group, we have a professional and I'm the peer facilitator and that seems to work pretty good. . . . Maybe the professional will pick out a subject for the day and they don't want to talk about it. But, I sort of have a feeling for what's going on with the whole group and I can bring out whatever they're feeling . . . In my other group, we just have a professional. I think we should have both.

In Background: Uh huh. (expressed by several participants)

Surprisingly, the focus group discussions also revealed that support groups for caregiving grandparents can be highly unstructured and lack goals even when they are professionally led. Moreover, there was a tendency for these grandparents to see themselves as so needy that they would tolerate poorly run groups. A startling example of this occurred in the focus group containing grandparents who were also human service professionals:

Participant 1: In looking at my own support group, I think that a focus on problem solving is a very important thing. Where we got bogged down was that each time we went, the leader had each of us tell our story, and by the time we each told our story again, it was time to go home (much laughter in background). I got really tired of it. It wasn't useful to me, and I was taking off from work to go to the meetings!

Participant 2: Did you have an idea before you went what the group was going to discuss? The idea just hit me that groups might be more attractive if grandparents were told in advance what would be covered. Of course, they could raise other issues too.

Participant 1: No, there was no agenda for any of the groups that I went to. I think it would be helpful to have them. But, at that point I was so grateful to have a support group that I would have gone for anything! Just to be able to talk to people who were in the same situation (laughter). . . . So, I found the things I needed somewhere else.

Participant 3: How big was your group?

Participant 1: Not large, about 5 or 6 people. But it changed each time, and then the leadership changed. So, it was a very unsettled group.

What Else Do Grandparents Want from Support Groups?

A key reason for including focus groups in the present study was to identify any additional aspects of support groups that were important to these caregiving grandparents that were not covered on the questionnaire. Two prominent themes that were absent on the questionnaire arose during the focus group discussions: (1) a desire to work on specific goals, and (2) a desire to involve grandchildren and other family members in support group activities.

Achievable Goals

Many statements were made throughout the focus groups revealing that grandparents valued support groups as an outlet to express the intense feelings they experience as a result of their caregiving circumstances: "You need to vent. You listen to the other grandparents talk about their problems and you say to yourself: 'Gee I thought I had it bad.' " "It's like a second family. Sometimes it's *really* your family. My own family doesn't have time to sit down and listen to what I'm going through, but a support group does."

Although these findings are consistent with clinical reports that what caregiving grandparents seem to want most from support groups is the chance to vent their frustrations (O'Reilly & Morrison, 1993; Vacha-Hasse et al., 2000), it is also evident, as noted earlier, that these groups frequently tolerate too much complaining beyond those beneficial levels that typically occur in the early stages of support groups and result in a sense of common emotionality (Strom & Strom, 2000; Szinovacz & Roberts, 1998). Caregiving grandparents typically believe that it is therapeutic to express disappointments and assume that the best listeners are peers who will not judge them (Strom & Strom, 1993). In turn, this belief may exacerbate a defensive posture that blunts internal processing of the events, resulting in their plight, and may make it difficult for caregiving grandparents to generate answers from within themselves (Brown-Standridge & Floyd, 2000).

According to Strom and Strom (1993), a remedy for this dilemma and a way to promote a sense of optimism within the support group is to ask participants to share their small victories, identify short-term goals, propose ways for overcoming obstacles, and become more cognizant of the good things in their lives. Consistent with this view, Robinson and Kensinger (1996) reported that the majority of caregiving grandparents in their study wanted support groups to be purposeful and not just an outlet to vent their frustrations. This same attitude toward support groups was repeatedly echoed by participants in the present study, as demonstrated by the following remark from one focus group participant: "I think support groups fall apart simply because nobody feels as though they've accomplished anything. If you want to come and just cheer each other up, that's one thing. But, if you really want to get something out of it, then you must set some goals and objectives."

Involving Grandchildren and Other Family Members

As noted earlier, the present study was part of a larger project in which the grandparents' views about support groups for the grandchildren in their care were also elicited (Smith, Savage-Stevens, & Fabian, in press). One specific question was whether grandchildren and grandparent support groups should be held simultaneously. This is an important issue because the lack of child care is a major barrier that prevents caregiving grandparents from attending their own support groups (Burnette, 1998; Cohen & Pyle, 1999; Minkler et al., 1993; Vacha-Haase et al., 2000), and simultaneously scheduled groups might alleviate this problem. The majority (69%) of the respondents preferred to have support groups for both themselves and their grandchildren held at the same time and place.

Unexpectedly, the desire to have occasional meetings or get togethers where both grandparents and grandchildren would be present together was also expressed in the focus groups. Said one grandparent, "I think the grandkids should be around the table, and we should just sound off. I think that would be splendid because they would at least have a chance to talk, and in a group you can pretty much say what you want to say and get a response back. Your grandchild might say something at the table that you didn't realize. I think this would be something great to be included in support groups."

Another grandmother added, "I like the idea of the grandchildren sitting around the table too . . . most times they would be separate. I also think that it should be very relaxed when the grandchildren are there. Almost as if it's not really a meeting, but a gathering such as a dance maybe. But, also make it talk."

A participant in the group containing grandparents who also were human services professionals said, "One other dimension for a support group might be to have the opportunity to bring grandchildren once in a while to observe the interaction between other grandparents and their grandchildren. Maybe they'd see someone who talked louder than their grandmother, or someone who was more demanding. Then, all of a sudden, you're the winner!"

The notion of occasionally involving other family members outside of the caregiving household in support groups was also brought up in the focus group discussions: "Another thing that support groups can be helpful with is when you care for a grandchild who has other brothers and sisters who are in different places. The group can help you work with other family members who have these children. So, you can bring them together as a group. I look at my grandson and realize that he doesn't even know his brothers. I don't want him to grow up not knowing who his brothers are! I think the support group could help with that by sometimes having the family members that do have the other children come in and sit with the support group and support one another."

CONCLUSION

The validity and generalizability of the findings from this modest exploratory study should be viewed with caution for several reasons. First, the sample of caregiving grandparents was small, self-selected, from one geographical area, and restricted to respondents who expressed positive attitudes toward support groups in a screening interview. Second, a small sample precluded the use of multivariate data analyses that are needed to rule out potentially confounded variables in group comparisons. Third, it should not be automatically assumed that grandparents' views of support groups are necessarily meaningful or appropriate from a clinical perspective. For example, the desire expressed by grandparents to have occasional joint sessions with grandchildren and other family members may be inappropriate when grandchildren are very young or have substantial emotional problems. Finally, this study should not be seen as comprehensive with respect to either the aspects of support groups that the grandparents were asked to contemplate or the particular group comparisons that were made regarding their views on support group content and leadership. Indeed, grandparents' views of support groups may be influenced by a host of factors that were not assessed in this study. Some possibilities include availability of informal support, other role demands, physical health, gender (of both grandparent and grandchild), race/ethnicity, and legal custody status.

Despite these limitations, this study provides insight into how caregiving grandparents view support groups as a way to help them cope with their caregiving responsibilities. Four general conclusions and recommendations for future research and practice emerge from the present findings:

First, although support groups for caregiving grandparents continue to grow in popularity, the quality and effectiveness of these groups in meeting the needs of this target population remain largely unknown. Regrettably, the findings of this study seem to corroborate the suspicions of some experts that these groups may even be harmful for some grandparents to the extent that they (1) can foster unproductive self-pity and complaining, (2) are loosely structured in the absence of skillful leaders, (3) place an overemphasis on self-help, and (4) lack clear objectives (Strom & Strom, 1993; Szinovacz & Roberts, 1998). In fact, there is recent evidence suggesting that participation in support groups may actually increase the overall level of stress and anxiety experienced by some caregiving grandparents (Sands & Goldberg-Glen, 2000). A clear objective for future research and practice is to develop viable interventions based on comprehensive theories that describe how and why they work, and then to evaluate these interventions through rigorous empirical studies.

A second conclusion arising from this study is that caregiving grandparents have diverse needs, not all of which can be properly addressed within the context of support groups. A surprising finding, for instance, was the number of grandparents who viewed support groups as an arena for working on such complicated family issues as uniting half siblings from different households. It was also evident within the focus groups that the level of anger and ambivalence expressed by some grandparents over their caregiving situation is so intense that these individuals would be poor candidates for support group membership. It thus appears that support groups may be best regarded as one component of a multimodal approach for working with grandparent-headed families that might also include individual counseling or therapy for grandparents, individual work with the grandchild, and conjoint family sessions (O'Reilly & Morrison, 1993). Other components of a multimodal approach for this target population might include respite, health care, and emergency assistance. As Szinovacz and Roberts (1998) have noted, there is also the danger that support groups reinforce an erroneous belief among caregiving grandparents that other forms of assistance are either unavailable or inappropriate.

Third, the potential content areas that grandparents were asked to rank order in the present study were diverse and reflect a blend of peer support, information, stress reduction, and the learning of new coping and parenting skills. The fact that all of the content areas were highly ranked by at least some grandparents suggests that support groups involving a psychoeducational format may best meet the multiple needs of caregiving grandparents. In other words, it is clear that some grandparents want more from these groups than just the opportunity to vent their feelings and be around supportive others. An exemplary support group approach was described by Burnette (1998), for example, who combined elements of the Lazarus stress and coping model with a psychoeducational format to provide information, cognitive problem solving skills, and emotional support to caregiving grandparents.

Another model psychoeducational approach for use with grandparents raising grandchildren was recently reported by Vacha-Haase et al. (2000). Their intervention protocol consisted of eight weekly group sessions that covered topics such as parenting skills, personal well-being, relationships, financial management, and legal issues. Consistent with the need for structure and clear objectives noted earlier in this chapter, group leaders used a guide that provided background information for each topic, suggestions for lectures and activities, references for further reading, instructional guidance for each unit, and the expected outcomes for the grandparents who attended. A corresponding participant's notebook for the group members that included background information, exercises, and assignments, was also used.

Finally, the apparent reluctance of many caregiving grandparents to become involved with support groups and similar interventions may be countered by informing prospective participants that they will have a sense of ownership in both the development and implementation of the program (Emick & Hayslip, 1999; Smith, 1999). The present findings reinforce earlier observations by other researchers that participants in grandparent support groups feel that peers can understand them better than anyone else (Strom & Strom, 1993). They may also be reluctant to ask for help from professionals for fear of being judged as abusive to their grandchildren or outdated with respect to their child rearing practices (Strom & Strom, 2000). At the same time, however, grandparents revealed in the focus groups an awareness that they lacked the skills needed to keep a group focused and the resources required to run a group effectively (Monahan, 1994). Coled groups may be an ideal way to resolve this dilemma, and offer caregiving grandparents a sense of empowerment. Support groups with co-leadership depend on the professional for information, resources, and meeting arrangements and on the grandparent leader for mutual support and understanding. Coleadership provides a balance, helps the group leaders cope with member issues and crises, and may reduce the risk that grandparent-headed families are stigmatized as being a problem or deficit family structure (Cohen & Pyle, 1999; Landry-Meyer, 1999).

It is promising that support groups for caregiving grandparents have grown so dramatically in number and popularity. However, much work lies ahead for practitioners and researchers to evaluate the goals, structure, and outcomes of these groups from the perspective of both caregiving grandparents and the professionals who serve them.

REFERENCES

Bowers, B. F., & Myers, B. J. (1999). Grandmothers providing care for grandchildren: Consequences of various levels of caregiving. *Family Relations, 48,* 303–311.

Brown-Strandridge, M. D., & Floyd, C. W. (2000). Healing bittersweet legacies: Revisiting contextual family therapy for grandparents raising grandchildren in crisis. *Journal of Marriage and Family Counseling, 26,* 186–197.

Bryson, K., & Casper, L. M. (1999, May). Coresident grandparents and grandchildren: U.S. Bureau of the Census, Population Division Working Paper No. 26. Washington, DC: U.S. Bureau of the Census.

Burnette, D. (1998). Grandparents rearing grandchildren: A school-based small group intervention. *Research on Social Work Practice, 8,* 10–27.

Carey, M. A. (1994). The group effect in focus groups: Planning, implementing, and interpreting focus group research. In J. M. Morse (Ed.), *Critical issues in qualitative research methods* (pp. 225–241). Thousand Oaks, CA: Sage.

Cohen, C. S., & Pyle, R. (1999). Support groups in the lives of grandmothers raising grandchildren. In C. B. Cox (Ed.), *To grandmother's house we go and stay: Perspectives on custodial grandparents* (pp. 235–252). New York: Springer.

Cox, C. B. (Ed.). (1999). *To grandmother's house we go and stay: Perspectives on custodial grandparents.* New York: Springer.

Emick, M. A., & Hayslip, B. (1999). Custodial grandparenting: Stresses, coping skills, and relationships with grandchildren. *International Journal of Aging and Human Development, 48,* 35–61.

Fuller-Thomson, E., & Minkler, M. (2000). America's grandparent caregivers: Who are they? In B. Hayslip & R. Goldberg-Glen (Eds.), *Grandparents raising grandchildren: Theoretical, empirical and clinical perspectives* (pp. 3–21). New York: Springer.

Fuller-Thomson, E., Minkler, M., & Driver, D. (1997). A profile of grandparents raising grandchildren in the United States. *The Gerontologist, 37,* 406–411.

Hayslip, B., Silverthorn, R., Shore, J., & Henderson, C. (2000). Determinants of custodial grandparents' perceptions of problem behavior in their grandchildren. In B. Hayslip & R. Goldberg-Glen (Eds.), *Grandparents raising grandchildren: Theoretical, empirical and clinical perspectives* (pp. 255–268). New York: Springer.

Jendrek, M. D. (1993). Grandparents who parent their grandchildren: Effects on lifestyle. *Journal of Marriage and the Family, 55,* 609–621.

Knodel, J. (1993). The design and analysis of focus group studies: A practical approach. In D. L. Morgan (Ed.), *Successful focus groups: Advancing the state of the art* (pp. 35–50). Newbury Park, CA: Sage.

Landry-Meyer, L. (1999). Research into action: Recommended intervention strategies for grandparent caregivers. *Family Relations, 48,* 381–389.

Langus, L. J., Roosa, M. W., Schupak-Neuberg, E., Michaels, M. L., Berg, C. N., & Weschler, L. F. (1992). Using focus groups to guide the development of a parenting program for difficult-to-reach, high-risk families. *Family Relations, 41,* 163–168.

Minkler, M. (1999). Intergenerational households headed by grandparents: Contexts, realities, and implications for policy. *Journal for Aging Studies, 13,* 199–218.

Minkler, M., Driver, D., Roe, K. M., & Bedeian, K. (1993). Community interventions to support grandparent caregivers. *The Gerontologist, 33,* 807–811.

Monahan, D. J. (1994). Caregiver support groups: Efficacy issues for educators. *Educational Gerontology, 20,* 699–714.

Morgan, D. L., & Krueger, R. A. (1993). When to use focus groups and why. In D. L. Morgan (Ed.), *Successful focus groups: Advancing the state of the art.* Newbury Park, CA: Sage.

Morrow-Kondos, D., Weber, J. A., Cooper, K., & Hesser, J. L. (1997). Becoming parents again: Grandparents raising grandchildren. *Journal of Gerontological Social Work, 28,* 35–46.

O'Reilly, E. O., & Morrison, M. L. (1993). Grandparent-headed families: New therapeutic challenges. *Child Psychiatry and Human Development, 23,* 147–161.

Pinson-Millburn, N. M., Fabian, E. S., Schlossberg, N. K., & Pyle, M. (1996). Grandparents raising grandchildren. *Journal of Counseling and Development, 74,* 548–554.

Robinson, M., & Kensinger, J. L. (1996). *Final report with African American and Hispanic grandparents about issues related to caring for their grandchildren.* Washington, DC: American Association of Retired Persons.

Roe, K. M. (1999). Community interventions to support grandparent caregivers: Lessons learned from the field. In C. B. Cox (Ed.), *To grandmother's house we go and stay: Perspectives on custodial grandparents* (pp. 283–303). New York: Springer.

Roe, K., Minkler, M., & Saunders, F. (1995). Combining research, advocacy, and education: The methods of the grandparent caregiver study. *Health Education Quarterly, 21,* 458–475.

Rose, S. R. (1998). *Group work with children and adolescents: Prevention and intervention in school and community systems.* Thousand Oaks, CA: Sage.

Sands, R. G., & Goldberg-Glen, R. S. (2000). Factors associated with stress among grandparents raising their grandchildren. *Family Relations, 49,* 97–105.

Smith, G. C. (1999). Prevention and promotion models of intervention for strengthening aging families. In M. Duffy (Ed.), *Handbook of counseling and psychotherapy with older adults* (pp. 178–194). New York: Wiley.

Smith, G. C., Savage-Stevens, S., & Fabian, E. (in press). How caregiving grandparents view support groups for the grandchildren in their care. *Family Relations.*

Strom, R. D., & Strom, S. K. (1993). Grandparents raising grandchildren: Goals and support groups. *Educational Gerontology, 19,* 705–715.

Strom, R. D., & Strom, S. K. (2000). Goals for grandparents and support groups. In B. Hayslip & R. Goldberg-Glen (Eds.), *Grandparents raising grandchildren: Theoretical, empirical and clinical perspectives* (pp. 289–303). New York: Springer.

Szinovacz, M. E., & Roberts, A. (1998). Programs for grandparents. In M. E. Szinovacz (Ed.), *Handbook on grandparenthood* (pp. 171–201). Westport, CT: Greenwood.

Vacha-Haase, T., Ness, C. M., Dannison, L., & Smith, A. (2000). Grandparents raising grandchildren: A psychoeducational group approach. *Journal for Specialists in Group Work, 25,* 67–78.

Vardi, D. J., & Bucholz, E. S. (1994). Group psychotherapy with inner-city grandmothers raising their grandchildren. *International Journal of Group Psychotherapy, 44,* 101–122.

Zeller, R. A. (1993). Focus group research on sensitive topics. In D. L. Morgan (Ed.), *Successful focus groups: Advancing the state of the art* (pp. 167–183). Newbury Park, CA: Sage.

CHAPTER 7

Grandparent Caregivers to Children With Developmental Disabilities: Added Challenges

Jennifer M. Kinney, Kathryn B. McGrew, and Ian M. Nelson

Despite increased attention to grandparents raising grandchildren, researchers have not been particularly sensitive to custodial grandparents of "special population" grandchildren (e.g., racial/ethnic groups, secondary caregivers, grandparents raising grandchildren with AIDS) (Goldberg-Glen & Hayslip, 2000). Recent profiles of grandparent caregivers do not present data on custodial grandparents to grandchildren with mental retardation and other developmental disabilities (MR/DD) (e.g., Fuller-Thomson, Minkler, & Driver, 1997), and when published accounts do refer to special needs grandchildren, this category often simultaneously subsumes those from large sibling and/or minority groups, those with emotional and/or behavior problems, and those with MR/DD (Kolomer, 2000). Emick and Hayslip (1996) point to the need to document the prevalence, burden, and needs of custodial grandparents to grandchildren with medical, behavioral, and emotional problems; we recommend the addition of grandchildren with MR/DD to their list. As we become increasingly aware of custodial grandparents to grandchildren with MR/DD, we believe it is imperative that the formal service delivery system be prepared not only to respond to, but also to take the lead in helping to meet the complex needs of these families.

In this chapter, we focus specifically on one category of special needs grandchildren being raised by grandparents: grandchildren with MR/DD. Force, Botsford, Pisano, and Holbert (2000) identify three reasons this group warrants special consideration. First, because of medical advances that have resulted in decreased mortality rates at early ages among individuals with MR/DD, these individuals are living far longer, with a corresponding increase in the length of time during which they will need care. Second, despite the increase in community-based services that have accompanied the deinstitutionalization of individuals with MR/DD, these services have not been particularly attentive to the needs of grandparents. Third, substance abuse and neglect, both of which contribute to custodial grandparenthood, also place grandchildren at increased risk for MR/DD. Echoing this theme of the need for increased attention to this caregiving arrangement, McCallion, Janicki, Grant-Griffin, and Kolomer (2000) maintain that many of the concerns experienced by grandparent caregivers are exacerbated for custodial grandparents of grandchildren with MR/DD. The legal status concerns faced by all grandparents are greater for those whose grandchildren will require care and support throughout their lifetime; children with MR/DD typically have difficulty accessing services; and there are greater numbers of children with MR/DD in minority or mixed-racial households, which typically are underserved by the formal service delivery system.

We begin this chapter by defining developmental disability and mental retardation. Next, we summarize what is known about this special population of grandparents and grandchildren. Then we discuss life planning as an important responsibility for grandparent caregivers to grandchildren with MR/DD. Drawing from published accounts and our own work in this area, we briefly explore some of the dynamics of the life planning process. Finally, we conclude with implications and recommendations for practitioners and policy makers.

WHAT IS A DEVELOPMENTAL DISABILITY?

The Developmental Disabilities Assistance and Bill of Rights Act of 1994 (Public Law 103-230), a federal statute, defines a developmental disability as

> a severe chronic disability of an individual 5 years of age or older that: a) is attributable to a mental or physical impairment or combination of mental and physical impairments; b) is manifested before the individual attains age 22; c) is likely to continue indefinitely; d) results in substantial functional limitations in three or more of the following areas of major life activity: self care, receptive and expressive language, learning, mobility, self-direction, capacity for independent living, and economic self-sufficiency; and e) reflects

> the individual's need for a combination and sequence of special, interdisciplinary, or generic services, supports, or other assistance that are lifelong or extended duration and are individually planned and coordinated, except that such term, when applied to infants and young children means individuals from birth to age 5, inclusive, who have substantial delay or specific congenital or acquired conditions with a high probability of resulting in developmental disabilities if services are not provided. [Section 103(8)]

State law often elaborates upon federal law; for example, the Ohio Revised Code (Section 5126.01) identifies specific examples of developmental disabilities including "autism, cerebral palsy, Down Syndrome, epilepsy, postpolio syndrome, spina bifida, mental retardation, and neurological impairments."

GRANDPARENTS RAISING GRANDCHILDREN WITH MR/DD: WHAT DO WE KNOW?

In general, research on custodial grandparents of grandchildren with MR/DD has focused on the role of grandparents in supporting their adult children/children-in-law who actually serve as primary caregivers for the child (e.g., Findler, 2000; Heller, Hsieh, & Rowitz, 2000; Hornby & Ashworth, 1994; Mirfin-Veitch, Bray, & Watson, 1997; Schilmoeller & Baranowski, 1998). With relatively few exceptions (e.g., Hastings, 1997; Janicki, McCallion, Grant-Griffin, & Kolomer, 2000; McCallion et al., 2000), far less attention has been dedicated to grandparents who are primary caregivers to these grandchildren.

Historically, grandparents have served as a "safety net" for grandchildren with MR/DD whose parents could not provide care (Janicki et al., 2000). Janicki et al. report that relatively little is known about this population of custodial grandparents, with the exception that it includes an overrepresentation of minority and/or mixed racial and inner-city dwelling families. These grandparents feel especially vulnerable because many of them believe that the MR/DD experienced by their grandchildren can be attributed to risk factors they were exposed to while in the care of their parents (Kolomer, 2000). Seligman (1991) has shown that grandparents of grandchildren with physical, emotional, and/or neurological disabilities often express bewilderment, guilt, and fear related to interacting with them.

The number and/or proportion of grandparent caregivers to grandchildren with MR/DD is not well documented. In an effort to gain a generalized view of the incidence of special needs grandchildren residing in kinship households in a high-risk, low-income community, Grant (2000) found that 60.4% of the households surveyed had no special needs grandchildren; 29.7% had one grandchild with special needs, 5.5% had two grandchildren with special needs, and 4.4% had three grandchildren with special needs. Grant's classification of grandchildren as having special needs includes more than just those with MR/DD; also, Grant's description of the distribution of grandchildren with special needs is likely not representative of custodial grandparents of grandchildren with special needs. Nonetheless, Grant's data highlight two important issues: there are some grandparents residing in high-risk, low-income communities who are raising more than one grandchild; and there is a proportion of these grandparents who are raising more than one grandchild with special needs.

It has been documented in the literature on grandparenthood that the challenges of raising grandchildren are even greater when these children have behavioral problems (Hayslip, Shore, Henderson, & Lambert, 1998). The level of disability, physical health, and functional abilities of adult children with MR/DD impacts the well-being of their older family caregivers (Greenberg, Seltzer, & Greenley, 1993). Burnette (2000) suggests that these characteristics, in addition to a child's age and gender, are likely predictors of stress among grandparents caring for young grandchildren with MR/DD. McCallion et al. (2000) report that custodial grandparents of grandchildren with MR/DD experience greater stress than their peers whose grandchildren do not have MR/DD. Additional research documents increased depressive symptomatology (Janicki et al., 2000) and social isolation (Kolomer, 2000) among grandparent caregivers to grandchildren with MR/DD. Although Force et al. (2000) found no difference between grandparents caring for grandchildren with MR/DD and those caring for grandchildren without MR/DD with respect to caregiving mastery or depressive symptomatology, they did find that grandparents to grandchildren with MR/DD had greater needs for services in areas such as transportation and help with school, and used more benefits such as food stamps and child care.

Accessing and navigating the formal service network presents a number of challenges for grandparent caregivers, in part because the formal service delivery system is neither particularly sensitive to, nor equipped to meet the unique needs of grandparents who care for grandchildren (Grant, 2000; Janicki et al., 2000; McCallion et al., 2000). For example, Janicki et al. (2000) found that, in part, grandparents had difficulty accessing the formal service delivery system because of issues surrounding guardianship of the grandchild. In a separate sample, guardianship was also identified as one of five problem areas in caregiving reported by 800 grandparent caregivers who telephoned the New York City Department of Aging's Grandparent Resource Center during the first nine months that it was in operation (McCallion et al., 2000). Three fourths of these grandparents (75%) were caring for a grandchild with a developmental disability/delay. Other problem areas identified by grandparent caregivers included financial issues, respite, emotional support, and navigating the formal service delivery system.

In telephone interviews with nine caregivers (seven grandparents, two "grand-aunts") about the experience of being a kinship foster caregiver to grandchildren diagnosed with MR/DD, Kolomer (2000) found that the caregivers had difficulty accessing psychological and counseling services for their grandchildren. In addition, caregivers, most of whom cared for more than one grandchild, reported that services and interventions were especially lacking for the grandchildren who had been diagnosed with MR/DD. Kolomer's findings are consistent with those reported by Burnette (2000) for custodial grandparents to grandchildren with diverse special needs.

Even when grandparents are able to access the formal service system, they worry that providers will think them incompetent and unable to raise their grandchildren (Janicki et al., 2000; McCallion et al., 2000). Janicki et al. and colleagues surmise that this fear results in grandparents overestimating their health status, a finding consistent with the experience of grandparents who were raising their nonspecial needs grandchildren (Jendrek, 1994). Several studies add to this general theme, reporting that grandparent caregivers are potentially at risk for physical, and well as emotional and social distress. For example, Fuller-Thomson and Minkler (2000) claim that grandparent caregivers tend to delay seeking medical attention, Grant (2000) offers that grandparent caregivers to grandchildren with MR/DD often place the children's needs before their own, and Shore and Hayslip (1994) report that custodial grandparents who have the poorest health and greatest problems in caregiving are the least likely to seek professional care.

LIFE PLANNING IN THE CONTEXT OF CARING FOR A RELATIVE WITH MR/DD

Caring for an individual with MR/DD presents a number of unique challenges. One particular challenge faced by aging caregivers is the dual strain of the caregiver's own aging and the possibility that the individual with the developmental disability very well might outlive his or her caregiver (Heller & Factor, 1991; Janicki et al., 2000; McGrew & Murray, 2000). This is a relatively new occurrence; it is only since the 1960s that the average life expectancy for an individual with MR/DD such as Down Syndrome has increased from approximately 30 to approximately 56 years (Braddock, 1998). As a result, older adult caregivers, typically parents, must plan for the time, either because of increasing physical frailty, illness, or death, when they are no longer able to meet the needs and desires of an (aging) individual with MR/DD.

These issues are compounded for older grandparents who are caring for grandchildren. Increasing attention is being given to the need for planning to prepare for these future challenges. Within the aging network, such planning is often described by the terms "care planning" and "long-term care planning"; in the MR/DD network, "permanency planning," "futures planning," and "life planning" are terms used to describe planning for the future life of an adult with MR/DD. In this chapter, we use the term "life planning" because of its inclusiveness.

Life planning includes legal, financial, and residential planning, as well as making arrangements to meet the medical, social, and cultural needs of the individual with MR/DD. Life planning increases the probability that the individual with MR/DD will have continuity of care beyond current caregiving arrangements. Life planning is not a static set of decisions, and a life plan is not a legal document. Rather, life planning is a fluid process, and the components of a life plan should be reviewed on a regular basis to assure that the plan is as responsive as possible to the needs and desires of the individual with MR/DD (Morris, n.d.). Although the primary purpose of a life plan is to prepare for the time when a particular caregiver is no longer able to fulfill his or her responsibilities, the information contained in a life plan can also be useful in the event of a temporary emergency situation (Morris).

Many families have not planned for the eventuality that their current caregiving arrangement cannot be maintained (e.g., Pruchno & Patrick, 1999; Smith, Fullmer, & Tobin, 1994; Wood, 1993). Additional research indicates that many older caregivers put off planning, neglect to plan, or begin the planning process but give up in frustration (Carswell & Hartig, 1979; Gold, Dobrof, & Torian, 1987; Turnbull, Brotherson, & Summers, 1985). Heller and Factor (1991) explored residential and financial life planning among 100 family caregivers to an older adult with mental retardation. Almost one in three caregivers (31%) had not had any discussions about what would happen should he or she no longer be able to provide care; another 26% reported that they were "in the discussion stage" of the planning process. However, approximately three fifths (63%) of these caregivers had made some kind of financial arrangement for their relative with mental retardation. Of those who had made financial plans, almost half (48%) had made the sometimes ill-informed decision to will money to other relatives to be used to support the individual with mental retardation, 21% had willed money directly to the individual with mental retardation, and the remaining 31% had established a trust for the individual with mental retardation.

It is imperative that family caregivers to an individual with MR/DD and the professionals who work with them understand that not all plans are equally good. For example, money willed to one adult child for the provision of care to an adult child with MR/DD might not be used for the intended purpose. Willing financial assets or property to an individual with MR/DD can disqualify that individual for Medicaid, SSI, and other benefits. It is not enough to establish a generic trust for an individual with MR/DD; there is state-by-state variation in types of trusts and what these trusts can accomplish. As such, it is important that professionals who work with custodial grandparents of grandchildren with MR/DD have the resources necessary to assist to the extent possible, and then make appropriate referrals to attorneys and financial planners who specialize in life planning for individuals with MR/DD.

Although families were more likely to have undertaken financial than residential planning, Heller and Factor's (1991) findings suggest that custodial family caregivers had done relatively little life planning. It is not clear whether these families had engaged in planning efforts in the other aspects of life planning. It also appears that these families had unmet needs in areas directly related to life planning.

Grandparents' difficulty in accessing services, coupled with the finding that many caregivers have not made plans for the future care for their relative with MR/DD, suggests that a more integrated service delivery system is needed, especially for the long-term needs of grandparent caregivers. Indeed, older adults typically do not plan for their own futures (High, 1993; Kulys & Tobin, 1980; McGrew, 2000). Despite the fact that planning is essential in order to avoid making decisions in the midst of a crisis, most older adults have not undertaken life planning in the areas of finances, health care, and living arrangements (Heller & Factor, 1991; McGrew, 2000). Grandparent caregivers especially need to plan for multiple "possible futures" related to themselves and their grandchildren.

OHIO'S DOUBLE JEOPARDY PROJECT AS A "CASE STUDY"

A number of efforts are currently underway to facilitate life planning by older families caring for baby boom generation adult children who have MR/DD. For example, a recent policy brief by the National Center for Family Support@HSRI (2000) describes specific programs designed to provide information on, and encourage the process of, life planning in British Columbia, Massachusetts, and Rhode Island.

Initiated in August, 1999, Ohio's Double Jeopardy project had as its goal the support of families in their efforts to plan for secure futures for family members with MR/DD and for their aging caregivers. "Double jeopardy" refers to the fact that older family members who care for a relative with MR/DD are at risk for needing both aging and MR/DD services (McGrew & Murray, 2000). The Double Jeopardy demonstration project was funded by the U.S. Department of Health and Human Services' Administration on MR/DD, and was a partnership among the Ohio Department of Aging, the Ohio Department of Mental Retardation and MR/DD, and the Ohio MR/DD Council. Three planning and service areas (PSAs) across the state served as demonstration sites for the project. Among the objectives of the project were to increase the knowledge about, and actual life planning behavior among, older family members who were caring for adult children with MR/DD; and to improve the coordination of services between the aging and MR/DD networks at both the state and local levels, as well as with other networks and organizations.

The Double Jeopardy project consisted of four distinct components: (1) training about life planning for family members, (2) training about life planning for professionals from both the aging and MR/DD networks, (3) cross-training of professionals from the aging and MR/DD networks about the populations that are served and how the networks operate, and (4) training for attorneys and financial planners about life planning. The kickoff to the project was a statewide, two-day training designed to prepare professionals from the aging and MR/DD service networks to serve as trainers for future Double Jeopardy training. Across the three PSAs that served as demonstration sites, nine 2–4-hour training sessions were held for family members, six 3–5-hour training sessions were held for professionals from the aging and MR/DD networks, and three 4-hour training sessions were held for attorneys and financial planners.

Presented below are pre- and posttraining data on participants' (both family members' and professionals') knowledge about, and self-evaluation of their abilities regarding life planning. In addition, four-month follow-up data on family members' life planning behaviors since the training sessions, and changes in professionals' involvement in assisting their clients with life planning activities are also presented. Results of the evaluation of the two other components of the Double Jeopardy project are presented in Kinney and McGrew (2001).

Summary of Findings From the Family Training

Across the state, 130 family members completed the Double Jeopardy training. Evaluation data were collected at approximately one-half of the trainings. Across all training sessions for family members, the average response rate for the pretraining/posttraining evaluation was 82.0%; the four-month follow-up response rate was 22.4% ($N = 29$).

The average age of participants was 58.93 years ($SD = 13.72$; range = 33–84). Approximately two fifths (40.4%) of the participants had graduated from high school; an additional 21.3% had completed some college; and 34.0% had graduate from college. Less than 5% of participants (4.3%) had not completed high school. Almost three fourths (70.2%) of participants were married.

Approximately three fourths (76.2%) of the participants had a child with MR/DD, and 11.9% had a sibling with MR/DD; approximately 5% had one or more grandchildren with MR/DD. The average age of the family member with MR/DD was 36.4 years (SD = 9.4; range = 17–57). Of the individuals with MR/DD whose family member(s) attended the training, slightly less than three fourths (69.2%) resided with the participant(s) who attended the training, 10.3% resided in group housing (with supervision), and 12.8% lived independently in the community. Almost one half (46.9%) of the family members with MR/DD received formal services, but nine tenths (90%) of participants had not attended any life planning training prior to the Double Jeopardy training session, and slightly more than one half (52.6%) had not engaged in any life planning for their family member with MR/DD.

As part of the pretest evaluation, participants were asked to identify concerns they brought with them to the training. Very few family participants identified concerns for specific information. The posttest responses differed in that family participants left the sessions with specific questions (e.g., "What are legal obligations after child's age 21?"). They also indicated that they were motivated to specific action (e.g., "Have a life planning check list," "Have a Family Survival Kit," "Write down a daily routine," "Get important documents into one place," "Find a competent attorney for the trust").

Evaluation after the training sessions showed that family members had a significantly better understanding of the basics of life planning for their relative with MR/DD than before ($p < .001$), and were, in fact, significant more knowledgeable about life planning ($p < .001$). However, following the training, family members did not feel any more comfortable about the process of life planning for their family member with MR/DD.

With respect to the evaluation completed four months after the training, 95.7% of family members who returned the follow-up survey indicated that they would recommend life planning training to other families who had a relative with MR/DD. More important, as part of the four-month follow-up, family members were asked whether they had actually engaged in each of 27 life planning activities (e.g., reviewed an existing life plan, expanded or changed a Circle of Support, established a Durable Power of Attorney for Health Care). Of the 29 family members who completed the four-month follow-up survey, all but one had engaged in at least one new life planning activity since attending the training; the average number of life planning activities undertaken since attending the training was 6.92 ($SD = 4.59$; range = 0–18). The percentage of family members who had engaged in each of the life planning activities is presented in Table 7.1.

Specifically, since attending a family training, seven in ten participants (70.8%) had talked with other family members about life planning, slightly more than one half (54.2%) had started the life planning process, and one half had talked with an MR/DD professional about life planning. In addition, 41.7% of participants had talked with their family member with MR/DD about life planning, the same percentage of participants had decided that they needed to appoint a guardian for their relative with MR/DD, and approximately one third of participants had spoken with an attorney (37.5%) or financial planner (33.3%) about the life planning process.

Family members who responded to an open-ended question on the follow-up survey overwhelmingly reported that their "biggest hurdles" in life planning are

TABLE 7.1 Percentage of Participants Who Had Engaged in Life Planning Activities in the Four Months Following the Double Jeopardy Family Training

Life Planning Activity	Percentage of Participants Who Had Engaged in the Activity
Talked with family members about life planning	70.8
Started the life planning process	54.2
Talked with an MR/DD professional about life planning	50.0
Decided whether a guardian was needed	41.7
Talked with the family member with a disability about life planning	41.7
Revised a life plan that had already been started	25.0
Talked with an attorney about life planning	37.5
Talked with a financial planner about life planning	33.3
Made arrangements for meeting the relative's future housing needs	29.2
Reviewed a life plan that had already been started	29.2
Wrote a Letter of Intent	29.2
Made arrangements for meeting the relative's future medical needs	25.0
Made arrangements for meeting the relative's future social needs	20.8
Made a will	20.8
Changed a will	20.8
Set up a Durable Power of Attorney for Health Care	20.8
Appointed a guardian	16.7
Expanded or changed a Circle of Support	16.7
Talked with an aging social service professional about life planning	12.5
Set up a Circle of Support	12.5
Set up a trust	12.5
Changed a trust	12.5
Started a Family Survival Kit	12.5
Attended additional life planning training	12.5
Changed a Letter of Intent	8.3
Changed or completed a Family Survival Kit	4.5
Chose three people who would be guardians or advocates	20.8

family decision issues. Apparently, family members left training with some sense of direction but encountered resistance or apathy from others. Specifically, family respondents mentioned a number of issues that superseded other concerns:

> "Choosing person(s) as trustee, advocate"
> "Dynamics of family"

"Getting my husband to understand how important it is to do this. Getting him to face up to what's needed as he won't look into anything"
"A father who does not fully recognize the needs of the one with special needs and to do what is best for that individual"
"Cooperation from other family members"
"Deciding how we want things set up"

Other issues identified in the training posttests, such as need for particular information or a list of qualified professionals, will not be relevant until consensus about planning objectives is reached among family members.

Summary of Findings from the Professional Training

Across the state, 302 professional staff completed the Double Jeopardy training. The average response rate for the pretraining/posttraining evaluation was 90.4%; unfortunately, the four-month follow-up response rate was only 13.9%. Results from the pretest evaluation tool indicated that almost three fifths (57.1%) of participants were employed in the MR/DD services network; the remainder were employed in the aging services network. Participants from the aging services network averaged 11.4 years of employment (*SD* = 7.5, range = 1–40 years); participants from the MR/DD services network averaged 13.4 years of employment (*SD* = 2.12, range = less than 1 year–35 years).

Prior to the training, almost three fourths of all professional participants (71.8%) had received some aging-specific training, and 65.2% had received MR/DD-specific training. Almost one fourth of participants (22.3%) had a family member or other person close to them who had mental retardation or another developmental disability. In the six months prior to the training, 23.8% of participants had provided life planning services for an older person with MR/DD and/or their family members. Of the professional participants who had assisted with life planning during this time, their average number of clients was 7.1.

As part of the pretest evaluation, participants were asked to bring questions or concerns to the training sessions. There was wide variability in issues raised by the professionals. Many came to the training sessions with a need for information and skills (e.g., "I know nothing! Teach me!") and with concerns about the service system. These included concerns about:

the status of less privileged families ("What can families do that have no assets?")
families unknown to the system ("How do we find hidden cases?")
staffing resources ("How can we get a life planner in our county?")

service resources ("How can we overcome local roadblocks to more accessible, available congregate housing?")

Professionals also came to the training concerned about ethical issues (e.g., "parents who want their child to have guardians to make themselves feel better, but this takes independence away from the individual"; "ethical issues regarding using public funds to support a person whose parents have money to pay for the support"), as well as skills that they need to communicate with families and motivate them to plan (e.g., "how to establish a rapport with principal families"; "how to help families who do not trust anyone else with their adult child's care"; "how to convince parents to take action early on"; "direction to take in approach to parents to encourage financial planning").

Upon completion of the training, professionals still identified the need for additional information and skills, ethical concerns, and service system problems as issues that remained. In addition, professionals commented liberally about the effect of training on their personal sense of confidence, motivation, and direction. Several suggested a need for ongoing training. Results of the pretraining/posttraining evaluation indicated that professionals had a better understanding of the basics of life planning ($p < .001$), objectively demonstrated more general knowledge about life planning ($p < .001$) and showed increased knowledge about legal/financial aspects of life planning ($p < .001$). In addition, professionals felt significantly more prepared than before training to assist families with life planning ($p < .001$).

With respect to the four-month follow-up evaluation, professionals reported that they were not seeing significantly more clients with MR/DD-related issues than they were prior to the training, although they continued to indicate that the Double Jeopardy training had enhanced several aspects of their work with families with MR/DD. Specifically, 52.7% of the professionals who returned the follow-up survey indicated that they had an increased ability to identify life planning needs in families in their case load, and 30.2% of the professionals indicated that they were better able to provide life planning advocacy for families in their caseload.

Approximately one half of the professional staff wrote responses to two open-ended questions in the follow-up survey. They were asked "to identify three major areas of information or skills that would improve your ability to serve families," and "to identify other information that we should be aware of." In general, the responses identified a variety of needs such as "grant money," "community resources books," "forms," and "pamphlets/handouts on services for the elderly." Several respondents also mentioned the need for a list of contact persons and planning experts. However, the overarching theme of most written responses was the need for conditions that foster planning work in everyday practice (e.g. "the need for trust," "how to have the older generation accept your help/information without bruising their egos," "more communication with MR/DD staff," "lack of residential options," and "more options available for our clients"). Finally, several respondents declared a need for a designated Life Planner in their service area.

CONCLUSIONS AND IMPLICATIONS

Taken together, the results from the Double Jeopardy family and professional training reveal that even a brief (i.e., two hour) training program can lead to increased understanding of, and knowledge about, life planning for both family members and professionals. However, although professionals felt more prepared to assist families with life planning after the training, this was not the case for family members. They did not feel any more comfortable about the process of life planning. These findings have several implications. First, providing families with knowledge is necessary, but not sufficient. Knowledge about life planning must be supplemented with advice about how to negotiate decisions among family members/the informal network, as well as how to navigate the formal service system to accomplish the various goals for the individual with MR/DD.

Second, by its very nature, life planning is a complex process that involves a multitude of individual decisions that must be made and actions that must be taken. As such, each individual life planning activity that is undertaken is important. Data from the Double Jeopardy project show that, despite the complexity of the process, caregivers did engage in a number of life planning activities in the four months following the Double Jeopardy training. Such life planning activities need to be acknowledged and encouraged.

Just as other aspects of caregiving are exacerbated among custodial grandparents for grandchildren with MR/DD, such is most likely the case with life planning. Life planning is a process that is ongoing and rarely completed. Recommendations to review life plans annually (Morris, n.d.) may be especially important for grandparent caregivers, as they and the grandchildren for whom they care all undergo physical, psychological, and emotional health changes. Also, relationships between custodial grandparents, their own adult children, and the grandchildren for whom they care can and do change.

Because of the difficulties associated with life planning and its ongoing nature, the role of professionals in the process is especially important. Professionals from the aging and MR/DD networks who attended the Double Jeopardy training also had questions about information and skills, the service delivery system, and ethics. In fact, professionals came to the training with more questions than did family members and, despite gains in knowledge about life planning and their ability to work with clients on life planning, a number of these questions remained unanswered at the completion of the training and in the months following. These findings underscore the need for ongoing training for professionals about life planning.

In the absence of a coordinated service delivery system, the needs of custodial grandparents, particularly those who care for grandchildren with MR/DD, are at risk for being overlooked (McCallion et al., 2000). As such, cooperation among multiple components of the formal service delivery system—the aging, MR/DD and mental health networks—have the potential to make services available that are optimally responsive to these caregivers' unique needs (Hayslip, Silverthorn, Shore, & Henderson, 2000). It has been suggested that state agencies on aging might be targeted to take the lead in this initiative (Janicki, McCallion, Force, Bishop, & LePore, 1998), as was the case with the Double Jeopardy project. Regardless of who assumes the lead role in these efforts, collaboration, coordination, and cooperation among components of the formal service delivery system are essential to the success of any such undertaking.

It is important to acknowledge that the findings from the Double Jeopardy project might represent the "best possible" scenario, in that they derive from family members and professionals who were sufficiently interested, concerned, and motivated to attend a training on life planning and to participate in an evaluation, including a four-month follow up survey. Nonetheless, both family caregivers and professional participants identified continuing barriers to life planning. Overcoming these barriers will require the active participation of the formal service delivery network.

In light of claims that professionals in the aging and MR/DD networks are often unprepared to help families with an MR/DD relation (McCallion & Tobin, 1995; Sutton, Sterns, Schwartz, & Roberts, 1992), and that services offered by the aging and MR/DD networks are not well coordinated (McCallion et al., 2000), it is critical that researchers and practitioners alike respond to pleas for programs that are specifically designed to help custodial grandparents who are raising grandchildren (Chenoweth, 2000), and continue to conduct research that explores the special needs of custodial grandparents of grandchildren with MR/DD (Kolomer, 2000). The need for life planning among these caregivers affords an excellent point of departure for collaboration between academic researchers and policymakers.

REFERENCES

Braddock, D. (1998, September 18). Testimony before the Senate Select Committee on Aging, Committee on Aging Forum. *Can we rest in peace? The anxiety of elderly parents caring for baby boomers with disabilities.*

Burnette, D. (2000). Latino grandparents rearing grandchildren with special needs: Effects on depressive symptomatology. *Journal of Gerontological Social Work, 33,* 1–16.

Carswell, A. T., & Hartig, S. A. (1979). *Older developmentally disabled persons: An investigation of needs and social services.* Athens: University of Georgia, Georgia Retardation Center, Athens Unit.

Chenoweth, L. (2000). Grandparent education. In B. Hayslip, Jr. & R. Goldberg-Glen (Eds.), *Grandparents raising grandchildren: Theoretical, empirical, and clinical perspectives* (pp. 307–326). New York: Springer.

Emick, M. A., & Hayslip, B., Jr. (1996). Custodial grandparenting: New roles for middle-aged and older adults. *International Journal of Aging and Human Development, 43,* 135–154.

Findler, L. S. (2000). The role of grandparents in the social support system of mothers of children with a physical disability. *Families in Society, 81,* 370–381.

Force, L. T., Botsford, A., Pisano, P. A., & Holbert, A. (2000). Grandparents raising children with and without a developmental disability: Preliminary comparisons. *Journal of Gerontological Social Work, 33,* 5–21.

Fuller-Thomson, E., & Minkler, M. (2000). America's grandparent caregivers: Who are they? In B. Hayslip, Jr. & R. Goldberg-Glen (Eds.), *Grandparents raising grandchildren: Theoretical, empirical, and clinical perspectives* (pp. 3–21). New York: Springer.

Fuller-Thomson, E., Minkler, M., & Driver, D. (1997). A profile of grandparents raising grandchildren in the United States. *The Gerontologist, 37,* 406–411.

Gold, M., Dobrof, R., & Torian, L. (1987). *Parents of the adult developmentally disabled.* New York: Brookdale Center on Aging.

Goldberg-Glen, R. S., & Hayslip, B., Jr. (2000). Epilogue. In B. Hayslip, Jr. & R. Goldberg-Glen (Eds.), *Grandparents raising grandchildren: Theoretical, empirical, and clinical perspectives* (pp. 383–395). New York: Springer.

Grant, R. (2000). The special needs of children in kinship care. *Journal of Gerontological Social Work, 33,* 17–33.

Greenberg, J. S., Seltzer, M. M., & Greenley, J. R. (1993). Aging parents of adults with disabilities: The gratifications and frustrations of later-life caregiving. *The Gerontologist, 33,* 542–550.

Hastings, R. (1997). Grandparents of children with disabilities: A review. *International Journal of Disability, Development, and Education, 44,* 329–340.

Hayslip, B., Jr., Shore, R. J., & Henderson, C. E. (2000). Perceptions of grandparents' influence in the lives of their grandchildren. In B. Hayslip, Jr. & R. Goldberg-Glen (Eds.), *Grandparents raising grandchildren: Theoretical, empirical, and clinical perspectives* (pp. 35–46). New York: Springer.

Hayslip, B., Jr., Shore, R. J., Henderson, C. E., & Lambert, P. L. (1998). Custodial grandparenting and the impact of grandchildren with problems on role satisfaction and role meaning. *Journals of Gerontology, 53B,* S164–S173.

Hayslip, B., Jr., Silverthorn, P., Shore, R. J., & Henderson, C. E. (2000). Determinants of custodial grandparents' perceptions of problem behavior in their grandchildren. In B. Hayslip, Jr. & R. Goldberg-Glen (Eds.), *Grandparents raising grandchildren: Theoretical, empirical, and clinical perspectives* (pp. 255–268). New York: Springer.

Heller, T., & Factor, A. (1991). Permanency planning for adults with mental retardation living with family caregivers. *American Journal of Mental Retardation, 96,* 163–176.

Heller, T., Hsieh, K., & Rowitz, L. (2000). Grandparents as supports to mothers of persons with intellectual disability. *Journal of Gerontological Social Work, 33,* 23–34.

High, D. (1993). Why are elderly people not using advanced directives? *Journal of Aging and Health, 5,* 497–515.

Hornby, G., & Ashworth, T. (1994). Grandparents' support for families who have children with disabilities. *Journal of Child and Family Studies, 3,* 403–412.

Janicki, M. P., McCallion, P., Force, L. T., Bishop, K., & LePore, P. (1998). Area agency on aging outreach and assistance for households with older carers of an adult with a developmental disability. *Journal of Aging and Social Policy, 10,* 13–36.

Janicki, M. P., McCallion, P., Grant-Griffin, L., & Kolomer, S. R. (2000). Grandparent caregivers I: Characteristics of the grandparents and the children with disabilities for whom they care. *Journal of Gerontological Social Work, 33,* 35–55.

Jendrek, M. P. (1994). Grandparents who parent their grandchildren: Circumstances and decisions. *The Gerontologist, 34,* 206–216.

Kinney, J. M., & McGrew, K. B. (2001, May). *Evaluation of the Ohio Double Jeopardy Demonstration Project.* Oxford, OH: Scripps Gerontology Center.

Kolomer, S. R. (2000). Kinship foster care and its impact on grandmother caregivers. *Journal of Gerontological Social Work, 33,* 85–102.

Kulys, R., & Tobin, S. (1980). Interpreting the lack of future concerns among the elderly. *International Journal of Aging and Human Development, 11,* 111–126.

McCallion, P., Janicki, M. P., Grant-Griffin, L., & Kolomer, S. (2000). Grandparent caregivers II: Service needs and service provision issues. *Journal of Gerontological Social Work, 33,* 57–84.

McCallion, P., & Tobin, S. S. (1995). Social workers' perceptions of older parents caring at home for sons and daughters with developmental disabilities. *Mental Retardation, 33,* 153–162.

McGrew, K. B. (2000, April). *Impossible selves? Challenges and strategies for encouraging individual long-term care planning.* Oxford, OH: Ohio Long-Term Care Research Project, Scripps Gerontology Center.

McGrew, K. B., & Murray, A. (2000, February). *Life planning for older individuals with developmental disabilities: Lessons from a pioneer program.* Oxford, OH: Ohio Long-Term Care Research Project, Scripps Gerontology Center.

Mirfin-Veitch, B., Bray, A., & Watson, M. (1997). "We're just that sort of family": Intergenerational relationships in families including children with disabilities. *Family Relations: Interdisciplinary Journal of Applied Family Studies, 46,* 305–311. Allen Press/National Council on Family Relations.

Morris, K. (n.d.). *Life planning.* Hamilton, OH: Butler County Board of Mental Retardation and Developmental Disabilities.

National Center for Family Support@HSRI. (2000, Winter). *Family support policy brief #3: Aging family caregivers: Needs and policy concerns.* Salem, OR: Author.

Pruchno, R. A., & Patrick, J. H. (1999). Future worry about living arrangements among mothers of adults with developmental disabilities. *American Journal on Mental Retardation, 104,* 487–499.

Schilmoeller, G. L., & Baranowski, M. D. (1998). Intergenerational support in families with disabilities: Grandparents' perspectives. *Families in Society, 79,* 465–476.

Seligman, M. (1991). Grandparents of disabled children: Hopes, fears, and adaptation. *Families in Society, 72,* 147–152.

Shore, R. J., & Hayslip, B., Jr. (1994). Custodial grandparenting: Implications for children's development. In A. Gottfried & A. Gottfried (Eds.), *Redefining families: Implications for children's development* (pp. 171–218). New York: Plenum.

Smith, G. C., Fullmer, E. M., & Tobin, S. S. (1994). Living outside the system: An exploration of older families who do not use day programs. In M. M. Seltzer, M. W. Krauss, & M. P. Janicki (Eds.), *Lifecourse perspectives on adulthood and old age* (pp. 17–38). Washington, DC: American Association on Mental Retardation.

Sutton, E., Sterns, H. L., Schwartz, L., & Roberts, R. (1992). The training of a specialist in developmental disabilities and aging. *Generations, 16,* 71–74.

Turnbull, A. P., Brotherson, M. J., & Summers, J. A. (1985). The impact of deinstitutionalization on families: A family systems approach. In R. H. Bruininks & K. C. Lakin (Eds.), *Living and learning in the least restrictive environment* (pp. 115–140). Baltimore: Brookes.

Wood, J. B. (1993). Planning for the transfer of care: Social and psychological issues. In K. A. Roberto (Ed.), *The elderly caregiver: Caring for adults with developmental disabilities* (pp. 95–107). Newbury Park, CA: Sage.

CHAPTER 8

Why Support Groups Help: Successful Interventions for Grandparent Caregivers of Children With Developmental Disabilities

Stacey R. Kolomer, Philip McCallion, and Jenny Overeynder

INTRODUCTION

There have been longstanding recommendations from both the practice and research communities to utilize support groups to assist grandparents with the stresses and strains of caregiving for their grandchildren. This chapter reports on the components of an educational support group supported by an active case management strategy used successfully with grandparent caregivers of children with developmental disabilities. After six support group sessions, compared to control subjects, symptoms of depression were significantly reduced and grandparent carers' self-appraisal of empowerment and mastery over their caregiving situation significantly increased (see McCallion, Janicki, Grant-Griffin, & Kolomer, 2000). The grandparents involved were primarily female, African-American and drawn from inner city neighborhoods in New York City.

BACKGROUND

The success of the intervention offers a unique opportunity to examine the content of the support group sessions and to determine what were the issues for grandparent caregivers that were addressed and to determine if improvements can be made to the components of the intervention. Qualitative analysis of the transcripts of support group meetings and of leader interviews are used to describe emergent themes on needs for assistance, to examine effects of support group attendance, and to identify content areas that should be addressed for future groups.

In 1997, the Joseph P. Kennedy, Jr. Foundation, the University of Albany, the New York City Department for the Aging, the Bureau of Aging and Special Populations, and the Multi-Cultural Professional Development Institute of the New York State Office of Mental Retardation and Developmental Disabilities requested applications from community-based multicultural agencies in the New York City area to conduct a year-long demonstration project for grandparent caregivers of children with developmental disabilities. The funding initiative was designed to respond to the well-documented higher risk among grandparents for experiencing physical deterioration, emotional problems, and financial strain (Kelley, Yorker, & Whiteley, 1997; Minkler & Roe, 1993; Woodsworth, 1996) and builds upon the effectiveness being reported for grandparent support groups. It was also designed to address the additional stress of caring for a grandchild with a disability (Janicki, McCallion, Grant-Griffin, & Kolomer, 2000). Given that the most common reasons for placement of a child with a grandparent are substance abuse and child abuse and neglect, it should not be surprising that many children in these families have emotional difficulties and disabilities. In addressing these needs many grandparent caregivers report trying to access assistance from service agencies both with crises and for day-to-day care for their grandchildren. Despite their being eligible for many services, lack of coordination between agencies causes grandparent-headed families to be denied needed services and to fall through the cracks (McCallion et al., 2000). Case management and other support services appeared to be necessary and were important supplementary components of the support group intervention in this study.

Three community-based local service agencies serving two boroughs of New York City were selected to participate in the collaborative project hereafter referred to as the Grandparent Assistance Project. Representatives of these agencies were asked to locate grandparents living in their catchment areas who were caring for at least one child with a developmental delay or disability. The agencies used a variety of outreach methods, including posting notices at churches, libraries, hairdressing salons, convenience stores and bodegas, health centers, and human service agencies. They also employed word of mouth recruitment through local churches, cultural community organizations, and participant grandparents. A total of 101 grandparent families were recruited to participate. Four moved out of the area before completing the intervention, leaving 97 participants. The following brief vignettes describe typical families and the physical, emotional, social and legal difficulties they face.

Mrs. N. is a 77-year-old grandmother who raised her emotionally disturbed granddaughter and is now raising that granddaughter's three children, one of whom has been classified by the school district with multiple disabilities. Mrs. N. has never pursued establishing legal guardianship or benefits for her great-grandchildren. Her health is compromised by arthritis and several knee surgeries. Mrs. N. feels trapped because she lives in a second-floor apartment, waiting for a more accessible apartment to become available. However, she's not sure that she can afford what a new apartment would cost, and she is afraid that her landlord will evict her if he finds out that she is looking for alternative accommodations.

"They" took Mrs. G.'s grandson away from her daughter in the middle of the night and dropped him off with Mrs. G. All he had was the clothing he was wearing. It was an abuse case. The child protective worker made her all kinds of promises about the help she would receive. Mrs. G. says that she didn't see any of that help. When she wouldn't agree to help terminate her daughter's parental rights and become a kinship foster care provider, but wanted to keep her grandson, they told her she was on her own. "Don't they understand how hard it is to take a child away from your own daughter, to take away her hope . . . ?"

INTERVENTION

The intervention created for the grandparent families caring for children with a developmental disability or delay consisted of two parts: intensive case management and support/educational groups. This chapter focuses on the outcomes of the support groups. However, a description of the intensive case management provided to the families is presented.

The agencies were required to provide case management related to the problems raised by the participating grandparents. Each agency designated a staff person responsible for case management and counseling. Case managers assisted grandparents with such tasks as accessing emergency funds for heat, food, rent, and telephone services; adaption of the home environment; applications for more suitable housing; enrollment in summer camps for children with special needs; advocacy within the grandchildren's school system, Medicaid office, and hospitals; obtaining comprehensive assessment and diagnosis for the grandchildren; negotiating services through disability and foster care service agencies; and completion of documents for guardianship.

For the support/education group component of the intervention, each agency was required to identify an individual to lead its groups. Groups of 8–10 grandparents were offered a minimum of six support group meetings (mostly held every two weeks). To facilitate attendance, agencies offered in-home or on-site respite for the grandchildren and assistance with transportation. Group leaders were trained using the project's support group training manual (McCallion, Janicki, Grant-Griffin, & Kolomer, 2000), the contents of which were developed in response to the recommendations of focus groups of grandparents and grandparent advocates. The manual also made extensive use of existing grandparent support materials (see for example, Grandparent Resource Center, 1998a, 1998b; Samuel Sadin Institute on Law, 1997a, 1997b, 1998). Leaders were also encouraged to use supplemental resources that would be appropriate for their participating families. Topics not only included items the grandparents chose that addressed their grandchildren's needs, but also those that would help the grandparents take care of themselves (including stress reduction, relaxation, nutrition, and taking care of one's own health needs). Table 8.1 provides brief descriptions of the components of the support group intervention.

The premise for the support group intervention contents was the recognition that grandparent caregiving needs varied widely, the children being cared for were of all ages, and disability-related needs required educational as well as support components for the group. Support group leaders were encouraged to work with each group of 8–10 grandparents to identify the six sections of the manual they would be most interested in having presented in their sessions.

SAMPLE

Ninety-seven grandparents caring for at least one child with a developmental disability or delay participated in the education/support groups. The majority of grandparent carers were female (94%) with an average age of 60 (*s.d.* = 10 years; range: 40–82). Some 79% were African-American, 36% had an available spouse, 25% were educated beyond high school, and 31% were also holding a job. Most of the grandparents were low users of any formal services (such as case management, assistance with housing issues, and support groups), using on average only one of these services. However, perceived need for services was high; grandparents reported needing at least five additional different formal services. They cared for at least one grandchild for an average of seven years. Most grandparents were caring for one or two grandchildren, but some were caring for as many as seven. One hundred and seventy-

TABLE 8.1 Components of the Education/Support Group Intervention

Leader Checklist	This section provided useful information generalizable to any support group on establishing confidentiality among participants, checking availability of the room, making transportation and respite available, providing snacks and drinks for breaks, making arrangements for speakers or guests, reviewing information that would be discussed and following up on any previous meeting topics, and checking in with families between support group meetings, especially if a family is experiencing a crisis.
Running a Group	This segment provided additional helpful tips for the group leader; how the room should look, encouragement of grandparent leadership within the group, how to engage group members, and how to deal with the eventual ending of the group.
Developmental Delays and Disabilities	This section of the manual facilitated discussions with grandparents about developmental disabilities and delays. Simple definitions, incidence, causes, characteristics, educational implications, organizations, and resources were available on approximately 15 developmental delays and disabilities. Leaders were directed on how to access additional resources on disabilities or delays that were not included in the manual.
Caring for a Child With a Developmental Disability	This area's focus was on making the home environment safe for a child with a delay or disability: for example, posting emergency numbers so they are readily available during a crisis situation, having a first aid kit that is easily accessible, use of smoke detectors throughout the home, a plan for evacuation should an emergency occur within the home, suggestions for evacuation drills, especially when caring for a child whose disability compromises the ability to get out of a home independently, storage of medicine, prevention of falls, maintenance of bright light, use of night lights, checking of food and bath water temperature, and kitchen safety. Specific information on positioning, lifting, feeding, and toileting children with disabilities was also provided.
Skills for Helping Your Grandchild	Information in this section gave direction about helping a child with a developmental disability or delay to communicate using adaptive devices or basic sign language, and reinforcing skills the child learned in school in the home environment through modeling and repetition.
Problem Behaviors	Information in this section provided assistance on how to cope with problem behaviors in children with a developmental disability. Suggestions included use of praise for positive behavior and tips for disciplining a child with a developmental disability.

(continued)

TABLE 8.1 *(continued)*

Education	This section of the manual provided practical, thorough information for grandparents on dealing with their grandchildren's school system. Suggestions included how to stay connected with the grandchild's teacher, where to find help when trying to understand the school system, what information the school must provide to a family, family rights within the school system, what the labels schools create for children with difficulties mean, available alternatives to special education and how to access those alternatives.
Medical Issues	This area of the manual provided direction on ensuring that both the grandparents and the children in their care are able to access good health care. Detailed information included consent issues, locating medical care that participates in health plans, how to handle particular medical crises, and clear and specific advice on how to speak with a health care professional so that the information is understood and valuable to the consumer.
Custody and Guardianship Issues	Understanding the legal relationship of what it means to be a physical custodian versus a legal custodian is a key but often misunderstood concept for grandparent caregivers. This section of the manual directed group leaders on explaining the different laws and legal aspects of being a caregiver, and the benefits and disadvantages of being a physical custodian, legal custodian, legal guardian, kinship care provider, or informal caregiver.
Negotiating Systems	This section was a guide to empowering grandparent caregivers to become their own best advocates. Understanding systems and how to negotiate them successfully was the primary goal of this section. Suggestions for being organized, being prepared, being on time, taking notes, remembering names, and being persistent were discussed.
My Grandchild's Parent	The goal of this section was to get grandparent caregivers to discuss their relationship with the biological parent of the grandchild, and their concerns about maintaining a relationship with the parent. This section also empowered grandparents to take control of the situation and problem solve with one another to find solutions to problems in dealing with the parent of the grandchild.
Tips for Raising Siblings of Children With Developmental Delays or Disabilities	Suggestions were offered for helping the child without a disability successfully grow up despite the challenges of having a sibling with a disability.

TABLE 8.1 *(continued)*

Teen Years	This section discussed differences in raising a teenage child versus a teenage grandchild. Discussion included the life changes occurring in a teenager and recommendations for counseling a grandchild on serious issues such as dating, using the telephone, friends, peer pressure, sex, sexuality, and substance abuse. Specific suggestions were provided on how to help a grandchild who is coping with all the challenges of caring for a teenager who also has a developmental delay or disability.
Taking Care of Self	This section of the manual directed the group leader to devote support group time on the needs of the grandparents themselves. Important issues highlighted included exercise, good nutrition, information about health problems, stress reduction, and relaxation techniques. Grandparents were provided with relaxation audio tapes and their use was demonstrated and encouraged.

one children were being cared for by the 97 grandparent caregivers. Fifty-seven percent of the children were boys, with an average age of 11 years (*s.d.* = 4.9; range: 2–25). Five children were over 21 and represented long-term caregiving by grandparents. Although many grandparents reported that they had legal responsibility for their grandchildren (75%), actual legal status included legal adoption (12%), kinship foster care (8%), ongoing court involvement in establishing status (56%), and informal care (24%). Multiple problems or disabilities were identified for 55% of the children, intellectual and other developmental disabilities were noted for 73%, and learning problems and attention deficit and hyperactivity disorders were a diagnosis for 55% and 32% respectively. More complete information on the grandparents and children are reported elsewhere (see McCallion et al., 2000).

METHOD

The researchers used a case study design examining a variety of sources to better understand the process that occurred during the support group (Creswell, 1998; Denzin & Lincoln, 1994). Data collected consisted of focus groups of grandparent caregivers prior to the intervention, interviews with grandparent caregivers soliciting responses to project-specific questions and standardized questionnaires, pre- and postintervention interviews with agency and support group leaders, audio taping and transcribing of support groups, and in-person observations of the interventions. The benefit of this type of case study is that the examination of multiple sources of data enables the researcher to gain additional insight into a particular issue or theory (Denzin & Lincoln).

Participants at one of the three agencies gave permission for all sessions to be taped. Audiotapes for those sessions were transcribed by an individual independent of the project and checked against the tapes by the principal investigator (PI). Also, transcripts were examined of in-depth interviews conducted by the investigators with the support group leaders. As the researchers were personally in attendance (with participant permission) at several of the support group meetings, some of those observations were also incorporated into the final analysis. The PI and a co-investigator each independently examined the audiotape transcripts and the group leader interview transcripts for themes and selected quotations that exemplified those themes. There was largely agreement on those themes and then consensus was reached easily. The following themes emerged.

GRANDPARENT THEMES

Lack of Informal Supports

Much of the first meeting of the support group consisted of grandparents stating that they lacked informal supports. One great-aunt stated: "I'm here for the group, because I haven't had any support and this is very good for me. I hope to gain a lot from the group."

Often the group members searched for answers for one another:

Mrs. H.: Well, are those relatives that you have, is there anyone who can take them (the grandchildren) for at least half the day . . . ?

Mrs. W.: Well, my sisters work, one works at the hospital for 16 hours a day, and the other works 16 hours a day too. My mother just died last year, my father has been dead for a while. I'm not an outgoing person, I don't have a lot of friends, so, that's my life. So, I just deal with it. I used to rush, rush, rush, everything had to be done, but now I just say, Oh, didn't I do this today? Well, I'll write it on a piece of paper, maybe I didn't do this today, but maybe I'll have time for it tomorrow. . . .

Many of the grandparent caregivers were taking care of the grandchild(ren) alone and other family members were not available or were unwilling to help. As a result, many of the feelings expressed by the grandparent caregivers included frustration, fear, isolation, sadness, loss, anger, and being overwhelmed.

The Biological Parent

Despite the physical absence of the biological parents from the grandparents' home, they continued to affect the family unit. Many of the grandparents became caregivers because of their own child's substance abuse. Often this caused tension between the grandparent and the grandchild's parent. "He is a sick person. He needs a lot of help. He's not able to take care of her. They keep him back and forth from the hospital. There's a lot of animosity between him and myself about the child, coming from him. He gives us both a hard time" (grandparent referring to grandchild's father).

Even more problematic for the grandparents was the impact of the parent's behaviors on the grandchild's well being. "Part of the problem is my son. I'm telling her one thing to do. He tells her the opposite. She doesn't know how to differentiate between speaking to him and speaking to me."

Parents making promises to the children that they were unable to keep was a common experience of the grandparents. These promises often forced the grandparent to feel like the "bad guy," having to be honest with the child about the parent's unreliability or make excuses for the parent.

Another grandmother discussed a situation where her daughter made the decision to no longer see her own child. The grandmother reported that her granddaughter was very hurt. "She (her granddaughter) walked away and then when I went and walked over, Amanda was crying. She said, 'Just get away from me, nobody wants me. You care about me, but my mother just doesn't.' And she's an affectionate child. Now if I want to touch her, she goes 'leave me alone.' "

Many of the grandparents expressed their concerns about how to discuss the parent's behaviors with the grandchild. Often they were overwhelmed by the prospect of explaining what happened to the parent and finding the right language to open the discussion. They appeared to have a strong inclination to want to help their grandchildren with the pain and loss they are feeling but didn't know how to approach it. One grandmother described what she thought was happening to her grandchildren: "In my case, when I got custody of my grandsons, they came to me from their mother and father's house. Now, the mother and father found both of their own mates. And I feel this has affected them, (the grandchildren) but, you know, they're just not coming out with it. Probably they don't have the words to express it. Now we're in therapy with the 8-year-old. . . . "

Another grandmother expressed how her 11-year-old grandson was depressed because his mother signed over legal papers giving guardianship of him to her yet kept two of her other children. "He asks me 'What, grandma, what did I do?' He doesn't want to live with her, he just wants to get to know her. They want their mother, they really do. How do you tell a child that their mother rejects them . . . ?

The grandparents often expressed their frustration at having to maintain a delicate balance of their feelings when it came to the grandchild's parent. Frequently the grandparents said that they were angry with the child's parent for passing on the responsibility of raising the child to them, yet they had a strong inclination to hide the anger from the grandchild for fear the grandchild would feel even further rejection. At times maintaining that balance was a struggle for the caregivers, as stated by one grandmother of her grandson: "I try not to talk 'bad' about her to him. When I take him out, he acts up, and I tell him, don't give me a hard time, because I'm the only one left. . . . "

Need for a Male Role Model

Grandparents, particularly grandmothers raising grandsons alone, voiced concerns about the lack of a male role model in the lives of the children. Often there is no opportunity to encounter older adult males whom the grandparents perceive as positive role models for their grandchildren. One grandparent described how she felt about her grandson missing his father. "It was a sadness that I had in my heart. His dad has never been an active part of his life. But I need a male role model for him, because my father passed away. It gets to the point that the mechanic who fixes my car met him for the first time. He (her grandson) said 'I like Patrick (the mechanic). Can Patrick be my daddy?' "

Another grandmother expressed her fear that she did not know how to teach her grandson how to be a man. Several of the grandmothers recognized that there were agencies and programs that addressed this concern but they were fearful of having their grandchild experience even more disappointment. Some had already tried connecting their grandchildren to positive male role models and were disheartened by the outcome. "I had a male pastor who called for awhile but then it stopped. I don't want to go through that again."

Problems With Grandchild's School

As many of the grandparents have not had to deal with schools for some years, getting involved with the school system provided many challenges for them. Because these were caregivers of children with special needs, many of the described obstacles revolved around special education issues and lack of knowledge about the system. Grandparents also reported difficulties and frustrations in negotiating for services within a school. When a service was provided it would be for that year only and the process of advocating for the service had to be started up the following year. "Needs don't end in June . . . why do we have to start over?"

Grandparents said they got mixed messages about how they were to proceed in the schools, who could advocate for them, and how they could ensure that their grandchild's needs were being met. "My grandchild was supposed to take speech therapy and OT last year. They never gave it to her. They told me I should have a prescription from the physician. I got all that and I presented it to them. She (the superintendent) tried to push me off. So I made an appointment with her today. And even in taking things in, she told me that it's up to the Board of Education. If they decide whether he needs OT or speech therapy. . . . "

Another issue that continued to plague caregivers in the sessions was who was the expert on their grandchild's condition. Physicians and schools often had differing opinions on how to treat a child, which caused doubt and mistrust for the caregivers.

Need for Services and Resources

Despite the set agenda for the weekly support groups, conversation often turned to grandparent needs for resources and services. The most common service requested was affordable, quality housing. New York City housing tends to be very expensive, and affordable housing for individuals with limited income tends to be in neighborhoods that are perceived to be unsafe or where there are wait lists for the affordable units. An example of the critical housing shortage is the great-aunt who became a caregiver when her niece unexpectedly died leaving a child. The child, a 9-year-old girl with severe cerebral palsy, was confined to a wheelchair and used a device to communicate. The family was living in a fourth floor walk-up and the great-aunt struggled every day to bring the girl and her wheelchair down the stairs so that the girl could attend school.

GROUP LEADER THEMES

A number of themes also emerged from the interviews with the support group leaders.

Flexibility in Location, Supports, and Timing

Locations included agency offices, schools, a local community center with a playground for the children and, for one set of summertime group meetings, the outdoor patio of a local laundromat. Providing respite and transportation was found to enable grandparents to attend who would not have done so otherwise. Scheduling meetings to suit the grandparents' schedules (including renegotiating the day and time of each meeting to accommodate school and medical appointment schedules), making telephone calls reminding grandparents of the meetings and the transportation arrangements, providing snacks, and social time at the meetings all helped to encourage good attendance. The leaders reported 90% of participants attended all sessions.

All of the agencies originally intended to hold evening or weekend meetings. However, most found that daytime meetings worked better because the children were usually in school and grandparents were more open to doing something for themselves during this time. However, one agency did offer an evening group to accommodate grandparents who also worked. This agency provided on-site respite, as the grandparents in this group usually preferred to bring their grandchildren with them.

Open Discussion

Leaders commented on the openness of the discussions, including grandparents' willingness to discuss controversial topics like the use of corporal punishment. Many participants treated the groups as a safe place to talk about their concerns. It was also a place where leaders felt grandparents received support from their peers, and where they acknowledged feeling less alone in their caregiving when among others with the same experience. In addition, many of the grandparents offered specific advice and suggestions to their peers. Indeed, from their participation in the project, several grandparents were trained as peer volunteers who then accompanied other grandparents to reapply for benefits for which they were initially denied. One grandparent reconnected with her own training as a counselor and became the co-leader of a support group.

Every Group Is Different

The needs of groups varied and leaders appreciated having a manual that permitted choosing sessions that reflected the interests of a particular group of grandparents. For example, one group made extensive use of the materials on caring for teens. Others did not use this section because the grandparents in the group were all caring for very young children. Leaders also brought in additional material, for example, an educational piece on budgeting, to respond to specific needs raised by grandparents.

Children Are Harder Than Grandchildren

"I raised her to be church-going and hard-working, not to do drugs, not to hurt her baby." Problems with their own children, the grandchild's parents, were reported to be the most intractable. Group leaders reported that often the meeting was the only place where grandparents felt free to talk about the hurt they felt about their sons or daughters no longer being able to care for their own children. Reappearances of that son or daughter were often disruptive to caregiving for the grandchild and were brought up. In the meetings, grandparents discussed their reluctance to utilize legal remedies, whereas others (usually informal grandparent caregivers) pointed out they did not have such remedies available.

Grandchildren Are Harder Than Children

"Schools are different now. . . . I'm older, I can't run as fast and do as many things. . . . What's this hair thing? She gets real upset when I just brush it and send her to school. . . . Yeah there's a PTA but I don't see other people with grey hair there. . . . " These are some of the concerns group leaders remembered grandparents bringing up about the challenges of raising grandchildren that were different from their first experience of parenting. They also noted fears about being able to keep up, the teenage years, and worries about the potential consequences of their own health needs, something they acknowledged they did not think about the first time around as parents.

DISCUSSION

It should first be acknowledged that these were a resilient group of grandparent caregivers who, despite pressing caregiving and personal health concerns, were enthusiastic about pursuing their responsibilities to their grandchildren and who offered assistance to each other as much as they sought assistance from the group. All of the families had pressing needs for services; many discussed stresses and strains from caregiving, reporting that coming to the sessions was difficult. The themes that emerged from the support group leader interviews support these conclusions. Discussion did, at times, turn to concrete service needs, despite the particular support session agenda. Flexibility in choice of agenda, location, and timing of meetings were critical to good attendance, and offering transportation and respite services made the difference for many participants in being able to attend. Often, resources available to underwrite support groups are limited and there are reports of low attendance for different types of support groups in the community. This intervention study illustrates that the provision of transportation and respite, choice among session topics, and the flexible scheduling of sessions will not only lead to steady attendance, but will also attract and retain the most needy caregivers.

The pressing need for services found among these grandparents does raise the question of the appropriateness of offering support group services without service connection and other case management functions. For many of the caregivers, needs for new housing, additional services for their grandchild, and health interventions (grandchild and grandparent) were at times life and health threatening. In one case, a family with many complex service needs and an unresolved immigration status simply disappeared before appropriate services were found. Support group providers for this population should at least be connected with other providers of services if they are not able to provide those services themselves. Finally, as was found here, grandparents themselves are often able and interested in being peer supports, and the mutual exchange of "caregiving and service access wisdom" should be encouraged during sessions.

The most troubling finding was the enormous toll reported for both grandparents and grandchildren resulting from negative interactions and fears associated with the biological parent. In the support group manual, one session was dedicated to these issues and all groups in the project utilized this session. However, the issues raised often influenced discussions in other sessions and for many participants remained unresolved, albeit a little less burdensome, by the end of the sessions. More attention should be paid to these issues during support group interventions. Some grandparents may benefit from individual counseling; grandchildren should also be targeted for assistance, and some families may benefit from interventions that include all involved generations.

Finally, this project was also unusual in that it utilized local community-based multicultural agencies to deliver the intervention to a largely African-American and Latino group of grandparent caregivers. More has been written elsewhere on how this was achieved and the benefits of this approach (see McCallion et al., 2000). However, the value cannot be overstated of using agencies and staff invested in the community they are serving. It proved critical in locating families who, because of their informal caregiving, immigration, or other status preferred to "hide" from larger, more formal agencies. The agencies also proved very adept in engaging peer, church, and other local resources in support of the grandparents. These are resources that all support group providers should include or cultivate.

REFERENCES

Creswell, J. W. (1998). *Qualitative inquiry and research design: Choosing among five traditions.* Thousand Oaks, CA: Sage.

Denzin, N. K., & Lincoln, Y. S. (Eds.). (1994). *Handbook of qualitative research.* Thousand Oaks, CA: Sage.

Grandparent Resource Center. (1998a). *The grandparent raising grandchildren book: Support services resource guide.* New York: New York City Department for the Aging.

Grandparent Resource Center. (1998b). *For grandparents raising grandchildren: A series of workshops to help you COPE.* New York: New York City Department for the Aging.

Kelley, S. J., Yorker, B. C., & Whiteley, D. (1997). To grandma's house we go . . . and stay. *Journal of Gerontological Nursing, 25,* 13–20.

Janicki, M. P., McCallion, P., Grant-Griffin, L., & Kolomer, S. R. (2000). Grandparent caregivers I: Characteristics of the grandparents and the children with disabilities they care for. *Journal of Gerontological Social Work, 33*(3), 35–56.

McCallion, P., Janicki, M. P., Grant-Griffin, L., & Kolomer, S. R. (2000). Grandparent caregivers II: Service needs and service provision issues. *Journal of Gerontological Social Work, 33*(3), 57–84.

Minkler, M., Driver, D., Roe, K. M., & Bedeian, K. (1993). Community interventions to support grandparent caregivers. *The Gerontologist, 33,* 807–811.

Minkler, M., & Roe, K. M. (1993). *Grandmothers as caregivers: Raising children of the crack cocaine epidemic.* Newbury Park, CA: Sage.

Samuel Sadin Institute on Law. (1997a). *Help for grandparent caregivers: A guide to legal custody, foster care, kinship foster care, guardianship, standby guardianship, adoption (Vol. I).* New York: Brookdale Center on Aging of Hunter College.

Samuel Sadin Institute on Law. (1997b). *Help for grandparent caregivers: A guide to visitation, housing, education, medical consent (Vol. II).* New York: Brookdale Center on Aging of Hunter College.

Samuel Sadin Institute on Law. (1998). *Help for grandparent caregivers: A guide to the family assistance program, New York State's temporary assistance to needy families program (TANF) (Vol. III).* New York: Brookdale Center on Aging of Hunter College.

Woodsworth, R. S. (1996). You're not alone . . . you are one in a million. *Child Welfare, 75*(5), 619–635.

CHAPTER 9

Psychological Distress and Physical Health Problems in Grandparents Raising Grandchildren: Development of an Empirically Based Intervention Model

Susan J. Kelley and Deborah M. Whitley

INTRODUCTION

A body of literature has emerged in the past decade that addresses the growing phenomenon of grandparents raising grandchildren. Much of what has been published relates to trends and demographics, reasons for becoming custodial grandparents, and the impact of this role on caregivers. This chapter describes findings from an

---

Portions of this chapter were previously published in: Kelley, S. J., Whitley, D. M., Sipe, T. A., & Yorker, B. C. (2000). Psychological distress in grandmother kinship care providers: The role of resources, social support and physical health. *Child Abuse & Neglect, 24,* 311–321.

ongoing research and community service project with grandparents raising grandchildren in the Atlanta area. The development and implementation of an empirically based, interdisciplinary intervention for grandparents raising grandchildren is described. The purpose of this chapter is to: (1) compare the physical and psychological status of African-American grandparents who are raising grandchildren to national norms, (2) determine predictors of psychological distress among African-American grandparents who are raising grandchildren, and (3) describe an intervention to improve the well-being of grandparents raising grandchildren.

PSYCHOLOGICAL DISTRESS

Researchers consistently find that assuming full-time parenting responsibilities for grandchildren is associated with increased emotional health issues in grandparent caregivers (Dowdell, 1995; Emick & Hayslip, 1999; Kelley, 1993; Kelley, Whitley, Sipe, & Yorker, 2000; Minkler & Roe, 1993). Higher rates of depression and psychological distress are the mental health issues reported most often. Using a nationally representative sample, researchers found that custodial grandmothers were more likely than noncustodial grandmothers to have significant levels of depressive symptomatology (Fuller-Thomson & Minkler, 2000). Minkler, Fuller-Thomson, Miller, and Driver (1997) reported that caregiving grandmothers were almost twice as likely to be categorized as depressed as noncaregiving grandparents. In a study using data from the National Survey of Families and Households, Minkler and Fuller-Thomson (2001) compared the mental and physical health status of grandparents who were divided into five groups based on the amount of time they spent caring for grandchildren. The highest rates of depressive symptoms, using the Center for Epidemiological Studies-Depression (CES-D), were found in the two groups spending the greatest amount of time with grandchild responsibilities (grandparents who were raising grandchildren and those who provided extensive care to grandchildren), defined as 30 hours or more of caregiving per week or having the children overnight for at least 90 days in the past year. An interesting finding was that the rates of depression were comparable between custodial grandparents and those who were not full-time caregivers but yet provided extensive care. The investigators raise the possibility that the comparable rates of depression in extensive caregivers could be related to issues that are similarly faced by custodial grandparents, including feelings of entrapment or resentment and having a dysfunctional adult child.

A number of factors have been identified as potential sources of increased psychological distress in grandparent caregivers. Some of the most well documented issues are poor physical health, social isolation, and financial difficulties. Other contributing factors include the circumstances involving the onset of assuming full-time parenting responsibilities for grandchildren, changes in role demands, conflict with the children's parents, behavior problems of grandchildren, and issues related to public policies and legal issues (Caliandro & Hughes, 1998; Dowdell, 1995; Emick & Hayslip, 1999; Kelley & Damato, 1995; Minkler & Roe, 1993; Yorker et al., 1998).

The disruptive family events that precede grandparents' assuming care of their grandchildren is typically a source of significant stress. These events can occur suddenly (e.g., incarceration of the parent; removal of the children due to abuse or neglect), or after a long and difficult period (e.g., death of the parent from AIDS, mental illness, addiction). Grandparents often express feelings of shame, guilt, and anxiety over their child's drug addiction, incarceration, or death due to AIDS (Roe, Minkler, Saunders, & Thomas, 1996; Waldrop & Weber, 2001). Feelings of anger and resentment are also common as a result of assuming an unexpected and unwanted role (Kelley & Damato, 1995; Minkler & Roe, 1993; Waldrop & Weber).

PHYSICAL HEALTH

Studies of grandparents raising grandchildren indicate that they are at increased risk for poor physical health, with some health problems serious enough to jeopardize their ability to parent. Using a national sample, researchers found that grandmothers raising grandchildren were more likely than noncaregiving grandmothers to report their health as very poor to fair (Fuller-Thomson & Minkler, 2000). Grandmothers raising grandchildren were also more likely to report physical limitations in performing daily living activities. Using a qualitative approach to study issues confronted by custodial grandparents, Waldrop and Weber (2001) report that almost one third experienced heightened health problems since assuming full-time caregiving responsibilities for their grandchildren. Roe et al. (1996) report that whereas one half of the custodial grandparents in their study reported that their physical status interfered at times with their parental duties and responsibilities, many had a high sense of perseverance and determination to continue their responsibilities in spite of any physical limitations or symptoms. Thus, the literature emphasizes the potentially vulnerable physical status of custodial grandparents. Relative to the grandchildren, these health issues raise concerns about the quality of the family environment when grandparents with failing health raise young, active children.

THE STUDY

Participants

The findings reported in this chapter are based on data obtained during the first two years of an ongoing intervention study designed to support grandparents raising grandchildren. Data reported here were collected prior to the grandmothers receiving an interdisciplinary, community-based intervention that is described later in this chapter. Participants were eligible for enrollment in the study if they were raising one or more grandchildren in parent-absent households. Grandmothers, grandfathers, as well as great-grandmothers and great-grandfathers, were eligible for inclusion in the study. If there was more than one grandparent caregiver in the household, the grandparent who provides the majority of caregiving was selected as the research participant.

Of the 102 participants, most were grandmothers (95.1%); however there were five great-grandmothers (4.9%). Although not an inclusion criterion, all participants were African-American. The demographic characteristics of the sample are summarized in Table 9.1. It can be noted that, overall, the mean educational attainment for the sample is 11.24 years with a range of 1–19 years. Only 18% were married or living with a partner. The mean number of grandchildren being raised by the participants was 2.52 with a range of 1–7. The age of the children they were raising ranged from one month to 18 years, with a mean age of 8.7 years.

TABLE 9.1 Demographics

Grandparent (n = 102)	
Age (years)	
M	56.17
SD	8.94
Range	38–78
Marital Status (%)	
Married	15.7
Separated/divorced	32.0
Living with partner	2.0
Single, never married	8.8
Widowed	21.6
Paid job (%)	29.4
Grandparent receives TANF (%)	16.7
Grandchild(ren) receive TANF (%)	67.6
Grandparent receives SSI/disability	25.5
Grandparent receives RSDI/ retirement	20.6
Retired (%)	21.6

From "Psychological Distress in Grandmother Kinship Care Providers: The Role of Resources, Social Support and Physical Health," by S. J. Kelley, D. M. Whitley, T. A. Sipe, & B. C. Yorker, 2000, *Child Abuse & Neglect, 24,* pp. 311–321. Reprinted with permission.

The primary reasons that the grandchildren (n = 223) were being raised by the participants in this study are as follows: substance abuse, 38.2%; incarceration, 17.5%; abandonment, 16.1%; removal of children by child protective services, 11.2%; parent(s) deceased, 6.3%; and other, 10.8%. It is important to note that there is considerable overlap among these categories.

Procedure

Participants were referred to the project staff by professionals from a variety of agencies including primary care clinics, day care centers, public schools, and child protective services. The research staff contacted potential participants and explained the purpose of the study. All participants signed letters of informed consent. Participants were compensated for their time with $20 at each of the two preintervention data collection sessions. Data were collected in the participants' homes by trained research assistants and registered nurses. Questionnaires were read to all participants because of the low educational attainment of the sample.

Measures

Brief Symptom Inventory (BSI)

The Brief Symptom Inventory (Derogatis, 1983) was used to assess psychological distress in participants. The BSI is a 53-item self-report symptom inventory designed to measure the psychological symptom patterns of psychiatric and medical patients as well as community nonpatient respondents. It is a shorter version of the Symptom Checklist-90-R (Derogatis). Each item of the BSI is rated on a five-point scale of distress (0–4), ranging from "not at all" (0) to "extremely" (4). The BSI is scored and evaluated in terms of nine primary symptom dimensions and three global indices of distress. The nine primary symptom dimensions are (1) somatization, (2) obsessive-compulsive disorder, (3) interpersonal sensitivity, (4) depression, (5) anxiety, (6) hostility, (7) phobic anxiety, (8) paranoid ideation, and (9) psychoticism. The three global indices are Global Severity Index (GSI), Positive Symptom Total (PST), and Positive Symptom Distress Index (PSDI). The Global Severity Index (GSI) combines information about numbers of symptoms and intensity of distress and is considered the best summary score for psychological distress. Thus the GSI is used to measure psychological distress in the multiple regression analysis.

The BSI has shown high levels of both internal consistency reliability and test–retest reliability. Derogatis (1983) reports alpha coefficients for all nine dimensions of the

BSI as very good, ranging from a low of .71 on the Psychoticism dimension to a high of .85 on Depression. Test–retest reliability coefficients range from a low of .68 for Somatization to a high of .91 for Phobic Anxiety. Reanalysis of previous studies has confirmed that reduction in the length of the Symptom Checklist-90-R (SCL-90-R) dimensions has not had a significant effect on their validity. Correlations between the BSI and the SCL-90-R on a sample of 565 outpatients show very high correlations on all nine symptom dimensions. The BSI has been used widely with a variety of culturally diverse populations, including African Americans. Of the group on which the SCL-90-R/BSI was normed, 31% were African-American. The reliability coefficient for this sample is .94.

Family Resource Scale (FRS)

The Family Resource Scale (FRS) (Dunst & Leet, 1987; Dunst, Trivette, & Deal, 1988) was chosen to measure caregivers' perceptions regarding adequacy of family resources. The FRS is a 31-item self-report Likert-type scale and is derived from a conceptual framework that predicts that inadequacy of resources will negatively impact personal well-being and parental commitment. Items refer to specific resources and are rated on a 5-point scale from (1) does not apply to (5) almost always adequate. The total score is obtained by adding the scores for each item, with higher scores indicating more resources.

In a sample of 45 mothers, internal consistency was estimated to be .92 and split-half reliability was .95. Test–retest reliability with an interval of two to three months was .52. Factor analysis revealed 8 factors: Growth and Financial Support, Health and Necessities, Nutrition, Physical Shelter, Intra-Family Support, Communication and Employment, Child Care, and Independent Source of Income. The criterion validity was determined through correlational analysis with personal well-being; four of the seven subscales were significantly related to well-being and all seven predicted parental commitment. A total score is obtained by adding the scores for the items. The FRS has been used by numerous researchers examining the resources available to low-income African-American families with children. The reliability coefficient for this sample is .90.

Family Support Scale (FSS)

The Family Support Scale (Dunst & Trivette, 1989) was used to assess participants' level of social support. The FSS measures the helpfulness of sources of support to families raising children. The FSS includes 18 items that are rated on a 5-point scale from (1) not at all helpful to (5) extremely helpful. A total score is obtained by adding the scores for each item. Higher scores are indicative of increased social support. Reliability and validity were assessed in a sample of 139 parents of preschool retarded, handicapped, and developmentally at-risk children. Internal consistency reliability was .77, split-half reliability was .75, test–retest reliability (one month apart) was .75. Factor analysis yielded six factors that accounted for 62% of the variance. Factors were Informal Kinship, Social Organizations, Formal Kinship, Immediate Family, Specialized Professional Services, and Generic Professional Services. Criterion validity was established in several studies by correlating the total scale score with various parent and child outcomes. The FSS has been used by numerous researchers examining social support in low-income African-American families with children. The reliability coefficient for this sample is .70.

Short Health Form-36

Physical health was assessed with the Short Form-36 General Health Survey (SF-36) (Ware & Sherbourne, 1992) and by registered nurses who collected physical health data on each grandmother, including measurements of blood pressure, weight, cholesterol count, and glucose levels.

The SF-36 measures eight health attributes using multi-item scales. The scales are (1) physical functioning, (2) bodily pain, (3) role limitations resulting from physical health problems, (4) general mental health (psychological distress and psychological well-being), (5) role limitations due to emotional problems, (6) social functioning, (7) vitality (energy/fatigue), and (8) general health perceptions. The scales are scored on a Likert-type scale; the higher the score, the better the functioning. Validity testing on the instrument has been conducted in the United States and the United Kingdom. In general, researchers have found precision in the SF-36 instrument and there is evidence of good reliability and validity. Several studies have shown estimates of score reliability for the SF-36 scales exceed accepted standards for measures used in group comparisons (McHorney, Ware, Lu, & Sherbourne, 1994). Validity with other widely used health surveys also has been established (McHorney, Ware, & Raczek, 1993). Normative data for the SF-36 scales are available for noninstitutionalized females in the U.S. general population, which was used as a comparison with the sample group (Ware, 1993). The instrument has been widely used with diverse population groups, including African Americans. The reliability coefficient for this sample is .89. Because the Physical Functioning Scale is considered to have the best validity of the physical health scales (Ware), it was used as the measure of physical health for the multiple regression analysis.

Results

Psychological Distress

Results of the comparison of sample mean psychological distress scores to the national norm mean scores for nonpsychiatric females are displayed in Table 9.2. To avoid

TABLE 9.2 Brief Symptom Inventory General Severity and Dimension Scores

Scale	Sample	Norms	p
General severity index	.59 (.49)	.35 (.37)	.001
Interpersonal sensitivity	.53 (.71)	.40 (.55)	.037
Depression	.54 (.69)	.36 (.56)	.006
Anxiety	.56 (.61)	.44 (.54)	.025
Hostility	.53 (.56)	.36 (.45)	.001
Somatization	.65 (.69)	.35 (.46)	.000
Obsessive-compulsive disorder	.81 (.77)	.48 (.54)	.000
Phobic anxiety	.29 (.53)	.22 (.44)	.096
Paranoid ideation	.87 (.71)	.35 (.49)	.000
Psychoticism	.41 (.41)	.17 (.34)	.000

Note: Numbers in parentheses next to mean scores are standard deviation scores.

the problem of inflated error rates because of the number of analyses conducted (10 total), the Bonferoni technique was applied and the alpha level was set at .005. It can be noted that overall distress as measured by the General Severity Index (GSI) is significantly higher for this sample than the national normative data, indicating greater psychological distress in this sample. And five of the nine symptom dimensions mean scores in this sample were significantly higher than national norms. On the GSI, 28.4% of participants scored at or above the 90th percentile, which is considered in the clinical range.

Physical Health

Results of a comparison of sample mean scores to normative mean scores are displayed in Table 9.3. Because the national norms on the SF-36 are only available in transformed scores, it was necessary to transform the raw data to a 0–100 scale for comparison purposes as suggested by the SF-36 manual for scoring items and scales, with 100 indicating the most favorable health status (Ware, 1993). To avoid the problem of inflated error rates because of the number of analyses conducted (8 total), the Bonferoni technique was applied and the alpha level was set at .006. The sample mean score on Physical Functioning, considered the best SF-36 scale indicator of physical health (Ware), is significantly lower than the mean score for the normative group. Other scales where statistically significant differences were found include bodily pain, role functioning (physical), social functioning, and general health. These significantly lower scores indicate poorer health in this sample of grandmothers.

TABLE 9.3 Short Form 36 General Health Survey (N = 100) Transformed Scores: Sample and General Population

Sample M	General population M	t value	Significance
69.05	81.47	−4.700	.000
63.36	73.59	−3.590	.001
30.75	77.77	22.660	.000
70.84	73.25	−1.190	.234
72.33	79.47	−1.760	.081
72.70	81.54	−3.320	.001
56.25	58.43	.968	.335
61.80	70.61	−3.910	.000

From "Grandmothers Raising Grandchildren: Are They at Increased Risk of Health Problems?" by D. M. Whitley, S. J. Kelley, & T. A. Sipe, 2001, *Health & Social Work, 26*(2), pp. 105–114. Adapted with permission.

Results of data obtained by registered nurses identified the following health problems in the participants: diabetes, 23%; hypertension, 54%; high cholesterol (240 or greater), 22%; and marked obesity (> 20% overweight for height and frame), 80%. When asked to describe their health status, participants reported their health as follows: excellent, 7%; good, 48%; fair, 41%; and poor, 4%.

Predictors of Psychological Distress

Hierarchical regression was used to determine if social support, resources, and physical health improved prediction of psychological distress beyond that attributed to differences in grandparent age, employment status, number of grandchildren in their care, and ages of grandchildren. Evaluation of assumptions and the regression analysis were conducted using the enter method in SPSS Version 8.0.

Results of evaluation of assumptions for multivariate statistics led to transformations of two variables to reduce skewness in their distributions and improve the normality, linearity, and homoscedasticity of residuals and thereby improve the robustness of the hierarchical regression. The dependent variable of psychological distress was positively skewed and transformed with a square root transformation. The independent variable (IV) of physical health that was negatively skewed was reflected, which converted the negative skewness to a positive skewness, and transformed with a square root transformation. Consequently, the direction of the physical health variable was changed from negative to positive. The IV of family support was positively skewed without transformation and negatively skewed with it; thus, it was not transformed. The IV of family resources was normally distributed. The IVs of grandparent age and number of grandchildren were positively skewed but not transformed as the scale of measurement for these variables is meaningful and transformation would hinder interpretation. No outliers among cases were identified with the use of a $p < .001$ criterion for Mahalanobis distance (Tabachnick & Fidell, 1989).

Because of the likelihood that certain extraneous variables (age and employment status of grandmother, age and number of children in her custody) would influence the dependent variable, they were entered first as a block to control their effect in Step 1. Resources and social support were entered simultaneously in Step 2. These were entered simultaneously for two reasons. First, social support can be viewed as a type of resource. Second, the theoretical model used in this study, family adaptation model (McCubbin, Thompson, & McCubbin, 1996), does not indicate whether social support or resources are more likely to moderate psychological distress. Physical health was entered in Step 3.

Table 9.4 displays the unstandardized regression coefficients (B) and intercept, the standardized regression coefficients (β), and the semiparital correlations (sr^2) for each step, and the multiple correlation coefficient (R), the squared multiple correlation coefficient (R^2), and the adjusted squared multiple correlation (adjusted R^2) after entry of all seven independent variables. R was significantly different from zero at the end of each step. After Step 3, with all seven independent variables in the equation, $R = .64$, $F(7, 94) = 9.42$, $p < .001$.

After Step 2 with number of grandchildren, grandparent age, employment status, children < 5 years old in the equation, $R^2 = .15$, $F\ (4, 97) = 4.15$, $p < .01$. After Step 2 with social support and family resources added to the equation $R^2 = .32$, $F\ (6, 95) = 7.42$, $p < .001$. Social support and family resources add significant increment in R^2. After Step 3 with the square root of physical health in the equation, $R^2 = .41$, $F\ (7, 94) = 9.42$, $p < .001$. Addition of the square root of physical health reliably improved R^2.

DISCUSSION

The compromised psychological and physical health of custodial grandparents reported in this chapter are consistent with the findings of other researchers (Fuller-Thomson & Minkler, 2000). The finding in the current study that close to 30% of participants scored in the clinical range on a standardized measure of psychological distress is of serious concern and suggests that as a population, grandparents raising grandchildren are at significant risk for psychological distress, often serious enough to warrant

TABLE 9.4 Hierarchical Regression of Background, Social Support, Physical Health, and Resource Variables on Psychological Distress (n = 102)

Variables	B	β	Step	sr^{2a} (incremental)
Number of grandchildren	.015	.07	1	.15*
Age	−.152	−.25	1	
Employment status	.097	.14	1	
Children < 5 yrs old	−.152	−.23	1	
Social support	.002	.07	2	.17**
Family resources	−.006	−.37	2	
Physical health (transformed)	.104	.33	3	.09**
Intercept	1.424			
				R^2 = .41
				R^2 = .41
				Adjusted R^2 = .37
				R = .64**

*p < .01, **p < .001
[a]incremental change in R^2

From "Psychological Distress in Grandmother Kinship Care Providers: The Role of Resources, Social Support and Physical Health," by S. J. Kelley, D. M. Whitley, T. A. Sipe, & B. C. Yorker, 2000, *Child Abuse & Neglect, 24,* pp. 311–321. Reprinted with permission.

psychiatric intervention. Identifying risk factors for psychological distress in custodial grandparents expands upon findings of previous researchers and provides direction for clinical intervention. Grandmothers who reported fewer resources, less social support, and poorer physical health tended to experience higher levels of psychological distress. While previous research has reported that financial burdens and social isolation can be sources of stress for custodial grandparents, these variables were not previously tested in a statistical model as predictors of psychological distress. Poor physical health was also found to be a predictor of psychological distress; however, it is possible that psychological distress, in turn, influences physical health.

Based on the results presented in this chapter, as well as results reported by other researchers, it is essential that strategies to decrease psychological distress in this population include affordable and accessible health care; basic resources, such as a stable income, housing, food and clothing; social support; and screening and treatment for psychological distress.

The findings reported in this chapter lend empirical support to an intervention being implemented and evaluated by the authors. The goal of the intervention is to improve the well-being of families in which grandparents are raising grandchildren in parent-absent households.

The Present Intervention

Project Healthy Grandparents (PHG) was established in 1995 in response to the critical needs of the growing numbers of grandparents raising children who have been abused, neglected, or abandoned by birth parents. Sponsored by Georgia State University, PHG works to strengthen intergenerational families and to improve their quality of life by providing grandparents and grandchildren with comprehensive services and improved access to community resources.

Over the past five years, PHG has provided services to more than 270 Atlanta families, including 675 children. Core services offered by Project Healthy Grandparents include health care services, social work case management services, parenting classes, grandparent support group meetings, legal assistance, specialized mental health services for the grandchildren, and early intervention services. Project Healthy Grandparents is currently supported by funds provided by Georgia State University, the Children's Bureau at the U.S. Department of Health and Human Services, the Georgia Department of Human Resources, and numerous national and local foundations.

PHG Intervention Model

Although many of PHG's families endure numerous economic and social constraints (e.g., poverty, dangerous home environments, lack of social connections), it is recognized that they also possess strengths to be used as resources for change. PHG provides the necessary supports for grandparents to acknowledge their personal strengths and to use them to address the challenges they are encountering in order to feel secure and confident about parenting a second time around. The intended outcome is to have grandparents gain a sense of competence that they can take care of themselves and their families, and can interact effectively with other systems, including their communities. Specific service components include the following:

Social Work Services

Each family is assigned a social worker who conducts a minimum of two home visits per month. Using the strengths-based approach, social workers provide individualized case management services. During the initial home visit with the social worker, grandparents are asked to identify and prioritize their needs, goals, and strengths. Emphasis is placed upon using those personal, familial, and community strengths that could facilitate problem resolution and goal achievement. Social workers confer with families on issues that may impede the family's stability, including access to resources such as public assistance, housing, child care, and respite care. During individual monthly visits, social workers monitor the grandparents' progress to sustain or improve their social functioning. They also serve as the lead staff person to ascertain the legal relationship between the grandparent and the grandchild. Our research with this population has found that often the grandparents have no legal relationship with their grandchildren (Yorker et al., 1998), a fact that impedes family stability and causes emotional distress for grandparents. If a grandparent has no legal relationship with the grandchild, steps are taken to direct the grandparent to obtain guardianship, at a minimum. If a grandparent wishes to adopt his or her grandchildren, the social worker can facilitate the process, working through the Atlanta Legal Aid Society and Kilpatrick Stockton, an Atlanta-based law firm that provides pro bono legal services to assist grandparents in the adoption process. To date, 90 children in PHG have been adopted by their grandparents.

Nursing Services

Each family receives at least one home visit per month by a registered nurse. The home visit consists of a health assessment of the grandparent, including measurement of blood pressure, weight, cholesterol, glucose levels to screen for diabetes, and vision screening. The nurse also checks medications, monitors health needs, and educates grandparents about any health challenges they may be encountering. Referrals for additional health care are made as needed. The nurse also monitors the physical health status of grandchildren, including assessment of their height, weight, and head circumference for children less than one year of age. The nurse also determines if the childhood immunizations are current. Grandparents who have serious or chronic health conditions receive additional visits by a nurse whose primary responsibility is to manage high-risk clients.

Support Group Meetings

Grandparents have the opportunity to participate in monthly support group meetings. Participation in support groups has the potential to lessen the social isolation many grandparents experience. Facilitated by a master-level social worker, the meetings provide a physical and emotional respite for the grandparents. Topics of discussion are dictated by the grandparents' needs and interests. The support groups also provide a socialization outlet; for some grandparents attendance at the meeting may be one of only a few opportunities to associate with peers. Support group meetings are held at a time and location convenient for the grandparents.

Parent Education Classes

Grandparents in PHG may attend monthly parent education classes. Topics have included how to discipline a child, managing the difficult adolescent, relating to the birth parent, raising grandchildren with special needs, and the adoption process.

Transportation is provided to all group meetings. Whereas social service and nursing support are provided on a one-year basis, grandparents may attend support group and parenting education meetings indefinitely.

Children's Services

In the past two years, we have expanded our services to include programming for the grandchildren. For children who are trying to cope with parental abandonment, substance abuse issues, and violence, the area of greatest need is mental health services. A recent study of 242 PHG children revealed that 38% had emotional problems, and virtually all children being raised by their grandparents could benefit from support and counseling from mental health professionals. In March 2000, we launched the PHG Saturday Youth Academy to provide children ages 5–16 with psychoeducational group therapy and cultural/recreational activities. The Youth Academy also gives the children time to socialize with each other and helps them to build a positive self-image and reduce their sense of isolation. Since the pilot program was launched in spring 2000, we have served 150 children in the Saturday Youth Academy program.

In October 2000, PHG launched a second offering for grandchildren, the Early Childhood Intervention Program. This program provides intervention services to young children (ages 0 to 5 years) who are at risk for developmental delay due to maternal substance abuse and/or HIV/AIDS. Through a formal partnership with the Marcus Institute for Development and Learning, an affiliate of Emory University, we are providing assessments for children who show signs of developmental delay, as well as intensive services for these families.

Staffing

PHG is staffed by eight full-time professionals, two half-time professionals, and one administrative staff person. Additionally, the program utilizes the talents and skills of registered nurses and social workers seeking advanced degrees, as well as graduate students from the Colleges of Education, Business, Arts and Sciences, and Law.

The project is based on a cross-sector collaboration model that involves numerous community agencies, including hospitals, substance abuse treatment facilities, day care centers, and juvenile court systems.

Intervention Efficacy

The PHG model was initially pilot-tested with the first 25 families in the program (Kelley, Yorker, Whitley, & Sipe, 2000). Participants included grandparents raising grandchildren in parent-absent households The intervention included home visitation by registered nurses, social workers, and legal assistants; services from an attorney; and monthly support group meetings. The duration of the intervention was six months. The mean number of grandchildren per household was 2.6, with a range of 1 to 7 children. The participants were African-American, predominately low income, with a mean age of 55.7 years. Thirty-two percent of grandparents were 61 years of age and older, with 12% over the age of 70. Most participants were grandmothers (84%); however there were three great-grandmothers (12%) and one grandfather (4%). Most subjects (92%) were maternal grandparents and two (8%) were paternal grandparents.

A pre-posttest design was used to determine the efficacy of the intervention. Measures included the Short Form-36 General Health Survey (SF-36), Brief Symptom Index (BSI), Family Resource Scale (FRS), and Family Support Scale (FSS). One participant was lost to attrition and thus 24 participants comprised the final sample. Statistically significant results included improved mental health scores as measured by the SF-36, decreased psychological distress scores as measured by the BSI, and increased social support scores as measured by the FSS. There were no statistically significant changes in physical health or family resource scores. Participants also experienced improved levels of public benefits and legal relationships with their grandchildren. Thus, findings from the pilot study suggest that the intervention was effective in decreasing psychological distress, increasing social support, and improving mental health.

Results are available from a recently completed federal demonstration project conducted from 1996 to 2001 (Kelley, Whitley, Sipe, & White, 2002). Outcome data are available for 92 PHG participants including 84 grandmothers (91.3%), six great-grandmothers (6.5%), and two grandfathers (2.2%). Participants were African-American and the primary caregivers of one or more grandchildren in parent-absent households. The mean age of the participants was 57.1 years, with a range of 28–78. The mean educational attainment was 11.5 years, with a range of 0–20 years. The mean number of grandchildren per family was 2.4, with a range of 1–7. While the core services remained the same as during the pilot study, the duration of intervention was changed from six to twelve months.

Major findings related to grandparent outcomes are presented here. Statistically significant results included improved family resources as measured by the FRS, decreased psychological distress scores as measured by the BSI, and increased social support scores as measured by the FSS. There were no statistically significant changes in physical health. It is, however, possible that the intervention prevented further deterioration of the health of participants. These results support and extend the findings of the pilot study.

Program Replication

The Georgia Department of Human Resources has recognized the impact of PHG and is funding replication of the PHG model in three Georgia locations: the University of Georgia (Athens), the Medical College of Georgia (Augusta), and Valdosta State University (Valdosta). Because these three replication sites serve predominantly rural clients, it was necessary to demonstrate that the model can be adapted to various populations of grandparent caregivers. By operating the program through universities, we focus on conducting research crucial to understanding the needs of intergenerational families; however, the PHG model can easily be adapted by other community service agencies.

National Center on Grandparents Raising Grandchildren

We are currently launching a National Center on Grandparents Raising Grandchildren. The goal of the National Center is to support replication of the PHG model in communities outside of Georgia, enhance the knowledge of professionals who work with grandparents raising grandchildren, foster collaboration among researchers in the field, and inform policy makers of current research and practices related to the needs of grandparent caregivers. The University of Maryland, at Baltimore, will be the initial national replication site.

REFERENCES

Caliandro, G., & Hughes, C. (1998). The experience of being a grandmother who is the primary caregiver for her HIV-positive grandchild. *Nursing Research, 47*(2), 107–113.

Derogatis, L. R. (1983). *SCL-90 administration, scoring, and procedures: Manual II.* Towson, MD: Clinical Psychometric Research.

Dowdell, E. B. (1995). Caregiver burden: Grandmothers raising their high risk grandchildren. *Journal of Psychosocial Nursing, 33,* 27–30.

Dunst, C. J., & Leet, H. E. (1987). Measuring the adequacy of resources in households with young children. *Child Care, Health, and Development, 13,* 111–125.

Dunst, C. J., & Trivette, C. M. (1989). Toward experimental evaluation of the family, infant and pre-school program. In H. Weiss & F. Jacobs (Eds.), *Evaluating family programs* (pp. 315–346). New York: Aldine.

Dunst, C. J., Trivette, C. M., & Deal, A. G. (1988). *Enabling and empowering families: Principles and guidelines for practice*. Cambridge, MA: Brookline Books.

Emick, M. A., & Hayslip, B., Jr. (1999). Custodial grandparenting: Stresses, coping skills, and relationships with grandchildren. *International Journal on Aging and Human Development, 48,* 35–61.

Fuller-Thomson, E., & Minkler, M. (2000). The mental and physical health of grandmothers who are raising their grandchildren. *Journal of Mental Health and Aging, 6,* 311–323.

Kelley, S. J. (1993). Caregiver stress in grandparents raising grandchildren. *Image: Journal of Nursing Scholarship, 25,* 331–337.

Kelley, S. J., & Damato, E. G. (1995). Grandparents as primary caregivers. *Maternal Child Nursing, 20,* 326–332.

Kelley, S. J., Whitley, D. M., Sipe, T. A., & White, K. (2002, January). *Neglected children in intergenerational care: Final report submitted to Office of Child Abuse and Neglect, Children's Bureau, U.S. Department of Health and Human Services.*

Kelley, S. J., Whitley, D. M., Sipe, T. A., & Yorker, B. C. (2000). Psychological distress in grandmother kinship care providers: The role of resources, social support and physical health. *Child Abuse & Neglect, 24,* 311–321.

Kelley, S. J., Yorker, B. C., Whitley, D. M., & Sipe, T. A. (2000). A multimodal intervention for grandparents raising grandchildren: Results of an exploratory study. *Child Welfare, LXXX,* 27–50.

McCubbin, H. I., Thompson, A. E., & McCubbin, M. A. (1996). *Family assessment: Resiliency, coping, and adaptation.* Madison, WI: University of Wisconsin Press.

McHorney, C., Ware, J., Lu, J., & Sherbourne, C. (1994). The MOS 36-item short form health survey (SF-36): Tests of data quality, scaling assumptions, and reliability across diverse patient groups. *Medical Care, 32,* 40–66.

McHorney, C., Ware, J., & Raczek, A. (1993). The MOS 36-item short form health survey (SF-36): Psychometric and clinical tests of validity in measuring physical and mental health constructs. *Medical Care, 31,* 247–263.

Minkler, M., & Fuller-Thomson, E. (2001). Physical and mental health status of American grandparents providing extensive child care to their grandchildren. *Journal of the American Medical Women's Association, 56,* 199–205.

Minkler, M., Fuller-Thomson, E., Miller, D., & Driver, D. (1997). Depression in grandparents raising grandchildren: Results of a national longitudinal study. *Archives of Family Medicine, 6,* 445–452.

Minkler, M., & Roe, K. M. (1993). *Grandmothers as caregivers: Raising children of the crack cocaine epidemic*. Newbury Park, CA: Sage.

Roe, K. M., Minkler, M., Saunders, F., & Thomas, G. E. (1996). Health of grandmothers raising grandchildren of the crack-cocaine epidemic. *Medical Care, 34,* 1072–1084.

Tabachnick, B. G., & Fidell, L. S. (1989). *Using multivariate statistics* (2nd ed.). New York: Harper Collins.

Waldrop, D., & Weber, J. A. (2001). From grandparent to caregiver: The stress and satisfaction of raising grandchildren. *Families in Society: The Journal of Contemporary Human Services, 82,* 461–472.

Ware, J. E. (1993). *SF-36 Health Survey: Manual and interpretation guide.* Boston: Health Institute, New England Medical Center.

Ware, J. E., & Sherbourne, C. D. (1992). The MOS 36-item short-form health survey (SF36). *Medical Care, 30,* 473–483.

Whitley, D. M., Kelley, S. J., & Sipe, T. A. (2001). Grandmothers raising grandchildren: Are they at increased risk of health problems? *Health & Social Work, 26*(2), 105–114.

Yorker, B. C., Kelley, S. J., Whitley, D. M., Lewis, A., Magis, J., Bergeron, A., & Napier, C. (1998). Custodial relationships of grandparents raising grandchildren: Results of a home-based intervention study. *Juvenile and Family Court Journal, 49,* 15–25.

CHAPTER 10

A Stress and Coping Model of Custodial Grandparenting Among African Americans

Martha Crowther and Rachel Rodriguez

The 1990 Census reported a 44% increase over the preceding decade in the number of children living with their grandparents or other relatives (Saluter, 1992). In one third of these homes, neither parent was present, typically making the grandparent or other relative the primary caregiver. In 1997, it was estimated that 3.9 million children, or 5.5% of all children under age 18, were living in homes maintained by their grandparents (Bryson & Casper, 1999). Custodial grandparents were 60% more likely than noncustodial grandparents to report incomes below the poverty line and to live in the South (Fuller-Thomson, Minkler, & Driver, 1997). African Americans had 83% higher odds of being custodial grandparents than respondents from other races (Fuller-Thomson et al.). In fact, almost 30% of African-American grandmothers and 14% of African-American grandfathers reported being the primary caregiver for a grandchild for at least six months (Szinovacz, 1998), compared to 10.9% of all grandparents (Fuller-Thomson et al.). In sum, the research implies that grandparents who raise their grandchildren are more likely to be African American, female, poor, and live in the South. Because an increasing number of children are being cared for by their grandparents, considerable research has focused on the stress experienced by these caregivers, who have been repeatedly found to suffer from a host of physical and psychological problems, financial burdens, and the loss of social support (Burton, 1992; Joslin & Brouard, 1995; Joslin & Harrison, 1998; Minkler & Fuller-Thomson, 1999; Minkler & Roe, 1993; Minkler, Roe, & Price, 1992; Sands & Goldberg-Glen, 2000).

The extent to which custodial grandparents perceive and/or experience stress and interference with their other activities because of grandparenting is often noted in the literature (Burton, 1992; Dilworth-Anderson, 1994; Sands & Goldberg-Glen, 2000; Strom, Collinsworth, Strom, & Griswold, 1993). The stress grandparents experience takes various forms and affects them differentially. For example, a report by the American Association for Retired Persons (1994) suggests that financial stress may confront many custodial grandparents. Of the 405 custodial grandparents who contacted the Grandparents Center, 61% of the African-American grandparents were on fixed incomes. In contrast, 41% of white grandparents were in a similar financial situation. Pinson-Millburn, Fabian, Schlossberg, and Pyle (1996) also found that grandparents in their sample experienced "severe economic" hardship.

Sands and Goldberg-Glen (2000) explored stress factors among grandparents raising their grandchildren in the context of stress theory. In their study, which included African Americans and Caucasians, they found that younger grandparents, those who had been providing care longer, and those who were without resources/support reported more stress (depressive symptoms, heightened psychological anxiety). The researchers did not find that race or income was significantly associated with stress among the grandparent caregivers. Pruchno (1999), using telephone interviewing, did find differences with respect to race, with white grandmothers indicating that they felt more burdened with caregiving than African Americans. Minkler, Fuller-Thompson, Miller, and Driver (1997) found higher psychological distress among grandparents who raised their grandchildren than among those who did not. Other researchers have identified stress-producing factors for grandparent caregivers such as competing roles of work (Jendrek, 1994), caring for grandchildren with special needs (Burton, 1992; Dilworth-Anderson, 1994; Minkler & Roe, 1993), and grandchildren's anxiety and relationship with grandchildren's parent (O'Reilly & Morrison, 1993).

Research findings exploring the extent to which grandparents' roles and relationships with their grandchildren interfere with their other activities, health, and well-being are somewhat contradictory. For example, several studies report that grandparents providing primary care, like caregivers in general, tend to delay or do not obtain health care for themselves (Joslin & Brouard, 1995; Minkler & Roe, 1993); experience a decline in social activities with friends and other family members (Burnette, 1999; Burton, 1992; Minkler & Roe, 1993); and have interruption in the labor force (Jendrek, 1994). Baydar and Brooks-Gunn (1998), on the other hand, report that similar caregiving among the grandmothers in their sample did not interfere with their social roles, which included employment, caring for a person with a disability, household chores, and participation in social organizations.

The existing literature includes a number of findings on the manifestations of stress among custodial grandparents. The studies have also found that African Americans are more likely to be custodial grandparents. However, variation in the stress process among African-American caregivers has been little studied. In the present chapter, we applied a stress process model to investigate the nature, impact, and consequences of custodial grandparenting among African Americans.

THE CONCEPTUAL MODEL: STRESS AND COPING PROCESSES

The stress and coping model presented is similar to other caregiver stress models in that stress is viewed as a process (Pearlin, Mullan, Semple, & Skaff, 1990). Caregiver stress is viewed in terms of the relation among many conditions, and the ways these conditions develop and change over time. There are two types of stressors that are discussed in this model: primary and secondary (Pearlin et al., 1990). Primary stress encompasses the nature and magnitude of the demands of caregiving. It is the catalyst that initiates the subsequent stress process. Secondary stress is defined as those issues that arise as a result of the caregiving situation. This model emphasizes the importance of the adaptational processes, a term referring to appraisal of caregiving, social support, and coping as moderators of stress. The proposed model delineates the possible relation between the background and context of custodial grandparenting, the stressors, the mediators of stress, the moderators of stress, and the outcomes or manifestations of stress. The model presented below (Figure 10.1) is described using four components to capture the essence of this unique caregiving situation.

The first component of the model examines the background and context of custodial grandparenting. The sociodemographics of custodial grandparents such as age, gender, marital status, education, employment status, length of caregiving, presence in home of the substance abusing child, type of caregiving arrangement (formal/informal), number of children being cared for, physical and/or psychological problems with the grandchildren, and age at which caregiving began may impact the outcomes of caregiving. According to Pearlin et al. these are key characteristics of the caregiver and influence virtually all aspects of the caregiving role. This background information specifies the strengths and weaknesses, experience, privileges, disadvantages, responsibilities, and preexisting stressors that custodial grandparents bring to the caregiving situation. The characteristics of the caregiver are present throughout the stress process and may predict how the caregiver will respond to the caregiving

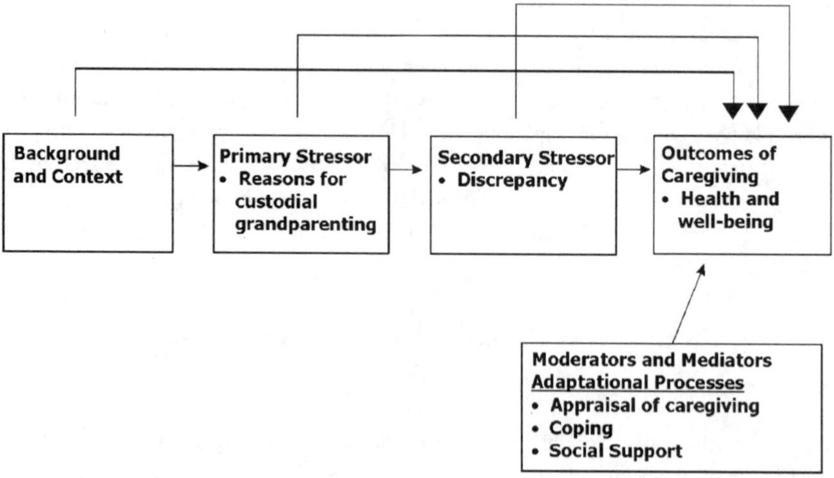

FIGURE 10.1 Using four components to capture caregiving situation.

arrangement. The background and context of the caregiver are expected to be threaded throughout the stress process and subsequently impact the manifestations of stress.

The second component adds the primary stressor, reasons for custodial grandparenting. The model hypothesizes that there is a relation between the reasons for caregiving and health and well-being. To adequately examine stress it is important to know how and why the conditions arise. Therefore, the reasons for custodial grandparenting must be explored. In this chapter we examine the differences in caregiving between grandparents who are raising their grandchildren because of the crack cocaine use of the child's parent and those who are raising them for reasons other than substance abuse. The two groups presume different environmental and social circumstances, which may alter the function of the stress process. The model presented here examines health and well-being among noncustodial African-American grandparents and two groups of custodial grandparents. Noncustodial grandparents may report higher levels of health and well-being.

The third component, the secondary stressor, postulates that custodial grandparents are performing an expected role by providing generational continuity, but they can no longer rely on the instrumental and emotional support they once received from their families and the community. The sociohistorical influences and perspectives of the African-American community compel many grandparents to become surrogate parents even when the role is not desired, the resources are not present to support the primary caregiving arrangement, or both. Additionally, the attitudes toward caregiving have changed for many of the caregivers due to increased opportunities in their lives and the feeling that they no longer want to delay personal gratification. The potential stress that may arise from performing a role that is expected but no longer supported and/or desired may lead to adverse psychological and physical health and impairment of the subjective well-being of the caregiver. This discrepancy is conceptualized to function as the secondary stressor in the stress process. As a result of the caregiving situation, many custodial grandparents are in the process of adjusting the expectations between their anticipated roles and activities and their actual roles and activities at this point in their lives. The model hypothesizes that the discrepancy between the expected versus their actual roles and activities will mediate the relation between custodial grandparenting and the outcomes of caregiving, that is, high discrepancy scores will be related to poorer outcomes.

The fourth component includes the adaptational processes: appraisal of caregiving, coping, and social support. These factors may reduce the feelings of isolation and the negative effects of role discrepancy on the health and well-being of custodial grandparents. The caregiving literature focused on adults taking care of the dependent elderly utilizing these constructs has demonstrated that the adaptational processes are often mediators of the stress process. In this project they have been hypothesized to function as moderators as a result of the inclusion of the discrepancy construct and a different caregiving population.

The proposed model therefore hypothesizes that the background and context of custodial grandparenting and the reasons for caregiving will affect the health and well-being of the grandparents. The magnitude of the effect will be mediated by the degree of discrepancy between anticipated and actual roles and activities. Greater discrepancy will be associated with more adverse outcomes. The adaptational processes of the caregivers (appraisal of caregiving, coping, and social support) will moderate this relation.

A TEST OF THE CONCEPTUAL MODEL

Participants

A sample of custodial and noncustodial grandparents was recruited. Grandparents were considered eligible for inclusion in the study if they met all of the following criteria: resided in the Triangle or Piedmont areas of North Carolina, at least 25 years of age at the time of entry into the study, and noninstitutionalized. The resultant sample included 55 custodial grandparents and 37 noncustodial grandparents.

Procedure

After meeting eligibility criteria, each participant was interviewed in a neutral location chosen by the interviewer and the participant, usually the home. One 2-hour testing session was conducted. The purpose and requirements of the study were explained to the participants and any questions were answered. Participants were ensured of the confidentiality of their responses. Participants were then interviewed and asked to complete standardized and open-ended questionnaires. Incentives included $20 and a four-week skills-building support group at the conclusion of data collection.

Measures

Quantitative and qualitative methods were used to examine the impact of caregiving on African-American custodial grandparents. The items presented below measure components of the stress process model presented in this chapter: background and context, primary stressor, secondary stressor, adaptational processes, and the outcomes of caregiving.

Sociodemographics

Sociodemographic characteristics of the sample provided a basis for understanding the personal context of custodial grandparents. The format included both closed and open-ended questions and covered the following topics: demographic information, religious affiliation and practices, household composition, family composition, number of care recipients, and physical and psychological status of the custodial grandchildren.

Discrepancy

A new scale was developed by the first author to determine the discrepancy in expected and actual roles and activities. This scale was developed using a subset of items adapted from a study of African-American grandparents (Burton, 1992). The discrepancy scale assesses the different roles and activities relevant to this population of African-American caregivers. The interviewer-administered scale consists of 35 items. Respondents were asked if they expected to be involved in the roles and activities listed. If they stated that they expected to be involved in the role or activity a second question was asked: how they feel about their involvement or lack of involvement in the roles and activities. The questions were asked in a Likert scale format. The choices for the first part of the question were: more than expected, about the same as expected, less than expected, and not applicable. The choices for the second part of the question were: negative, neutral, positive, and not applicable.

For the purposes of this project negative discrepancy the discrepancy between expected and actual roles and activities, was used to measure the impact of custodial grandparenting. Negative discrepancy is the sociobehavioral mechanism by which custodial grandparenting leads to negative outcomes. The discrepancy score was obtained by summing up the responses that had "negative" valence. The value could range from 0–35. The following is a sample of some roles and activities that are on the scale: (1) starting a job training program, (2) spending time on hobbies, and (3) taking more time for yourself. The scale was used to assess the secondary stressor (discrepancy) in the stress process model. Reliability coefficients (Cronbach's alpha) were calculated for the 35-item measure. The reliability coefficient for the overall instrument was 0.88, indicating very good internal consistency.

Coping

An instrument developed by Pearlin et al. (1990) was used to assess coping. The scale is composed of three components that address coping in response to life problems: management of the situation causing stress, management of the meaning of the situation such that its threat is reduced, and management of the stress symptoms that result from the situation. The components are specific to the study of caregivers. The items used to measure management of the situation are not factored; they are intended to be single items. Those that measure management of the meaning of the situation have three factors: reduction of expectations (alpha coefficient = 0.48), use of positive comparisons (alpha coefficient = 0.63), and a search for a larger sense of meaning (alpha coefficient = 0.49). Pearlin et al. acknowledge that the reliability coefficients are not "robust." Given this, these subscales should be interpreted with caution. The items that measure management of distress are to be analyzed separately. The response categories for the subscale items range from 1–4; the higher the score, the higher the coping. Because the coping scale was designed primarily for use with Alzheimer's caregivers, the subscales were slightly modified. The coping scale was used to assess a component of the adaptational process described in the stress process model.

Social Support

The Duke Social Support Index was used as a multidimensional measure of social support. The index consists of 35 items that measure four dimensions of social support: subjective social support, frequency of social interaction, size of social network, and instrumental support. The total score is the sum of the individual items; the higher the score the greater the social support for each scale. In a biracial community sample of approximately 3,000 adults aged 18 and over the subjective social support scale was found to be the best predictor of health outcomes among the four subscales and produced an alpha coefficient of 0.79. The social support scale was used to assess a component of the adaptational process described in the stress process model.

Appraisal of Caregiving

Scales developed by Pearlin et al. (1990) were used to assess appraisal of caregiving. Appraisal was measured by economic and intrapsychic strain questionnaires. Economic strain is composed of three items measuring the following dimensions: reduction in household income, increase in expenditures related to the care and treatment of the care recipient, and assessment of whether there is enough money to subsist month to month. The following scales measure intrapsychic strain: role captivity, loss of self, caregiving competence, and personal gain. Role captivity is a four-item scale that measures the reluctance of the caregiver to perform the role (alpha coefficient = 0.83). Loss of self is assessed by a two-item scale that measures the sense of personal identity the caregiver may have lost because of the caregiving role (alpha coefficient = 0.76). Caregiving competence is measure by a four-item scale, and asks caregivers to rate their level of competence in the caregiving role (alpha coefficient = 0.74). Personal gain is a four-item scale that assesses whether the caregiver has "grown" from the caregiving experience (alpha coefficient = 0.76). The intrapsychic scales may appear dependent because they are a closely linked construct; however the intercorrelations between them are not very high. The strongest relation is between role captivity and self-loss ($r = 0.35$); the next strongest correlation is between role competence and role gain ($r = 0.32$). The correlation between role captivity and caregiving competence is –0.17, and between loss of self and caregiving competence is –0.13. There is no correlation between loss of self and personal gain. The response categories are continuous for each item and range from 1–4; the higher the score, the higher the appraisal of caregiving. This scale has not been used previously with an African-American population. Psychometrics will be examined to determine validity with this population. The appraisal of caregiving scale was used to assess a component of the adaptational process described in the stress process model.

Physical Health

The presence and severity of health problems and the possible exacerbation of existing health problems were measured through closed and open-ended questions and the physical functioning section of the Medical Outcomes Study 36-Item Short-Form Health Survey (SF-36) (Ware & Sherbourne, 1992); the scale has also been called the Rand Health Survey. Reliabilities for the physical functioning section of the SF-36 were found to be good in subgroups of patients with different chronic conditions and in a general population; internal consistency reliability coefficients were reported to be 0.86 for physical functioning to 0.87 for health perceptions. The Rand Health Survey items and scales are scored using the Likert method of summated ratings. The health questions that pertain only to custodial grandparents are binary yes/no responses. The closed and open-ended questions have been used in studies examining African-American caregivers (Burton, 1993; Dilworth-Anderson, personal communication; Minkler & Roe, 1993). Physical health was used to assess one of the outcome variables described in the stress process model.

Psychological Health

Psychological health was assessed using the Symptom Checklist-90-Revised (SCL-90-R). The SCL-90-R is a 90-item self-report measure that uses a five-point Likert scale to assess psychological distress along nine dimensions: somatization, obsessive compulsive disorder, interpersonal sensitivity, depression, anxiety, hostility, phobic anxiety, paranoid ideation, and psychoticism (Derogatis, 1983). The Global Severity Index (GSI) will also be computed. It is considered a summary score of the SCL-90-R that serves as an index of current level or depth of psychological disorder. The reliability and validity of the SCL-90-R has been demonstrated in numerous studies. The coefficient alpha for the nine dimensions ranged from 0.77 for psychoticism to 0.90 for depression. The SCL-90-R was used to assess one of the outcome variables described in the stress process model.

Subjective Well-Being

Subjective well-being was assessed using three single-item measures relating to evaluations of life satisfaction, happiness, and goal attainment. The items combined represent the affective and cognitive dimensions of subjective well-being (Tran, Wright, & Chatters, 1991). Additionally, these items arrive at global versus domain-specific evaluations of life quality. When the items were combined, the scores ranged from 3–9 ($M = 7.44$, $SD = 1.40$), with higher scores indicating greater subjective well-being. The three items in this study have been used with African-American participants in the past and were found to be predictive in determining health, stress, and psychological resources (Tran et al., 1991). The subjective well-being scale was used to assess one of the outcome variables described in the stress process model.

RESULTS

The demographic characteristics of the sample are shown in Table 10.1. The data is presented using the following distinctions: "CC" refers to grandparents raising their grandchildren due to the crack/cocaine use of the children's parents, "OR"

TABLE 10.1 Demographic Characteristics of Grandparents

Characteristic	Crack/cocaine	Other Reasons	Control
Sample size	28.0% (26)	32.0% (29)	40.0% (37)
Gender			
Female	100% (26)	93.0% (27)	97.0% (36)
Male	—	7.0% (2)	3.0% (1)
Age			
30–39	3.8% (1)	10.3% (3)	—
40–49	38.5% (10)	31.0% (9)	22.9% (8)
50–59	30.8% (8)	41.4% (12)	40.0% (14)
60–69	23.1% (6)	13.8% (4)	8.6% (3)
70–79	3.8% (1)	3.4% (1)	20.0% (7)
80+	—	—	8.6% (3)
Median Age	52	50	54
Education			
< 12	26.9% (7)	24.1% (7)	5.4% (2)
12	15.4% (4)	20.7% (6)	24.3% (9)
Some college	34.6% (9)	48.3% (14)	40.5% (15)
≥ College	23.1% (6)	6.9% (2)	29.7% (11)
Marital status			
Married	46.2% (12)	28.6% (8)	29.7% (11)
Separated	3.8% (1)	17.2% (5)	—
Widowed	26.9% (7)	6.9% (2)	29.7% (11)
Divorced	11.5% (3)	34.5% (10)	37.8% (14)
Single	11.5% (3)	10.3% (3)	2.7% (1)
Other	—	3.5% (1)	—
Number of Grandchildren Being Cared for			
1	42.3% (11)	58.6% (17)	
2	23.1% (6)	34.5% (10)	
≥ 3	34.6% (9)	6.9% (2)	

refers to grandparents raising their grandchildren for reasons other than the substance use of the children's parents, and "Control" refers to the noncaregiving grandparents. To determine if there were statistically significant differences the Wilcoxon test and the Chi-square test were used.

A total of 92 participants were included in the study. Within the sample, 26 grandparents were raising their grandchildren because their children were crack/cocaine users (28%), 29 grandparents were raising grandchildren for reasons other than substance abuse (30%) and there were 37 noncaregiving controls (40%) (2%

missing). Grandmothers constituted the majority of the sample (97%). There was no median age difference among the three groups ($Median_{GP/CC}$ = 52; $Median_{GP/OR}$ = 50; $Median_{GP/Control}$ = 54; $p = .13$). The age range of the participants was 34–90 years, with a mean age of 55. There were three outliers in the control group who had a mean age of 84 years. There were no statistically significant education differences among the three groups (Median $response_{GP/CC}$ = high school; Median $response_{GP/OR}$ = high school; Median $response_{GP/Control}$ = high school; $p = .10$). Education ranged from less than high school to an advanced degree (JD, Ph.D., MD), with close to two thirds of the sample (62%) having some college education or more. More noncustodial grandparents had some college education. The custodial grandparents had similar educational attainment: 58% of the grandparents in the CC group had some college or more, 55% in the OR group had some college or more, and 70% of the Control group had some college or more. There were no significant marital status differences among the three groups ($p = .28$), although in the married category, there were more married grandparents in the CC group than in the other two groups. Forty-six percent of the grandparents in the CC group were married compared to 29% of grandparents in the OR group, and 30% in the Control group.

Stress and Coping Model

Component 1

The model viewed the reason for custodial grandparenting as a primary stressor and postulated that there would be variation in the caregiving outcomes based on the reasons for caregiving. This was not supported by the data. Overall, the grandparents reported high levels of health and well-being. Eighty-two percent of the grandparents rated their health as excellent, very good, or good. The other 18% stated that their health was fair or poor. When asked to compare their health to a year ago, 90% of the grandparents stated that their health was about the same or better than a year ago. Seventy-three percent of the grandparents rated their subjective well-being between 7 and 9. The remaining 23% reported SWB scores that ranged from 4 to 6 (4% missing). The Global Severity score (GSI) of the SCL-90-R was used to determine the level or depth of the grandparents' psychological distress. All of the grandparent groups fell within normal limits. There was individual variation. Seventy-seven percent of the grandparents had discrepancy scores ranging from 0 to 4. The remaining 23% had scores that ranged from 5 to 18. Multiple regression analyses revealed that there were no significant differences in health and well-being among the grandparents ($p > .05$).

Component 2

The second component of the model hypothesized that the reasons for caregiving would affect the caregiving outcomes. The reasons for caregiving did not affect the results. However, there were some interesting similarities and differences in the caregiving groups. There were more grandparents in the CC group (35%) who were raising three or more children than there were in the OR group (7%). Many grandparents were the caregivers for other persons in addition to their grandchildren (e.g., elderly parents). Since caregiving began, 32% of the custodial grandparents stated that they developed health problems. Although no significant differences were found among the grandparents based on their caregiving reasons, during the open-ended portion of the interview many expressed that the caregiving situation was stressful. They could not add their grandchildren to their health care plans and were therefore paying out of pocket for their grandchildren's medical care. Thus, caregiving resulted in a decrease in financial status for many of the caregivers. Many of the grandparents indicated that they did not know how to obtain the services they needed for their grandchildren. Additionally, many expressed ambivalence regarding their caregiving role.

Component 3

Discrepancy was viewed as the secondary stressor and mediator in the stress process. As presented in Table 10.2, discrepancy did arise as a result of the caregiving situation. However, it was not a mediating variable as hypothesized, although it was a main effect, indicating that it is an independent predictor of subjective well-being ($p = .001$). The results demonstrated that higher levels of discrepancy were associated with decreased subjective well-being. During the open-ended portion of the interview many of the grandparents stated that they had expected to be doing other things with their lives than primary caregiving. The following are examples of the discrepancies grandparents are experiencing: "I have to wait until (granddaughter) grows up to do the things I want to do. I have to put my life on hold again." "I have no social life, my social engagements have changed, I have no recreation myself, and my law school goals have changed, and I have more financial stress."

Component 4

The model also addressed the relation between discrepancy and the adaptational processes (appraisal of caregiving, coping, and social support) and the outcomes of caregiving. The only significant relation was found between discrepancy and coping in the prediction of subjective well-being. Multiple regression analyses, presented

TABLE 10.2 Results of Multiple Regression of Caregiving Outcomes on Discrepancy

PREDICTOR	b	P-VALUE
Multiple Regression of Subjective Well-Being on Discrepancy		
Age	0.16	.15
Education	0.03	.84
Marital Status	0.35	.18
Group Status	0.13	.43
Discrepancy	−0.11	.001
Multiple Regression of Overall Rating of Physical Health on Discrepancy		
Age	0.12	.23
Education	−0.10	.38
Marital Status	−0.22	.37
Group Status	−0.08	.59
Discrepancy	0.01	.65
Multiple Regression of Change in Health Status Over the Past Year on Discrepancy		
Age	0.13	.12
Education	−0.04	.66
Marital Status	−0.11	.61
Group Status	−0.15	.22
Discrepancy	0.04	.09
Multiple Regression of Psychological Health on Discrepancy		
Age	−0.78	.11
Education	1.19	.05
Marital Status	−0.04	.97
Group Status	−1.06	.15
Discrepancy	0.09	.49
Multiple Regression of Health Problems Before Caregiving on Discrepancy		
Age	−0.78	.02
Education	−0.49	.11
Marital Status	0.23	.72
Group Status	0.41	.50
Discrepancy	−0.020	.76
Multiple Regression of Development of Health Problems Since Caregiving Began on Discrepancy		
Age	−0.14	.68
Education	−0.24	.44
Marital Status	−0.34	.60
Group Status	0.67	.28
Discrepancy	−0.02	.80

in Table 10.3, indicate a significant interaction between discrepancy and several dimensions of the coping scale on health and well-being. After controlling for the sociodemographic variables in the model, examiners found a significant interaction between discrepancy and trying to be firm in directing the grandchild's behavior that was significant in the prediction of well-being ($p = .03$). Custodial grandparents with low levels of discrepancy and high levels of management of the grandchild's behavior had the highest levels of SWB as expected.

There was a significant interaction between discrepancy and keeping the grandchild busy in the prediction of SWB ($p = .03$). Custodial grandparents with high levels of discrepancy and high levels keeping their grandchild busy as a way to manage the situation had the highest levels of SWB. In other words, grandparents who did not expect to be caregiving at this point in their lives but are able to cope with the situation by keeping the grandchild busy report the highest levels of well-being. Additionally, there was a significant interaction between discrepancy and smoking in the prediction of SWB ($p = .02$). Custodial grandparents with low levels of discrepancy and low levels of smoking as a way to manage distress had the highest levels of SWB. There was a significant interaction between discrepancy and drinking in the prediction of SWB ($p = .05$). Custodial grandparents with low levels of discrepancy and low levels of drinking as a way to manage distress had higher levels of SWB. Below are statements from the open-ended portion of the interview that illustrate the relation between the grandparents' coping and discrepancy and the subsequent effect on their health and well-being. "I am not free when I should be free, and I have developed hypertension." "I don't like it. I'm angry because my youngest child is getting ready to graduate and I was almost finished raising children but now I have to start again."

CONCLUSIONS

Results revealed that custodial and noncaregiving grandparents were very similar in terms of health and well-being. This finding was not anticipated. Thus, the first component of the model, that custodial grandparenting adversely affects health and well-being among African Americans, was not supported. There are several possible explanations for the finding. The first has to do with selection bias, wherein grandparents in poor health would be less likely to become custodial grandparents. Another explanation could be that grandparents would be reluctant to admit health problems for fear that their grandchildren would be taken away from them. Alternatively, there may be a tendency for the grandparents to deemphasize their health concerns, viewing them as less important and troubling than other issues they are dealing with. Finally, perhaps prior exposure to and mastery of life stress, or experience of

TABLE 10.3 Results of Multiple Regression of Subjective Well-Being on the Discrepancy Coping Interactions

PREDICTOR	b	P-VALUE
Multiple Regression of Subjective Well-Being on the Discrepancy by Management of Situation Interaction		
Age	0.20	.24
Education	0.14	.31
Marital Status	0.61	.06
Group Status	0.22	.45
Discrepancy Management of Situation (direct grandchild's behavior)	−0.10	.03*
Multiple Regression of Subjective Well-Being on the Discrepancy by Management of Situation Interaction		
Age	0.18	.27
Education	0.15	.29
Marital Status	0.58	.07
Group Status	0.12	.69
Discrepancy Management of Situation (keep grandchild busy)	0.10	.02
Multiple Regression of Subjective Well-Being on the Discrepancy by Management of Distress Interaction		
Age	0.14	.37
Education	0.14	.32
Marital Status	0.42	.17
Group Status	0.01	.97
Discrepancy Management of Distress (smoking)	0.07	.02
Multiple Regression of Subjective Well-Being on the Discrepancy by Management of Situation Interaction		
Age	0.20	.23
Education	0.17	.26
Marital Status	0.58	.07
Group Status	0.15	.61
Discrepancy Management of Situation (drink some alcohol)	0.16	.05

Note: b is the unstandardized regression coefficient; main effects that are components of an interaction are not interpretable as main effects.

caregiving may serve to better prepare African-American custodial grandparents for the demands of caregiving.

Although not statistically significant, one third of the custodial grandparents reported they developed new health problems since caregiving began. This trend is consistent with the literature on grandparents as caregivers (Burton, 1992; Minkler & Roe, 1993). Focus on this subgroup could be helpful in the development and implementation of intervention strategies such as support groups.

As expected, discrepancy scores and coping were associated with the differences noted in well-being among the grandparents. Grandparents who were not engaging in the roles and activities in which they expected to be engaging in (discrepancy) had lower levels of well-being than grandparents who reported less discrepancy. This finding suggests that the sociobehavioral mechanism by which grandparenting leads to lower levels of well-being is through discrepancy. Custodial grandparenthood may not have occurred for these grandparents as expected and therefore they are reorienting their expectations, a process that could adversely affect their well-being. Given that discrepancy was a significant predictor in subjective well-being, further theoretical discussion and empirical examination are warranted to determine how discrepancy functions. The construct may function as a type of cognitive appraisal or it could serve as one part of a larger cognitive process in which discrepancy influences future appraisals of the caregiving situation. There was also an interaction between discrepancy and two dimensions of the coping scale (management of distress and management of the situation) in the prediction of well-being. The relation suggests that discrepancy and coping are important predictors within this population. Future studies should expand on methods used by African-American grandparents to cope with the stress of caregiving.

There are four major study limitations. First, the study uses a convenience sample. The subjects sampled may not represent the general population. Second, coping and adjustment to caregiving is a process, one that cannot adequately be assessed at one point in time. A longitudinal design is the only way to capture adaptation to the caregiving situation. Given that the caregivers and the grandchildren are of different ages and at different developmental places in the life span, a longitudinal design could address the developmental process of the grandparents over time. Third, the information obtained on the discrepancy scale is retrospective. The custodial grandparents may have had recall bias, finding it difficult to disentangle what they expected to do from what they are currently doing. Additionally, the scale does not account for respondents who have an absence of expectations. Fourth, the primary stressor was not sufficient. There was not a direct relation between reasons for caregiving and changes in health and well-being.

The chapter indicates that a stress and coping conceptual framework is an effective tool to guide in the development of research questions, interpretation of results, and development of interventions for custodial grandparents. For example, the results from the test of the conceptual model helped guide several of the topics chosen during the support group, such as different coping strategies. The chapter also illustrates that the study of African-American grandparents is an interdisciplinary effort. Additionally, there is a clear need to examine the contexts and environments in which African-American custodial grandparents conduct their lives and the ways these conditions develop and change over time.

REFERENCES

Baydar, N., & Brooks-Gunn, J. (1998). Profiles of grandmothers who help care for their grandchildren in the United States. *Family Relations, 47,* 385–393.

Bryson, K., & Casper, L. M. (1999). *Coresident grandparents and grandchildren: U.S. Bureau of the Census current population reports* (Series P-23 No. 198). Washington, DC: U.S. Government Printing Office.

Burnette, D. (1999). Custodial grandparents in Latino families: Patterns of service use and predictors of unmet needs. *Social Work, 44,* 22–34.

Burton, L. (1992). African American grandmothers rearing children of drug-addicted parents: Stressors, outcomes, and social service needs. *The Gerontologist, 32*(6), 744–751.

Derogatis, L. R. (1983). *SCL-90 administration, scoring, and procedures: Manual II.* Towson, MD: Clinical Psychometric Research.

Dilworth-Anderson, P. (1994). The importance of grandparents in extended-kin caregiving to Black children. *Journal of Health and Social Policy, 5,* 185–202.

Fuller-Thomson, E., Minkler, M., & Driver, D. (1997). A profile of grandparents raising grandchildren in the United States. *The Gerontologist, 37*(3), 406–411.

Jendrek, M. P. (1994). Grandparents who parent their grandchildren: Circumstances and decisions. *The Gerontologist, 34*(2), 206–216.

Joslin, D., & Brouard, A. (1995). The prevalence of grandmothers as primary caregivers in a poor pediatric population. *Journal of Community Health, 20*(5), 383–401.

Joslin, D., & Harrison, B. (1998). The hidden patient: Older relatives raising children orphaned by AIDS. *Journal of the American Medical Women's Association, 53*(2), 65–71.

Minkler, M., & Fuller-Thomson, E. (1999). The health of grandparents raising grandchildren: Results of a national study. *American Journal of Public Health, 89*(8), 1–6.

Minkler, M., Fuller-Thomson, E., Miller, D., & Driver, D. (1997). Depression in grandparents raising grandchildren. *Archives of Family Medicine, 6,* 445–452.

Minkler, M., & Roe, K. M. (1993). *Grandmothers as caregivers: Raising grandchildren of the crack cocaine epidemic.* Newbury Park, CA: Sage.

Minkler, M., Roe, K. M., & Price, M. (1992). The physical and emotional health of grandmothers raising grandchildren in the crack cocaine epidemic. *The Gerontologist, 32,* 752–761.

O'Reilly, E., & Morrison, M. L. (1993). Grandparent-headed families: New therapeutic challenges. *Child Psychiatry and Human Development, 23,* 147–159.

Pearlin, L. I., Mullan, J. T., Semple, J. S., & Skaff, M. M. (1990). Caregiving and the stress process: An overview of concepts and their measures. *The Gerontologist, 30,* 583–594.

Pinson-Millburn, N. M., Fabian, E. S., Schlossberg, N. K., & Pyle, M. (1996). Grandparents raising grandchildren. *Journal of Counseling & Development, 74,* 548–554.

Pruchno, R. (1999). Raising grandchildren: The experiences of African American and white grandmothers. *The Gerontologist, 39*(2), 209–221.

Saluter, A. F. (1992). *Marital status and living arrangements: March 1991. U.S. Bureau of the Census current population reports* (Series P-20 No. 461). Washington, DC: U.S. Government Printing Office.

Sands, R. G., & Goldberg-Glen, R. S. (2000). Factors associated with stress among grandparents raising their grandchildren. *Family Relations, 49*(1), 97–105.

Strom, R., Collinsworth, P., Strom, S., & Griswold, D. (1993). Strengths and needs of Black grandparents. *International Journal of Aging and Human Development, 36,* 255–268.

Szinovacz, M. E. (1998). Grandparents today: A demographic profile. *The Gerontologist, 38*(1), 37–52.

CHAPTER 11

The Impact of a Psychosocial Intervention on Parental Efficacy, Grandchild Relationship Quality, and Well-Being Among Grandparents Raising Grandchildren

Bert Hayslip, Jr.

INTRODUCTION

Both public interest and research speaking to the phenomenon of grandparents who raise their grandchildren have grown exponentially over the last decade. While it is beyond the scope of the present chapter to review such work, there is no shortage of information on the challenges to one's way of life, future goals, health, and well-being that raising a grandchild brings to grandparents who are often in their 50s and 60s, whose world has been turned upside down by their newfound parental responsibilities. Those domains that seem to be most affected by custodial grandparenting are physical and mental health, role-specific responsibilities (e.g., role overload, role confusion), relationships with age peers (social isolation), relationships with those grandchildren one is and is not caring for, and parenting for the second time (Beltran, 2000; Burton, 1992; Cox, 2000; Emick & Hayslip, 1996, 1999; Hayslip & Shore, 2000; Hayslip, Shore, Henderson, & Lambert, 1998; Jendrek, 1994; Minkler & Roe, 1993; Minkler, Roe, & Price, 1992; Pruchno, 1999; Shore & Hayslip, 1994). In particular, many authors (Burton, 1992; Dowdell, 1995; Emick & Hayslip, 1999; Kelley, 1993; Kelley, Whitley, Sipe, & Yorker, 2000; Minkler & Roe, 1993) have documented higher rates of depression and psychological distress among custodial grandparents (grandmothers) than among noncustodial grandmothers (Fuller-Thomson & Minkler, 2000; Minkler, Fuller-Thomson, Miller, & Driver, 1997). This is underscored by feelings of entrapment or resentment reported by grandparent caregivers at having a dysfunctional adult child. Studies of grandparents raising grandchildren also indicate that they are at increased risk for physical health problems, with some health problems serious enough to jeopardize their ability to parent (Kelley and Whitley, chapter 9, this volume). For example, grandmothers raising grandchildren are more likely than noncaregiving grandmothers to report their health as very poor to fair (Fuller-Thomson & Minkler, 2000), and such persons are also more likely to report physical limitations in performing daily activities of living (Minkler & Fuller-Thomson, 2001; Minkler & Roe, 1993). While many such persons have a high sense of perseverance and determination to continue their responsibilities in spite of any physical limitations or symptoms, they rarely seek help for themselves, thus heightening their vulnerability (Hayslip & Shore, 2000; Shore & Hayslip, 1994).

A number of factors have been identified as sources of increased distress in custodial grandparents, potentially interfering with their willingness and ability to parent, or perhaps arising as a consequence of the demands of the newly acquired parental role, for example, poor physical health, social isolation, and financial difficulties (Kelley and Whitley, chapter 9, this volume). Other contributing factors include conflict with the children's parents (Wohl, Lahner, & Jooste, chapter 13, this volume), the behavior problems of grandchildren, and issues related to public policies and financial and legal issues (Caliandro & Hughes, 1998; Dowdell, 1995; Emick & Hayslip, 1999; Kelley & Damato, 1995; Minkler & Roe, 1993; Yorker et al., 1998).

Indeed, given the context of disruptive family events that precede grandparents' assuming the care of their grandchildren (e.g., divorce, drug use, incarceration, child and/or spousal abuse, alcoholism, teenage pregnancy, abandonment), the negative impact on such middle-aged and older persons is hardly surprising. With regard to parenting, though grandparents are anticipatorially socialized into their roles as such even prior to the birth of their grandchildren (Somary & Stricker, 1998), there is often no such preparation regarding the (re)development of parenting skills that may have been latent for some years. This is especially significant in that for many grandparents, a norm of noninterference (except in crisis situations) in the raising of their grandchildren has been established prior to the reassumption of the parental role (Thomas, 1990).

Given the sudden and often stressful circumstances that characterize custodial grandparenting, it is rare to find grandparents whose parental skills are well developed and anchored in current information about parenting practices (e.g., communication, discipline, modeling respect, conflict resolution, problem solving); normal developmental changes in their grandchildren's physical, cognitive, psychosocial, and emotional development; and abnormal childhood disorders such as depression, ADHD, drug use, aggression/acting out behavior, grief at the loss of a parent, self-destructive behaviors, or alcoholism. Complicating matters are middle-aged and older grandparents' relative unfamiliarity with issues such as sexually transmitted diseases, drug use, school violence, and peer influences on both children and adolescents, as well as their comparative lack of knowledge about and predisposition not to seek mental health care either for themselves or their grandchildren (Currin, Hayslip, Schneider, & Kooken, 1998; Hayslip & Shore, 2000; Silverthorn & Durant, 2000). Significantly, the events that make care of grandchildren necessary can occur suddenly (e.g., incarceration of the parent, removal of the children due to abuse or neglect), or after a long and difficult period (e.g., death of the parent from AIDS, mental illness, addiction), leaving grandparent caregivers unprepared for such instant parenting, as opposed to the normal nine-month waiting period most parents experience.

While the adverse emotional and physical health problems experienced by many such grandchildren may have predated such difficulties or were reactions either to the desolation of their family of origin or to the placement with grandparents, there have emerged two distinct subgroups of custodial grandparents: those raising grandchildren with minimal physical and psychosocial difficulties and those raising grandchildren who are suffering from such difficulties (Emick & Hayslip, 1999: Hayslip et al., 1998). Custodial grandparents in each parental situation are either beset by the effects of the above sets of forces that may undermine their existing parental skills, or are faced with the additional demands on their skills brought about by the difficulties (e.g., depression, poor health) that either they or their grandchildren are experiencing. Complicating matters, grandparents often express feelings of shame, guilt, and anxiety because of their adult child's drug addiction, incarceration, or death due to AIDS (Joslin, 2000), and, not surprisingly, feelings of anger, resentment, or failure as a parent are also common as a result of assuming this unexpected and unwanted role (Burton, 1992; Emick & Hayslip, 1999; Kelley & Damato, 1995; Minkler & Roe, 1993).

As Kelley and Whitley (chapter 9, this volume) point out, the above physical and mental health issues raise concerns about the quality of the family environment when such grandparents attempt to raise young, active children. Despite the many positive benefits of raising their grandchildren, grandparents report worries about their ability to care for their grandchildren as the former age and/or develop chronic illness and disability (Shore & Hayslip, 1994), and both the short-term and the long-term impact of custodial grandparenting on such persons' ability to raise their grandchildren competently is of concern (Hirshorn, 1998). While some grandparents may only require and/or seek minimal updating of their parenting skills, others whose child-rearing experiences with their own adult children are either more removed in time or more problematic, or who are raising children with physical or mental health difficulties, may need more information, support, and assistance. For such persons, parental skills training that also incorporates support and information about adjustment to one's newly acquired parental role responsibilities, self-care/time management skills, and information about legal, financial, and health-related services and their accessibility, are likely to be most beneficial. This is because these parental role-adjustment and personal issues do not occur in isolation (see Kelley, Whitley, Sipe, & Yorker, 2001; Smith, chapter 6, this volume; Wohl et al., chapter 13, this volume).

PURPOSE OF THE PRESENT STUDY

In light of the above documented personal, health-related, interpersonal, and role-specific difficulties identified in the literature, there is ample reason to make available some form of supportive, educative, informational, or interventive assistance to custodial grandparents. In spite of this obvious need, there is little published work, over and above that dealing with grandparent caregiver support groups (see Smith, chapter 6, this volume), that speaks to the design, implementation, and efficacy of psychosocial interventions to assist grandparents who are raising their grandchildren. Consequently, the purpose of this chapter is to present findings explicitly dealing with the impact of a treatment program whose emphasis is on parental skills training and psychosocial adjustment, on custodial grandparent parental efficacy, grandchild relationship quality, and grandparent well-being. In light of the lack of efficacy data relating to such interventions, their availability is critical to mental health, nursing, support groups, social work, social service, legal assistance, and educational professionals who deal with custodial grandparents and the grandchildren for whom they care.

METHOD

Participants and Measures

Participants for the present study (N = 36) were recruited from the Dallas–Ft. Worth Metroplex, where announcements regarding the program were made in the local newspaper and in church bulletins, in senior centers, and through grandparent caregiver support groups. This program was described as educational in nature, offering grandparents who were raising their grandchildren on a full-time basis the opportunity to learn more about both normal and problematic issues with their grandchildren, to develop new and more effective ways of communicating, to enhance their self-care skills, and, most important, to not only develop more effective ways of coping with stress, but to enhance their knowledge and skills regarding the parenting of young children and adolescents.

After contacting the author, participants were randomly assigned to a parental skills training/psychosocial treatment group ($N = 18$, M age = 54.82, 4 males, 14 females, M Level of Education in Years = 13.41), or to a waiting list control group ($N = 18$, M age = 57.85, 4 males, 14 females, M Level of Education in Years = 13.51), where the latter were told that the current discussion/parenting skills group was full, and that in approximately two months, they would be contacted, after which they would begin their participation. Participants were brought together to form the treatment group, where two such group programs ($n = 8$–10 in each case) were presented (see below), after which those waiting list control participants who wanted it ($n = 12$) were provided skill training. Those waiting list control persons who did not wish to participate in parental/psychosocial skills training were nevertheless mailed copies of the materials provided to training group participants.

Before and after skills training, participants completed a questionnaire that assessed a variety of dimensions of custodial grandparenting. Waiting list control participants also completed these same questionnaires approximately six weeks apart (the length of the parenting skills training program), but before taking part in the optional skills training or receiving by mail training materials in the event they did not wish to participate in the optional skills training. This instrument consisted of a variety of questions asking about sociodemographic characteristics (e.g., age, gender, level of education, annual income, number of grandchildren, extent and duration of caregiving, legal custody status, reason for the assumption of caregiving, extent of contact with the grandchild's parents).

Grandparent caregivers also completed a number of self-report measures assessing numerous dimensions of the experience of caregiving: *Feelings Regarding Role Assumption*, assessing the grandparent's positive/negative attitude toward the resumption of the parental role (Emick & Hayslip, 1999); the *Parenting Stress Index/Short Form* (Abidin, 1990); *satisfaction with grandparenting* (Thomas, 1988); *psychological distress/depression* (Center for Epidemiologic Studies Depression Scale-CES-D) (Radloff, 1977); the *Positive and Negative Affect Index*, assessing aspects of one's perceptions of the relationship with the grandchild (i.e., extent of mutual trust, respect and understanding; affection for the grandchild versus negative feelings about irritating behaviors of the grandchild) (Bence & Thomas, 1988); *parental role strain* (Pearlin & Schooler, 1978); *financial role strain* (Pearlin & Schooler, 1978); *extent of life disruption* (Jendrek, 1994); *parental empowerment* (assessing attitudes toward, knowledge about, and behaviors specific to the [grand]parent's ability to appropriately solve problems with the child), where slight modifications were made to fit grandparent caregivers (Koren, DeChillo, & Friesen, 1992); *situational parental efficacy*, wherein grandparents rate the extent of confidence they have in their ability to manage the child's behavior in a variety of situations (e.g., at home, in the car, in the store, in the presence of family, friends or company at home), reflecting several underlying dimensions (suitability, communication, discipline) (Bachicha, 1985, 1997); *parental self efficacy* (rated self-confidence regarding time management skills, sensitivity to the child's feelings, handling of situations when a mistake has been made, ability to solve problems with the child, ability to perform one's duties as a parent and spouse, ability to take credit for one's own and the child's good and bad behavior) (Bachicha, 1997); *psychological well being* (Liang, 1985); and single ratings of the *quality of, and satisfaction with, the relationship with the grandchild* (Emick & Hayslip, 1999).

With the exception of the above indices of parental efficacy/parental empowerment that were derived from the measures developed and validated by Bachicha (1985, 1997) and by Koren et al. (1992), all of the above self-report scales and/or ratings have been successfully utilized in previous custodial grandparenting research by the author and colleagues (Emick & Hayslip, 1999; Hayslip & Shore, 2000; Hayslip et al., 1998; Shore & Hayslip, 1994) to differentiate custodial grandparents by the extent of problems in their grandchildren, to explore the determinants of well-being and role satisfaction in grandparent caregivers, and to examine relationships to mental health service attitudes in such persons. All parts of this latter set of scales have more than adequate reliability (see Emick & Hayslip, 1999; Hayslip et al., 1998). In each case, higher scores indexed more positive feelings about the parental role, greater parental self-efficacy and empowerment, greater well-being, greater role satisfaction, more depression, more role strain, greater grandchild relationship quality and satisfaction, and greater life disruption. Each questionnaire required approximately an hour to complete and, as mentioned above, was administered at equal time intervals for treatment and waiting list control participants.

The Parental Skills/Psychosocial Skills Training Program

The programmatic intervention consisted of six (90 to 120 minutes in length) sessions held on Saturday mornings, the first of which dealt with the development of parenting skills in the context of communication, the goals of discipline, modeling of desirable behaviors and everyday task completion, fostering positive self-worth, developing responsibility, parenting styles, differentiating the effects of positive discipline and logical consequences from punishment, developing cooperation, and understanding the function of child misbehavior. This was followed by four sessions dealing with grief, depression, and anger in the grandchild (and in some cases as they related to the grandparent); talking with children about sex and sexually transmitted diseases; drug use and abuse; and understanding and dealing with attentional and school-related problems as well as with learning difficulties and disabilities (see also Wohl et al., chapter 13, this volume). In each case, an equal emphasis was placed on how (grand)parents might handle such issues and on the imparting of information about content per se, the latter of which was often deemphasized so that grandparents could openly discuss each issue under the guidance of the group leaders (who were all doctoral level students in Counseling Psychology who had been educated about custodial grandparenting by the author), as well as share feelings and experiences with one another. Generally speaking, an emphasis was placed on providing grandparents the opportunity to raise any issues, such as getting needed social services, dealing with the school system and Child Protective Services, coping with their feelings about the uncertain nature of their relationship with the adult child whose child they were raising, and any concerns they had about the impact of their new roles on their personal well-being, health, and relationships with one another or with family and friends. A last session, led by a custodial grandmother, dealt with self-care, legal and financial issues, and solutions to each.

Results and Discussion

Table 11.1 presents the means and standard deviations for the above dependent variables for each group before and after training. Data were analyzed via a 2 (group: skills training versus waiting list control) X 2 (occasion: pre- versus postprogram) multivariate analysis of variance (MANOVA), wherein post hoc tests to decompose group by occasion interactions were carried out as appropriate. While this analysis yielded no main effects for group membership at the multivariate level, a multivariate main effect for occasion was obtained (F 15,15 = 4.47, $p < .01$) and was particular to Parental Role Strain (F 1,29 = 7.36, $p < .01$) and Situational Parental Efficacy (F 1,29 = 39.04, $p < .01$), wherein at posttraining, irrespective of group membership, participants experienced somewhat greater role strain and less situational parental efficacy (see Table 11.1), each relative to the initial assessment.

Of interest of course, was the group by occasion interaction, wherein such was obtained at the multivariate level (for the linear combination of measures as a set) (F 15, 15 = 4.19, $p < .01$). This was particular to: Parental Role Strain (F 1,29 = 22.56, $p < .01$), CES-D (depression) (F 1,29 = 4.73, $p < .04$), and Parental Self Efficacy (F 1,29 = 5.75, $p < .02$), and approached statistical significance for Negative Affect (F 1,29 = 3.14, $p < .08$), Financial Strain (F 1,29 = 3.25, $p < .08$), and Rated Quality of the Relationship with the Grandchild (F 1,29 = 3.60, $p < .07$).

TABLE 11.1 Means and Standard Deviations for Training and Control Groups

Variable	Training (*N* = 18)				Waiting List Control (*N* = 18)			
	M^1	SD^1	M^2	SD^2	M^1	SD^1	M^2	SD^2
Feeling[3]	33.12	6.06	32.50	6.30	31.20	5.95	32.66	5.42
PSI[4]	79.18	25.54	79.56	26.85	75.20	19.77	78.66	25.22
GP Sat[5]	59.37	8.21	57.75	9.86	57.60	7.27	56.73	11.41
Empower[6]	49.00	7.41	49.50	6.33	47.53	9.65	48.20	10.49
P Affect[7]	39.81	4.13	39.75	6.32	39.06	3.61	38.66	7.16
N Affect[8]	34.25	5.19	32.12	5.66	30.93	4.20	31.66	5.83
P Role Strain[9]	26.25	6.16	30.43	8.02	32.26	7.20	31.13	6.14
Fin. Strain[10]	6.62	2.60	6.75	3.02	8.13	4.45	7.00	3.09
Life Disrupt[11]	54.06	18.85	51.56	19.77	57.06	14.87	52.13	13.20
CESD[12]	37.31	6.70	39.75	6.22	38.46	6.33	36.80	7.90
Life Sat[13]	42.68	6.47	43.06	5.91	48.06	5.87	44.93	6.39
Sit. Par. Eff[14]	304.50	55.80	248.75	64.03	309.33	49.16	258.46	66.63
Parental Eff[15]	243.00	36.36	256.50	32.65	243.60	47.28	234.73	46.44
Quality[16]	4.56	.63	4.69	.60	4.66	.62	4.33	1.05
Satisfaction[17]	4.31	.79	4.43	.89	4.40	.74	4.06	1.22

Note:

1. Pretest
2. Posttest
3. Feelings About Role Assumption
4. Parental Stress Index
5. Grandparent Role Satisfaction
6. Parental Empowerment
7. Positive Affect
8. Negative Affect
9. Role Strain
10. Financial Strain
11. Life Disruption
12. Depression
13. Life Satisfaction
14. Situational Parental Efficacy
15. Generalized Parental Efficacy
16. Quality of Grandchild Relationship
17. Satisfaction with Grandchild Relationship

Inspection of means (see Table 11.1) suggested for training participants, relative to controls: Negative Affect scores (irritation/difficulty with the grandchild's negative behaviors) decreased over time (pre- versus postprogram), Parental Self-Efficacy increased over time, as did the rated Quality of the Relationship with One's Grandchild, while Parental Role Strain increased over time, as did both Financial Strain and Depression.

Though the magnitude of these effects is modest and impacted by the comparatively small sample sizes in each group, affecting the statistical power of the analyses, and in some cases somewhat surprising, they do document the extent to which the parental skills and psychosocial adjustment of grandparents can be effected by purposefully designed interventions targeting for many grandparents heretofore unspoken issues regarding the demands of raising a grandchild. For many grandparents, it may be that the use of the skills they acquired in the program made matters at home somewhat more tense, as might be the case when issues regarding the impact of their parenting roles on their marriages; relationships with friends; frustrations with service providers, social service agencies, school personnel, or with the adult child are aired for the first time, or when they became aware of the difficulty in changing their grandchild's behavior. It may also be that some grandparents were reactivating previous parenting styles that were somewhat traditional and/or authority-oriented, and therefore may have made their interactions with their grandchildren more difficult. This may explain the small yet reliable increases in parental role strain, financial strain, and depression over time in training participants relative to waiting list controls. The program may have brought to the surface previously ineffective ways of interacting with their adult children when the latter were young, heightened grandparents' awareness of the child-rearing task before them, or allowed them the freedom to discuss their negative feelings and frustrations at having to parent again. Indeed, many sessions lasted well over two hours because participants wanted more time to discuss concerns that the discussions elicited in them. In terms of consciousness-raising, so to speak, the program helped bring to the surface feelings of anger, shame, guilt, or frustration that participants felt uneasy about sharing in less supportive contexts. Therapeutically, this was advantageous, as many grandparents were able to test the validity of assumptions they had previously held about parenting, and were able to see their advantages and disadvantages in the context of their daily interactions with their grandchildren and weekly interactions with one another.

At the same time, within the training group, there were reliable increases in the tolerance for the negative, irritating, or disruptive behaviors that often might lead to arguments, cause resentment of one another, bring about futile attempts to change a grandchild, or undermine communication. Moreover, training participants expressed greater personal self-efficacy in their ability to deal with their grandchildren's behavior through the use of both verbal and physical (hugs, kisses) praise. They expressed greater self-confidence in their time management and self-care skills; communication with their grandchild; and understanding of their grandchild's wishes, feelings, and behaviors. They became better able to change their grandchild's behavior when necessary, carry out their parental responsibilities and solve problems with little fear of failure, and understand the limits of control over and responsibility for their grandchild's good and bad behavior. Not surprisingly in light of these findings, training participants also felt that their relationships with their grandchildren had improved qualitatively. Comparatively speaking, there is some indication (see Table 11.1) that those who lacked the presumed benefits of parental skills/psychosocial adjustment training actually worsened over time in the areas of parental efficacy, quality and satisfaction with grandchild relationships, life satisfaction, and negative affect.

These findings underscore the double-edged sword of intervening with grandparent caregivers, given that the issues dealt with in each session were inexorably linked to deeper, interwoven concerns that many grandparents in the groups expressed great frustration over. It could be argued that in some respects, the program made grandparents more attentive to the difficulties of raising a grandchild, but was less effective in providing easily implemented solutions to such problems, especially when the sources of the difficulties were beyond the ability and resources of many grandparents to control (e.g., difficulties with the school system, legal uncertainties over custody, unresponsive child protective services, grief over a broken family system). Significantly, in this respect, grandparents felt no greater sense of empowerment after training. Yet, in spite of such forces, grandparent caregivers who received training reported greater efficacy in their abilities to parent and improved relationships with their grandchildren.

On the one hand, having the opportunity to discuss one's feelings about the difficulties, sense of unfairness, isolation, guilt, or frustration in raising a grandchild under oftentimes adverse circumstances may lead to feelings of depression, being overwhelmed, or an awareness of the uncertainty of the future, given one's anticipated poorer health, possible widowhood, financial stress, or the entrance into school or puberty of one's grandchild. In this respect (see Smith, chapter 6, this volume), it could be argued that parental/psychosocial skills training, like support groups, can be counterproductive for some persons. This parallels in part the findings discussed by Roberto and Qualls (chapter 2, this volume) on caregiver respite programs. Yet, there is much benefit in the discomfort one feels when existing beliefs are challenged and previously unspoken feelings are aired. Indeed, some grandparents seemed to become more open to change over the course of the six sessions, but the data here indicate that such openness is not without its costs (see Wohl et al., chapter 13, this volume).

Alternatively, skills training group members reported greater personal parental efficacy, improved grandchild relationship quality, and greater tolerance for negative grandchild behaviors, indicating that the program was clearly effective with regard to targeted parental skills efficacy. Understandably, broader constructs such as generalized well-being, role satisfaction, life disruption, and life satisfaction did not respond to programmatic efforts whose focus was more limited by design, though means for some of the variables (e.g., life satisfaction) declined over time (though not in a statistical sense) among waiting list control participants. An analysis by situational specificity regarding parental efficacy might, however, prove more advantageous in revealing programmatic impact. As participants in both groups were not followed up over time, the long-term effects, if any, of the intervention, remain unverified.

The self-selected nature of this sample needs to be considered in evaluating these data as many grandparents were raising grandchildren with emotional and behavioral problems. Previous work (Emick & Hayslip, 1999; Hayslip et al., 1998) indicates that such grandparents are at risk for psychosocial distress and lessened role satisfaction. This is underscored by the fact that nearly 80% of the grandparents in this study were women, who bear the principal burden of raising the grandchildren in most cases (see Burton, 1992; Fuller-Thomson & Minkler, 2000; Hirshorn, 1998; Minkler & Roe, 1993). Many such women had sought professional help for themselves or their grandchildren, were single, and were living on a minimal fixed income. At least a third of the sample asked for and received a referral for either an individual assessment of their grandchildren or family counseling therapy, or specifically asked for and received assistance in gaining access to legal help, needed social services, or resources to help them come to grips with their own sense of grief over the losses they had experienced (see Baird, chapter 5, this volume). In light of these findings, much needs to be learned about males who raise their grandchildren, especially in the context of their marriages, careers, and health.

It is also important to reflect on the self-selected nature of the sample as it relates to the fact that nearly all participants were Caucasian, who, comparatively speaking, may lack support (especially if they are women) in the raising of their grandchildren. Thus, our data may paint a somewhat different, more dismal, picture than that gathered from African-American or Hispanic custodial grandparents (Burnette, 1999; Burton, 1992; Minkler, Roe, & Robertson-Beckley, 1994; Toledo, Hayslip, Emick, Toledo, & Henderson, 2000; Wilson, 1986; Wilson, Tolson, Hinton, & Kiernan, 1990) who may have more assistance from an extended family network (see also Unger, McAvay, Bruce, Berman, & Seeman, 1999).

While no single intervention can be expected to impact all of the interrelated difficulties our grandparents voiced, these pilot data nevertheless hold promise for the potential of appropriately designed intervention research with custodial grandparents. However, attention to the long-term efficacy of such efforts, the selective nature and size of the sample of volunteer participants here, and perhaps to a longer and/or more in-depth psychoeducational intervention to deal with some of the byproducts of confronting one's negative feelings toward a son or daughter or toward a grandchild, or activating previously ineffective and/or unchallenged assumptions and behaviors is certainly warranted.

If such programs have no other effect than to offer these grandparents hope and arm them with needed parental, role adjustment, and self-care skills, as well as creating a network of support involving other custodial grandparents upon which to draw, then the data here indicate that such interventions hold promise for positively affecting those grandparents' and their grandchildren's future well-being.

REFERENCES

Abidin, R. R. (1990). *Parenting stress index* (3rd ed.). Charlottesville, VA: Pediatric Psychology Press.

Bachicha, D. (1985). *The parental self-efficacy scale and its relationship to maternal variables in a triadic model for parent training*. Unpublished master's thesis, New Mexico Highland University, New Mexico.

Bachicha, D. (1997). *A validation study of the parental self-efficacy scale*. Unpublished doctoral dissertation, University of New Mexico, New Mexico.

Beltran, A. (2000, Summer). Grandparents and other relatives raising children: Supportive public policies. *The Public Policy and Aging Report, 1,* 3–7.

Bence, S. L., & Thomas, J. L. (1988, November). *Grandparent–parent relationships as predictors of grandparent–grandchild relationships*. Paper presented at the Annual Scientific Meeting of the Gerontological Society of America, San Francisco, CA.

Burnette, D. (1999). Social relationships of Latino grandparent caregivers: A role theory perspective. *The Gerontologist, 39,* 49–58.

Burton, L. M. (1992). Black grandparents rearing children of drug-addicted parents: Stressors, outcomes, and social services. *Gerontologist, 3,* 744–751.

Caliandro, G., & Hughes, C. (1998). The experience of being a grandmother who is the primary caregiver for her HIV-positive grandchild. *Nursing Research, 47*(2), 107–113.

Cox, C. (2000). *To grandmother's house we go and stay*. New York: Springer.

Currin, J., Hayslip, B., Schneider, L., & Kooken, R. (1998). Cohort differences in attitudes toward mental health services among older persons. *Psychotherapy, 35,* 506–518.

Dowdell, E. B. (1995). Caregiver burden: Grandmothers raising their high risk grandchildren. *Journal of Psychosocial Nursing, 33,* 27–30.

Emick, M. A., & Hayslip, B. (1996). Custodial grandparenting: New roles for middle aged and older adults. *International Journal of Aging and Human Development, 43,* 135–154.

Emick, M. A., & Hayslip, B. (1999). Custodial grandparenting: Stresses, coping skills, and relationships with grandchildren. *International Journal on Aging and Human Development, 48,* 35–61.

Fuller-Thomson, E., Driver, D., & Minkler, M. (1997). A profile of grandparents raising grandchildren in the United States. *The Gerontologist, 37,* 406–411.

Fuller-Thomson, E., & Minkler, M. (2000). The mental and physical health of grandmothers who are raising their grandchildren. *Journal of Mental Health and Aging, 6,* 311–323.

Hayslip, B., & Shore, R. J. (2000). Custodial grandparenting and mental health. *Journal of Mental Health and Aging, 6,* 367–384.

Hayslip, B., Shore, R. J., Henderson, C., & Lambert, P. (1998). Custodial grandparenting and grandchildren with problems: Impact on role satisfaction and role meaning. *Journals of Gerontology: Social Sciences, 53B,* S164–S174.

Hirshorn, B. (1998). Grandparents as caregivers. In M. Szinovacz (Ed.), *Handbook on grandparenthood* (pp. 200–216). Westport, CT: Greenwood.

Jendrek, M. (1994). Grandparents who parent their grandchildren: Circumstances and decisions. *The Gerontologist, 34,* 206–216.

Joslin, D. (2000). Emotional well-being among grandparents raising grandchildren affected and orphaned by HIV disease. In B. Hayslip & R. Goldberg-Glen (Eds.), *Grandparents raising grandchildren: Theoretical, empirical and clinical perspectives* (pp. 87–106). New York: Springer.

Kelley, S. J. (1993). Caregiver stress in grandparents raising grandchildren. *Image: Journal of Nursing Scholarship, 25,* 331–337.

Kelley, S. J., & Damato, E. G. (1995). Grandparents as primary caregivers. *Maternal Child Nursing, 20,* 326–332.

Kelley, S. J., Whitley, D. M., Sipe, T. A., & Yorker, B. C. (2000). Psychological distress in grandmother kinship care providers: The role of resources, social support and physical health. *Child Abuse & Neglect, 24,* 311–321.

Kelley, S. J., Whitley, D. M., Sipe, T. A., & Yorker, B. C. (2001, October). *Results of an interdisciplinary intervention to improve the well-being and functioning of grandparents raising grandchildren.* Paper presented at the American Public Health Association Annual Meeting, Atlanta, GA.

Koren, P., DeChillo, N., & Friesen, B. (1992). Measuring empowerment in families whose children have emotional disabilities: A brief questionnaire. *Rehabilitation Psychology, 37,* 305–321.

Liang, J. (1985). A structural integration of the Affect Balance Scale and the Life Satisfaction Index A. *Journal of Gerontology, 40,* 552–561.

Minkler, M., & Fuller-Thomson, E. (2001). Physical and mental health status of American grandparents providing extensive child care to their grandchildren. *Journal of the American Medical Women's Association, 56,* 199–205.

Minkler, M., Fuller-Thomson, E., Miller, D., & Driver, D. (1997). Depression in grandparents raising grandchildren: Results of a national longitudinal study. *Archives of Family Medicine, 6,* 445–452.

Minkler, M., & Roe, K. M. (1993). *Grandmothers as caregivers: Raising children of the crack cocaine epidemic.* Newbury Park, CA: Sage.

Minkler, M., Roe, K. M., & Price, M. (1992). The physical and emotional health of grandmothers raising grandchildren in the crack cocaine epidemic. *The Gerontologist, 32,* 752–761.

Minkler, M., Roe, K. M., & Robertson-Beckley, R. J. (1994). Raising grandchildren from crack-cocaine households: Effects on family and friendship ties of African-American women. *American Journal of Orthopsychiatry, 64,* 20–29.

Pearlin, L. I., & Schooler, C. (1978). The structure of coping. *Journal of Health and Social Behavior, 19,* 2–21.

Pruchno, R. (1999). Raising grandchildren: The experiences of Black and White grandmothers. *The Gerontologist, 39,* 209–221.

Radloff, L. S. (1977). The CES-D Scale: A self-report depression scale for research in the general population. *Applied Psychological Measurement, 1,* 385–401.

Shore, R. J., & Hayslip, B. (1994). Custodial grandparenting: Implications for children's development. In A. Gottfried & A. Gottfried (Eds.), *Redefining families: Implications for children's development* (pp. 171–218). New York: Plenum.

Silverthorn, P., & Durant, S. (2000). Custodial grandparenting and the difficult child: Learning from the parenting literature. In B. Hayslip & R. Goldberg-Glen (Eds.), *Grandparents raising grandchildren: Theoretical, empirical and clinical perspectives* (pp. 47–64). New York: Springer.

Somary, K., & Stricker, G. (1998). Becoming a grandparent: A longitudinal study of expectations and early experiences as a function of sex and lineage. *Gerontologist, 38,* 53–61.

Thomas, J. L. (1988, November). *Relationships with grandchildren as predictors of grandparents' psychological well-being.* Paper presented at the Annual Scientific Meeting of the Gerontological Society of America, San Francisco, CA.

Thomas, J. L. (1990). The grandparent role: A double bind. *International Journal of Aging and Human Development, 31,* 169–177.

Toledo, R., Hayslip, B., Emick, M., Toledo, C., & Henderson, C. (2000). Cross-cultural differences in custodial grandparenting. In B. Hayslip & R. Goldberg-Glen (Eds.), *Grandparents raising grandchildren: Theoretical, empirical and clinical perspectives* (pp. 107–124). New York: Springer.

Unger, J. B., McAvay, G., Bruce, M. L., Berman, L., & Seeman, T. (1999). Variation in the impact of social network characteristics on physical functioning in elderly persons: McArthur studies of successful aging. *Journals of Gerontology: Social Sciences, 54B,* S245–251.

Wilson, M. N. (1986). The black extended family: An analytical consideration. *Developmental Psychology, 22,* 246–258.

Wilson, M. N., Tolson, T. F. J., Hinton, I. D., & Kiernan, M. (1990). Flexibility and sharing of childcare duties in black families. *Sex Roles, 22,* 409–425.

Yorker, B. C., Kelley, S. J., Whitley, D. M., Lewis, A., Magis, J., Bergeron, A., & Napier, C. (1998). Custodial relationships of grandparents raising grandchildren: Results of a home-based intervention study. *Juvenile and Family Court Journal, 49,* 15–25.

Part III

The Pragmatics of Working With Grandparents Raising Their Grandchildren

CHAPTER 12

Grandparents Who Are Parenting Again: Building Parenting Skills

Carolyn W. Kern

INTRODUCTION

The number of children being raised by grandparents has increased substantially compared to previous decades (Harden, Clark, & Maguire, 1997). Research indicates that grandparents become the parent of their grandchild because of substance abuse, child maltreatment, HIV/AIDS, homicide, incarceration, or psychiatric illness of the birthparents (Dowdell, 1995). For these reasons, Child Protective Services (CPS) agencies favor placement of children with relatives. Many of these abandoned or seriously neglected children are cared for by grandparents through informal arrangements as opposed to a formal placement through CPS.

Grandparents who take on the role of parenting during their middle and later years often experience more stress than when they parented the first time. Not only do they have the responsibility of raising a grandchild, but their adult child is also often still involved (de Toledo & Brown, 1995). Moreover, custody issues with their adult child add another dimension to this ever-changing relationship. As most grandparent caregivers will clearly state, raising a grandchild changes one's lifestyle dramatically. When most grandparents are at the stage of life where they begin to enjoy more free time and less responsibility these grandparents' responsibilities multiply (Kelley, Yorker, Whitley, & Sipe, 2001). This chapter focuses on the grandparent–grandchild relationship and the development of effective parenting strategies.

By refreshing parenting skills, grandparents can be empowered to influence a young life to grow, mature, and take on responsibility. As a grandparent reflects on past parenting experience, overwhelming feelings can arise, and grandparents may question their parenting skills when they reflect on the life of the son or daughter who is the grandchild's parent. By dusting off old parenting strategies and adding new ideas, information, and skills, grandparents can gain new confidence as they take on this unexpected challenge.

KEYS TO EFFECTIVE PARENTING FOR GRANDPARENT CAREGIVERS

Children require more than new parents are often aware of. Even with the knowledge of what is required, grandparents can become overwhelmed. At the same time, grandparents have the opportunity to parent again with greater insight; they can take experiences when they were younger and less experienced and build on them to become more effective parents for a grandchild. Key elements in effective parenting include (1) understanding child and adolescent development, (2) building relationships, (3) teaching decision making and responsibility taking, and (4) setting limits and following through with consequences. One approach to the development of effective parenting that has proven effective is Positive Discipline. Principles of Positive Discipline can bring insight and new understanding to grandparent's roles as parents (Nelson & Lott, 2000). Positive Discipline relies on cooperation based on mutual respect and shared responsibility. Later in this chapter it will be discussed more fully.

CHILD AND ADOLESCENT DEVELOPMENT

Behaviors become less of a mystery when there is an understanding of developmental stages and tasks for children and adolescents. Developmental theorists have shown that children are easily influenced, and providing a healthy environment allows change and the opportunity to grow. Children can thrive and overcome early obstacles when a safe and nurturing environment surrounds them (Shaffer, 2002).

Normal growth in children and adolescents occurs in several stages. A key to successful development is building a sense of autonomy (Erikson, 1963). It is essential for children and adolescents to test limits and explore boundaries in that quest for autonomy. In turn, adults are challenged to be creative in setting boundaries and applying consequences (Faber & Mazlish, 1980). Failure of a child to develop a sense of independence and autonomy may result in children's doubting their abilities and feeling shame (Erikson). Grandparents can help children develop autonomy through a supportive and encouraging environment even when children have experienced negative involvement with adults in the past.

Havighurst (1952) believes that adolescents master nine developmental tasks in order to achieve healthy adjustment. They are:

1. Accepting one's physique and sexual role
2. Establishing new peer relationships with both sexes
3. Achieving emotional independence of parents
4. Selecting and preparing for an occupation
5. Developing intellectual skills and concepts necessary for civic competence
6. Achieving assurance of economic independence
7. Acquiring socially responsible behavior patterns
8. Preparing for marriage and family life
9. Building conscious values that are harmonious with one's environment

Each task brings new challenges for young people and provides opportunity to develop in areas with less conflict. Grandparents' knowledge of development is the foundation of the development of a healthy relationship with the grandchildren they parent.

KEYS TO DEVELOPING A RELATIONSHIP

A key component of parenting is the adult-child relationship. Warmth rather than parental aloofness or hostility engages a child's sense of belonging. A feeling of unconditional love and acceptance is particularly important when a child has experienced trauma of the loss of his or her nuclear family, as is the case for many children who are being raised by their grandparents. Affection, caring, and encouragement, as opposed to punishment, ridiculing, criticizing, or ignoring the child, build such a relationship (Hughes, 2002). When grandparents become the primary caregiver, a child needs to know that this relationship will survive hardship and struggle. As children who live in constant fear of rejection become angry, defiant, and withdrawn, grandparents need to communicate a sense of stability and emotional availability no matter at what age their grandchildren come to them. Teenagers are particularly in need of a secure and stable environment, even if the message being sent by the adolescent is "leave me alone" (Nelson & Lott, 2000). "No matter how often teenagers say they want to be left alone, in reality they need and want some guidance. They still need a copilot. Even though they act as if they would like to throw you out of the plane, they feel abandoned if you go" (Nelson & Lott, 2000, p. 61).

Creating an accepting environment where the child feels safe enough to explore thoughts and feelings is especially important. When grandparents increase their sensitivity to their grandchildren, by identifying emotional needs and responding to them empathetically, children experience trust and safety. In a nutshell, we are advising: Be sensitive to how the world is perceived by your grandchild. Listen to your grandchild with yours eyes as well as your ears. Moreover, do not ask questions that you already know the answers to. Questions go to the mind, while affirming statements go to the heart. In addition, the creative use of play with younger children can be valuable. Allow the child to lead in play activities and acknowledge behaviors and feelings that the child displays. As play is a child's natural medium of language, grandparents can learn more about their grandchild as well as develop the relationship through play (Landreth & Lobaugh, 1998).

Acceptance is a core element in communicating empathy and is also an essential condition for facilitating a child's development of positive self-worth (Bratton & Landreth, 1995). Grandparents can increase their ability to communicate acceptance of a grandchild's feelings and behaviors by learning to attend fully to the child, and by allowing their grandchild to lead in play rather than controlling or directing behaviors. By watching a child play, grandparents communicate confidence, belief, and approval of a child's ability. Children need to feel they are worth watching before they believe they are worthwhile as a person. Because observation requires time, watching represents approval. Children of all ages, including adolescents, respond very positively when a parent or grandparent comes to recitals, concerts, plays, athletic events, or special school programs. Persons that really matter to children are those to whom they belong. Consequently, genuine interest and involvement in children's lives can change their future choices. Children in whom this investment has been placed have more courage and strength to withstand pressures from outside sources. Indeed, grandparents can make a difference in a grandchild's life when the grandchild receives the message that they are there when the parent is unable to be.

Adult-Child Interactions

Grandparents can respond to grandchildren in a variety of ways. Helpful responses show understanding and give responsibility to the child; succinct messages without hidden meanings are most effective in this regard. For example, open body posture invites a child into your world. When one's arms are not crossed and you face children, they receive the message that you are ready to hear them and that their message is important to you. When you acknowledge their feelings, children feel heard and understood. When grandparents show interest and an attitude that tries to look at life through the child's experience, a child will respond more frequently and positively.

Grandparents should look for effective ways to interact with their grandchild to facilitate the maintenance of a good relationship. The difficult task is determining what a child needs when conflict arises. Such an approach has a better possibility for positive influence and a decreased possibility for rebellion (Nelson & Lott, 2000).

Children need to learn responsibility and to develop self-motivation. In today's world there are fewer opportunities to do so than in previous generations. For example, children are no longer needed as important contributors to the family's economic survival. It is for this reason that in today's family, children especially need opportunities to be responsible for specific tasks necessary for living. A child who has never had the opportunity to clean the kitchen grows up without gaining the skill and confidence that are developed by doing such a task. Many times, an adult's expectation is not met and adults decide to do the task themselves. While it may take extra time and energy for the grandparent to allow a child the opportunity to develop skill and gain a sense of accomplishment for doing a job well, when children experience such challenges, growth occurs. When conflict and disagreements arise, cooperation based on mutual respect and shared responsibility works better than an authoritarian, control-oriented approach to completing a task.

Styles of Parenting

Approaches to parenting affect adult-child interaction and take on different forms. Authoritative, laissez-faire, and authoritarian define such approaches (Baumrind, 1991). Positive discipline (Nelson & Lott, 2000) involves mutual respect and shared decision making between child and adult, and as such exemplifies an authoritative style in many respects.

The authoritarian style dictates that these are the rules and one must abide by them and that such-and-such is the punishment children will receive for violation of the rules. Importantly, the decision-making process regarding what the rules are and what will be the results of their violation does not involve the children.

Long-range results of such punishment include resentment, revenge, rebellion, or retreat. When a child experiences resentment the thought is, "This is not fair and I cannot trust adults." Revenge thoughts may be, "They're winning now, but I'll get even later." The thought, "I'll do just the opposite to prove I don't have to do it their way" is likely to occur with rebellion. When retreat is the reaction, sneakiness and reduced self-esteem result. With unreasonable and short-sighted punishment negative behavior may cease in the short term but long-term outcomes are not in anyone's best interest.

Permissiveness says there are no rules, and characterizes a laissez-faire style of parenting. "I am sure we will love each other and be happy, and you will choose your own rules later." Without any direction, a child experiences freedom without order, unlimited choices, and the message, "You can do anything you want" from the adult. Given such license, a child will fail to develop healthy boundaries and will experience confusion.

Positive disciple advocates involvement of the child in the process and allows the adult to include essential values about respect and decision making. Decisions about rules are decided on together for mutual benefit; solutions that are decided upon together are ones that will be beneficial to all. When the grandparent needs to use judgment without input from the grandchild, it is done firmly, but with dignity and respect for the child. In this way, a child who is involved learns to make decisions, to earn empathy for other family members, and to develop self-confidence (Nelson, 1987).

Principles of Positive Discipline

Positive Discipline guidelines provide a framework within which a grandparent can find direction and develop new tools for parenting. This approach uses the following six concepts to help describe children:

1. children are social beings
2. behavior is goal oriented
3. a child's primary goal is to belong and to be significant
4. a misbehaving child is a discouraged child
5. children want to interact with other children, and
6. all people have equal claims to dignity and respect (Walton & Powers, 1978).

Of these, the most basic principle is "misbehaving children are discouraged children." These children have mistaken ideas on how to achieve their primary goal, which is "to belong," and these mistaken ideas lead them to misbehavior. By using encouragement to help children feel a sense of belonging, misbehavior can be eliminated. One of the best ways to help children feel encouraged is to spend time with them doing something you can enjoy together. This may require some effort, but through finding a mutually enjoyable activity, children gain a sense of self-worth.

As most parents know, children and adolescents enjoy talking about themselves. By encouraging them to share times when they have felt very sad as well as those when they have been the happiest, grandparents can enhance relationships. When grandparents share with their grandchildren those same experiences, a level of trust can be developed. Family meetings can provide the opportunity for effective problem solving while helping children develop self-discipline, responsibility, and cooperation.

Children gain a sense of belonging when they know they have meaningful chores that contribute to the family. One suggestion might be to decide together what chores need to be done, and then put them in a jar, letting each person draw out a few each week. Thus, no one is left with the same chores all the time. Once a chore has been selected, it is important to take time for training, making sure, for example, that children understand what "clean your bathroom" means. They will probably not do a perfect job the first time, so look for ways to encourage and help them learn how to improve the outcome. In this context, it is important to ask oneself how one might feel after being humiliated. Children feel the same emotions.

Punishment Versus Logical Consequences

A key point to remember is that punishment may work if all one is interested in is eliminating misbehavior on a short-term basis. As noted above, teaching and modeling mutual respect by being kind and firm at the same time are more effective. Kindness shows respect for the child and firmness shows respect for oneself and an awareness of the needs of the situation. During conflict this may be difficult, so using cooling off periods may be necessary. Both the grandparent and the grandchild can go to separate rooms, do something to make themselves feel better, and then return to work on the problem with mutual respect. Importantly, using logical consequences when appropriate (consequences that are related to the behavior in question, respectful, and reasonable to the situation) is essential. Family meetings are a great place to have children involved in determining logical consequences for not keeping agreements; such meetings will be discussed in more detail later in this chapter.

Establishing routines helps avoid morning hassles. Have children choose clothes and lay them out the night before, and prepare books, lunches, and so on ahead of time. This helps children decide how much time they need to get ready and affords them the responsibility of getting up on time, using their own alarm clock. For an adolescent, this is very important for the development of responsible behavior. Both children and adolescents should be allowed to experience the consequences of their being late.

Winning Cooperation

Keeping in mind the following four steps of winning cooperation with children and adolescents makes the home a place of safety and security, promotes peace and calm, and minimizes the chances of destructive interactions taking place. First begin by getting into the grandchild's world, guess how he or she is feeling and check with the child to explore the accuracy of your impressions. Second, show understanding. One does not have to agree with or condone behavior to show understanding. Indeed, when the grandparent shares a time when he or she felt the same way, a child feels understood. A third way to win cooperation is by sharing one's feelings about the situation in a nonaccusing manner. When grandparents use "I" statements, children do not feel accused and thus they need not defend themselves. For example, "I am disappointed that you made that choice" might be an appropriate response. By helping work on ideas to avoid the problem in the future, responsibility can be developed. If the first three guidelines are expressed in a respectful manner, a child is ready for cooperation (Walton, 1990).

The last two guidelines can help young people grow and take healthy risks. Grandparents can 1) model recovery after they have made a mistake, for example, share with a grandchild what was disliked about a behavior and 2) ask for help in finding a better solution. Teaching children that mistakes are a wonderful opportunity to grow and learn is very important to modeling (Nelson, 1987).

PRINCIPLES FOR POSITIVE PARENTING

Parenting from a positive perspective reduces stress from both the grandparent's perspective as well as the grandchild's. Helping a child grow from weak to strong, from dependent to independent is the key to effective parenting. Through encouragement, children develop strong interpersonal skills (Glenn & Nelson, 2000).

Encouragement Versus Praise

Encouragement is defined as giving courage, hope, or confidence. It also includes being favorable to and supporting the grandchild, whereas praise sets a price or value on behavior. Children who are praised look for external evaluation from others. The message they receive is, "I do not count unless I perform in a certain manner." In contrast, children who are encouraged feel supported and favored. They have courage to take initiative and explore the world. Thus, there are underlying messages (see below) sent to a child when either encouragement or praise is given, and grandparents' understanding of the messages allows them to send the ones they really want heard.

Praise focuses on control and getting the child to meet an external demand, whereas encouragement focuses on building a child's character. A child develops the courage to be imperfect and a willingness to try when encouragement is used. When praised, however, a child learns to measure his or her worth by the ability to conform to other's expectations. Children learn to measure their worth in terms of how well they please others when praise is used. In contrast, with encouragement a child learns to self-evaluate progress and continue to make decisions.

As children are continually faced with making choices, if they don't have practice in decision making, they will be easily led by others. With praise given only for well done, completed tasks, children develop exceptionally high standards and learn to measure their worth by how well they approximate perfection, leading to "giving up" if they are unable to meet the standards set by others. When encouragement is given for improvement, children learn to accept themselves and their efforts. Children's strengths thus become known to them and they can evaluate themselves (Nelson, 1987).

Messages to Send

Encouragement sends the following messages: "I have faith in you," "You are doing just fine," "Your feelings and evaluation are important," "Set your own standards," "You do not have to be perfect. Effort and improvement are what really are important," "Your contributions count. I see your assets and I value you."

Praise sends these messages: "You are only acceptable when you do what I want," "To be worthwhile you must please me," "To be worthwhile you must meet my standards," "You must be superior to others to be acceptable."

Children can easily become discouraged when praise is the primary message they receive. Grandparents can challenge themselves to think of opportunities to encourage their grandchildren at any time. The response they receive from their grandchildren will no doubt surprise and delight them.

DEVELOPING RESPONSIBILITY

Taking responsibility is not innate in children; it must be taught. Grandparents should know what is normal development for the age of their grandchildren in order to prevent feelings of frustration and anger. While it is important to help children learn to do for themselves, it takes time for the training. For example, cleaning up messes happens to all of us. Letting the child clean up a mess and not verbally abusing the child or yelling are important points in this respect. When they are very young, children can help with a task, whereas challenging older children to think about what needs to be done to take care of a problem is important. Moreover, letting them know they can do something fun when the task is completed helps them learn a sense of order (Nelson, Lott, & Glenn, 1999).

Teenagers and older children are often consciously irresponsible. In these cases, it is best not to do things for them that they can do for themselves and not to nag. In addition, helping them explore the consequences of their choices through friendly discussions and nonconfrontative questions, and teaching problem-solving skills are essential to developing responsibility. Children are very often insightful when they have an opportunity to explore what they learn about misbehavior for the future. It is important that grandparents do not pamper grandchildren or help them avoid the pain of consequences. Providing supportive opportunities for accountability is crucial; children are usually motivated when given a second chance. This process is often slow to develop, so when grandparents maintain a sense of humor and focus on the task, it helps teens to stop taking themselves and others too seriously. Humor is a powerful tool that builds a bridge across relationships.

Specific methods for encouraging adolescents invite them to grow and gain confidence. For example, one might invite a grandchild to handle a task or problem previously handled by an adult. (e.g., running errands, purchasing groceries, gathering information about an expected family purchase). Dispense with the bedtime rule for teenagers and invite them to contribute opinions on family and current social topics. As with younger children, avoid conveying the notion that teenagers have to handle everything perfectly. Accepting mistakes and failures matter-of-factly is key here. Most important, emphasize strengths, enjoy your grandchild's friends and welcome them into your home, and be interested in their activities without smothering them. Having fun together and including the teenager in adult social gatherings whenever possible communicates the encouragement and support of adults outside the grandchild's primary family relationships.

Another important area in which to encourage an adolescent is financial responsibility, for example, estimating his or her clothing needs and budgeting money. Building on responsibility makes it possible for grandchildren to decide on what they want to purchase within their budget. As the grandparent, it is important to allow the child to experience the consequences when wants exceed budget. In this respect, part-time work helps a teenager experience self-sufficiency and independence, and brings the consequences of spending beyond one's means into sharp focus.

BUILDING COOPERATION

Several strategies can help grandparents build cooperation, including having family meetings, problem-solving sessions, and true dialogue; being nonjudgmental, being curious about friends, talking about friendship choices, and being reasonable about socialization. As grandparents consider what cooperation brings into a household, they can expect growth and harmony with children and adolescents.

Family Meetings

Holding family meetings where grandchildren have a voice and are active participants builds cooperation. Components of a family meeting can include: a chairperson, secretary, compliments, gratitude, the agenda, problem solving, planning activities, planning family fun, and discussion of chores. There are many advantages to having regular (weekly) family meetings. For example, they allow for steady involvement in one another's lives, troublesome situations can be addressed sooner, and everyone has a chance to feel a sense of belonging. Outcomes of such meetings include improved communication and problem-solving skills, with understanding and closeness developing in the process.

The role of chairperson and secretary should rotate on a regular basis, so that each family member has an opportunity for leadership and responsibility taking. Begin family meetings by having each person tell every other member of the family something he or she likes or appreciates about the others. This sets a tone of support and encouragement, and each person is more open to difficult situations that may arise.

The agenda can be displayed during the week so that family members can add items that they would like addressed at the meeting. It is important that planning activities and family fun be part of each family meeting; use of a timer and a designated timekeeper lets everyone know how long the meeting is expected to last.

During the meeting, take time to discuss concerns, including chores, and problem solving. Because it is important that each individual have freedom to express concerns, some issues may not get solved; they may simply be vocalized. Every family member needs to have the opportunity to be listened to with respect. In this context, children learn how to express themselves in an effective manner. Having time to brainstorm for solutions to a problem is important if the problem needs more than discussion. Moreover, choosing a solution everyone can live with, trying it for a week, and then reevaluating at the next meeting, if necessary, is an effective measure. In this context, it is helpful to discuss logical consequences and use the Three R's of Logical Consequences in Positive Discipline: (1) *Related* to the behavior, (2) *Respectful* to both child and adult, and (3) *Reasonable* to both child and adult (Nelson & Lott, 2000).

Logical Consequences Versus Punishment

Logical consequences do not happen naturally; adults or children determine them. They are reasonable when they are agreed on in advance by adults and children.

When it comes to discipline, the feelings behind what grandparents do are more important than what they actually do. By making a child feel worse, grandparents create a threatening environment, making it difficult for learning to take place. In this respect, the child's age is an important consideration in determining logical consequences, as they are designed to catch the child's attention so as to encourage him or her to construct positive change. When grandparents help children look at their experiences and identify what is significant in them, generalizations to other learning situations can occur. Logical consequences send the message to the child that "I trust you to learn and respect the rights of others," "I trust you to make beneficial decisions," "You are valid. You have the ability to make responsible choices," "You are able to take care of yourself," "I do not like what you're doing, but I still love you," and "You can decide. I accept your decision." In these ways, children learn the value of cooperation and mutual respect and thus, consequences make sense. A key outcome here is children's ability to become self-evaluating and self-directing. In addition, they feel loved and valued and, at the same time, they respect a grandparent who does not simply accept behaviors. A final outcome is children's increased ability for responsible decision-making.

Teaching children the value of logical consequences precludes punishment, which can result in rebellion, revenge, evasion of responsibility, and lack of self-discipline. Feelings of hurt, rejection, and guilt occur at the same time as wanting to get even. Punishment and threats can also cause children to feel unacceptable and that they can not make adequate decisions. For children to develop healthy respect and self-perceptions, logical consequences are effective means of dealing with misbehaviors. The long-range consequences of punishment can leave a child feeling one or all of the Four R's of punishment: Resentment, Revenge, Rebellion or Retreat—such children become sneaky or have reduced self-confidence (Walton, 1990).

COMMON GOALS OF MISBEHAVIOR

To understand children and adolescents, grandparents need to recognize that like adults, children and adolescents want to feel significant, to fit in and to belong. They want to count for something and to be important to somebody. Given the adverse changes in the nuclear family that bring them to their grandparents, children often feel a sense of isolation and insignificance. They become discouraged and unsure of their place in the world. A misbehaving child or adolescent is always discouraged (Walton, 1990; Walton & Powers, 1978). In this context, power struggles easily account for the majority of troubled relationships between adults and children.

Misbehavior can be dealt with effectively when viewed in the context of one or more of the goals of misbehavior: attention, power, revenge, inadequacy, and excitement. A child seeking attention says, "I am not the best but at least you will not overlook me." As adolescents are more concerned about attention from peers, these young people need to discover ways to gain recognition in useful ways so that they may be encouraged to let go of the negative attention, for example, finding ways to help others through volunteer work or through activities available in school, church, or in the community. Attention-getting behavior sends a message that grandparents need to address early to help a child or adolescent find significance within the newly constituted family system.

Struggles over power show themselves in defiance, aggression, withdrawal, and sexual promiscuity; such misbehavior continues and may even increase when correction is given in this context. When a grandparent intervenes to break this cyclic struggle, the message "I am not interested in fighting, but I want to help you deal with the problems life is giving you" is communicated.

Even with young children it is wise to avoid a power struggle. For example, stop making the child's behavior feel worthwhile to the child, show the child respect, and model cooperation. Avoiding hurt and anger, setting reasonable limits and logical consequences, and encouraging social participation, a desire for self-respect, and respect of others are all very important in this process (Walton & Powers, 1978).

A faulty belief of a child or adolescent whose goal is revenge is that he or she cannot be loved or accepted. The belief "I count only if I can hurt others when I am hurt" leads to violence or behaviors that are verbally or physically hurtful to others. Grandparents' reactions should be to maintain order with minimum restraint, avoid retaliation, and take time with the grandchildren, letting them know that there is no desire to hurt them. Many such grandchildren already have been hurt via divorce or abuse, and helping them to deal with such feelings in ways other than misbehaving is vital to their emotional well-being.

Inadequacy messages say "I can't measure up so I won't try. I count only when I am completely supported and consoled in my shortcomings." Children or adolescents whose behavior is directed toward inadequacy are highly concerned about failing; they have decided that it is better not to try at all than to try and then risk failure (Walton, 1990). Grandparents can help children recognize behavior that is positively helping children see mistakes as opportunities to grow, not as barriers to success. A message to send is that "anything worth doing is worth doing, even if it is less than perfect, when it leads somewhere and helps you to see what can be done to improve a situation."

Among adolescents, a fifth goal of misbehavior that can be troublesome is excitement. When teenagers are unable to find opportunities to make life interesting in a productive way or they are extremely limited in terms of opportunity, they often turn to irresponsible and even illegal activities to find excitement. It is important the grandparent elicit from their teenage grandchildren ways to make life interesting and exciting. This might be accomplished in family meetings by involving them in planning and in being in charge of family fun. Not only will they fill the need for excitement but they will also develop a sense of responsibility and leadership. The challenge for grandparents is to identify the goals of misbehavior and understand children's or young people's faulty belief systems, meeting them where they are emotionally without getting involved in a power struggle.

CONCLUSION

Through strengthening existing parenting skills and developing new ones grandparents can raise their grandchildren with confidence and determination. Taking on the task of parenting a second generation requires courage, and investing in the life of a young person who, without them, may be unable to maneuver through life successfully, is not an easy task. Although grandparents face many situations in which family and friends will question the wisdom of raising a grandchild, watching grandchildren grow and develop, knowing they are safe and happy, is worth the challenges grandparents face.

REFERENCES

Baumrind, D. (1991). Parenting styles and adolescent development. In R. Lerner et al. (Eds.), *Encyclopedia of Adolescence: Vol. 2* (pp. 746–758). New York: Garland.

Bratton, S., & Landreth, G. (1995). Filial therapy with single parents: Effects on parental acceptance, empathy, and stress. *International Journal of Play Therapy, 4*(1), 61–81.

De Toledo, S., & Brown, D. (1995). *Grandparents as parents.* New York: Guilford.

Dowdell, E. B. (1995). Caregiver burden: Grandmothers raising their high risk grandchildren. *Journal of Psychosocial Nursing, 33,* 27–30.

Erikson, E. (1963). *Childhood and society* (2nd ed.). New York: Norton.

Faber, A., & Mazlish, E. (1980). *How to talk so kids will listen & listen so kids will talk.* New York: Avon.

Geldard, K., & Geldard, D. (1999). *Counselling adolescents.* Thousand Oaks, CA: Sage.

Glenn, S., & Nelson, J. (2000). *Raising self-reliant children in a self-indulgent world.* Roseville, CA: Prima.

Harden, A., Clark, R., & Maguire, K. (1997). *Informal and formal kinship care: Findings from national and state data.* Washington, DC: U.S. Department of Health and Human Services, Office of the Assistant Secretary for Planning and Evaluation.

Havighurst, R. (1952). *Developmental tasks and education.* New York: David McKay.

Hughes, L. (2002). *Paving pathways: Child and adolescent development.* Belmont, CA: Wadsworth/Thomson Learning.

Kelley, S., Yorker, B., Whitley, D., & Sipe, T. (2001). A multimodal intervention for grandparents raising grandchildren: Results of an exploratory study. *Child Welfare, 80*(1), 27–24.

Landreth, G., & Lobaugh, A. (1998). Filial therapy with incarcerated fathers: Effects on parental acceptance of child, parental stress, and child adjustment. *Journal of Counseling & Development, 76,* 157–165.

Nelson, J. (1987). *Positive discipline.* New York: Ballantine.

Nelson, J., & Lott, L. (2000). *Positive discipline for teenagers* (2nd ed.). Roseville, CA: Prima.

Nelson, J., Lott, L., & Glenn, S. (1999). *Positive discipline A–Z* (2nd ed.). Roseville, CA: Prima Publishing.

Shaffer, D. (2002). *Developmental psychology: Childhood and adolescence* (6th ed.). Belmont, CA: Wadsworth/Thomson Learning.

Walton, F. (1990). *Winning teenagers over in home & school.* Columbia, SC: Adlerian ChildCare Books.

Walton, F., & Powers, R. (1978). *Winning children over.* Chicago, IL: Practical Psychology Associates.

CHAPTER 13

Group Processes Among Grandparents Raising Grandchildren

Elizabeth C. Wohl, Jessica M. Lahner, and Jane Jooste

INTRODUCTION

Custodial grandparenting is a growing trend in American society (Fuller-Thomson & Minkler, 2000; Pinson-Millburn, Fabian, Schlossberg, & Pyle, 1996). Given this fact, it seems imperative that we seek a greater understanding of the grandparents who comprise this group, the effects associated with parenting grandchildren, and what mental health professionals can do to assist these grandparents and grandchildren as they acquire and maintain these new roles.

Approximately 5.5 million grandparents report housing their own grandchildren (U.S. Bureau of the Census, 2000). Forty-two percent of these grandparents perceive themselves as the primary caretaker of these children of which 22% are under the age of one, 23% are between one and two years of age, 17% range from three to four years of age, and 35% are older than five years of age. Of all American children in the late 1990s, 6% were living in households maintained by grandparents (Fuller-Thomson & Minkler, 2000). Fuller-Thomson and Minkler consider this an underestimate, and, citing their own study utilizing data from a large, nationally representative sample, they estimated that more than one in 10 grandparents reported primary responsibility for raising a grandchild for at least six months. This custodial role was not usually a short-term commitment, with more than half the grandparents giving care for at least three years.

The majority of custodial grandparents are female, married, and reside in the Southern U.S. (Fuller-Thomson & Minkler, 2000; U.S. Bureau of the Census, 2000), and most categorize themselves as Caucasian (62%), followed by black (27%), Hispanic (10%), and, other (1%) (Fuller-Thomson & Minkler). Fifty-six percent hold jobs and 18.8% maintain incomes in the poverty range (U.S. Bureau of the Census). Although annual incomes of these grandparents vary, in general, they are below that of traditional, noncaregiving grandparents (Fuller-Thomson & Minkler, 2000; Hayslip, Shore, Henderson, & Lambert, 1998).

The circumstances under which grandparents find themselves in the caregiving role vary. Divorce, adult parent drug abuse, and child abuse appear to the be most common (Emick & Hayslip, 1999; Hayslip et al., 1998), but social factors such as teen pregnancy, incarcerated parents, and mental or physical impairment or death of a parent (Emick & Hayslip, 1999; Fuller-Thompson & Minkler, 2000; Hayslip et al., 1998; Pinson-Millburn et al., 1996) can also propel grandparents into this new role. Despite these circumstances, not all grandparents accept the task of providing primary care to their grandchildren. Those who choose to accept it report making this decision for differing reasons. Many do not want to see their grandchildren placed in foster homes and choose to provide care to prevent this outcome. Others perceive themselves as the only ones who are available to raise or care for the children. Some desire to provide these children with nurturance, believe that they can provide better care than the parent, or both. Others simply offer to care for their grandchildren in order to help their own adult children in times of crisis (Hayslip et al., 1998).

While these data give us a general overview of the custodial grandparent population, it is important to remember that it includes a diverse group of caretakers (Chenoweth, 2000). No two situations are exactly alike. Some grandparents have the means to provide financially for these children, while others are forced to leave retirement and reenter the workforce. Some may have legal custody of the children, others may have adopted the children, and some have no legal rights at all. Still others have some assistance from the adult parents, but in many cases, the adult parents are either unwilling or unable to share the responsibility. The diversity of this population highlights the need for mental health professionals to gather personal histories from the custodial grandparents with whom they work in order to understand their unique circumstances and to best provide them with resources that are tailored to meet their needs.

While most custodial grandparents who reflect on their experiences believe they would still choose to take responsibility for their grandchildren (Hayslip et al., 1998), doing so results in many negative consequences (Chenoweth, 2000; Emick & Hayslip, 1999; Fuller-Thomson & Minkler, 2000; Hayslip et al., 1998). Assuming the responsibility of raising a grandchild has been associated with declining physical health, increased psychological distress, decreased economic insecurity, and greater legal challenges. Specifically, many of these grandparents report feeling more isolated and less satisfied with their social lives than they were prior to caring for their grandchildren (Fuller-Thomson & Minkler, 2000; Hayslip et al., 1998). Often they feel as if they are alone in this situation, and the everyday tasks associated with child rearing prevent them from engaging in activities they once enjoyed or the plans they envisioned for themselves at this stage in their lives. Their caretaking responsibilities often take the time once reserved for their noncustodial grandchildren, which creates guilt when they cannot spend quality time with their other grandchildren (Emick & Hayslip, 1996). Furthermore, some grandparents believe that their relationship with their custodial grandchild deteriorates after entering this parenting role (Hayslip et al., 1998). In the same vein, many custodial grandparents experience grief over the various losses that have placed them in the caregiving role (Pinson-Millburn et al., 1996). They often grieve over the loss of their own child whether the adult child has died, is incarcerated, or has simply neglected to care for the child effectively. Having accepted the custodial role, they also lose their old role as a traditional grandparent as well as their former way of life. Furthermore, they fear for their grandchildren's well-being should they, themselves, become unable to provide care due to physical or mental incapacitation (Shore & Hayslip, 1994). Given these circumstances, it is not surprising that custodial grandparents suffer from depression at twice the rate of traditional grandparents (Minkler, Fuller-Thomson, Miller, & Driver, 1997). These negative consequences are even more severe when the child for whom they are caring displays problems such as hyperactivity, learning difficulties, resistance to authority, and depression (Emick & Hayslip, 1999; Hayslip et al., 1998; Hayslip & Shore, 2001).

Despite these negative consequences, many retain the positive meanings associated with being a grandparent (Emick & Hayslip, 1999; Hayslip et al., 1998). In fact, Hayslip and colleagues (1998) reported that when compared to traditional grandfathers, custodial grandfathers derived more meaning from their role. While in the minority, some grandparents welcome the chance to parent again (Hayslip et al., 1998). It appears they perceive themselves as more mature and capable than they may have been the first time around.

In recent years, more attention has been given to custodial grandparents. As psychologists, we are gaining a better understanding of who comprises this population and the effects this nontraditional family arrangement has on both grandchildren and grandparents. As a result, many researchers and other professionals have noted the need for interventions with this group and have recommended implementing support, educational groups, or both to assist custodial grandparents in coping with, transitioning into, and maintaining these new roles (Chenoweth, 2000; Cox, 2000; Emick & Hayslip, 1996, 1999; Hayslip et al., 1998; Heywood, 1999; Pinson-Millburn et al., 1996; Strom & Strom, 2000). Among other benefits, support groups provide the opportunity for catharsis, whereas education groups can offer information and training related to raising a child in today's society that is uniquely tailored to this population.

Many custodial grandparent support groups exist in the United States, but the benefits of these appear to be poorly documented (Strom & Strom, 2000). Anecdotal evidence suggests that custodial grandparents who have the opportunity to meet and interact with other custodial grandparents derive some comfort from meeting others in a similar situation. This form of social support likely mitigates some of the distress associated with their role. It is probable that this especially benefits custodial grandparents who raise children with emotional, behavioral, and learning difficulties, as these grandparents often receive less social support than those caring for normal grandchildren (Emick & Hayslip, 1999).

However, Strom and Strom (2000) note that support groups often fail because they tend to allow members to vent endless frustrations and complaints without moving on to a more positive and constructive focus. Although they are comforted to know that there are other custodial grandparents, members may acquire feelings of helplessness and defeat when caught up in a negative cognitive loop. Strom and Strom (2000) believe it is important to introduce balance to these groups by emphasizing messages of hope, and celebrating some smaller successes of fellow members along with the members' needs for catharsis. Much more is likely to be gained through learning from others' strengths than dwelling on angry, bitter emotions.

Although many mental health professionals recommend education and training for custodial grandparents, few published sources discuss specific interventions of this nature (e.g., Cox, 2000), and none to date have disclosed validation data on their efficacy. Nonetheless, the need for these grandparenting groups has been noted. Hayslip and colleagues (1998) point out that appropriate models of child-rearing behavior may not exist for these grandparents. Therefore, it seems especially important to educate them about contemporary child-rearing issues. These may include, but are not limited to, drug and alcohol use and issues related to sexual relations and preferences. For many grandparents, the content of these topics has changed dramatically since they raised their own children. Furthermore, custodial grandparenting is a role for which one is seldom prepared. Many aspects, such as the duration of care or the boundaries with other family members, may be very unclear and may require new learning (Chenoweth, 2000).

Both Chenoweth (2000) and Strom and Strom (2000) recommend that aspects of support and education be combined in a concurrent group. In contrast, Cox

(2000) recommends that custodial grandparents attend two separate groups simultaneously. As the caregiving role often leaves these grandparents with little unscheduled time, it is our belief that membership in two groups simultaneously places an undue burden on them and may be unnecessary. It is our experience that aspects of a support group, if facilitated properly, can be present in an education group. Many of the benefits associated with both groups can be achieved in one well-managed group. Although this combination would likely benefit many custodial grandparents, it may be especially helpful for those grandparents raising children who have emotional, behavioral, or learning difficulties. Information and skills training may help remedy problems and prevent future ones (Hayslip et al., 1998), and the support provided may help mitigate the greater distress experienced by these caregivers.

To attain this end, it is necessary to balance content and education with appropriate support. When designing custodial grandparent training, areas of content that are recommended include (1) parenting skills such as discipline styles, setting limits and consequences, and other contemporary lessons on raising children (Emick & Hayslip, 1999; Hayslip et al., 1998; Pinson-Millburn et al., 1996; Strom & Strom, 2000); (2) communication skills on topics such as how to talk to a teenager, and how to talk to a child's teacher (Chenoweth, 2000; Pinson-Millburn et al.); (3) advocacy issues that include legal/custody questions, and becoming knowledgeable about one's rights (Chenoweth; Cox, 2000); (4) contemporary issues such as drug use and sexual issues (Cox; Pinson-Millburn et al.); and (5) grief and related issues of loss (Cox; Pinson-Millburn et al.). Because many grandparents are raising children with psychological and behavioral difficulties, sessions focusing on learning disabilities and hyperactivity would also be beneficial.

Although parenting skills appears to be one of the more widely recommended educational interventions, Pinson-Millburn and colleagues (1996) warn that this training may be met with resistance by grandparents because it implies they may not have adequately parented their adult children, and thus require parent training. However, prefacing this training with a caveat that describes how times have changed, as has the importance of gaining access to professional knowledge regarding parenting issues, may help decrease grandparents' defensiveness about this issue, and may help them understand how any caretaker would benefit by gaining greater awareness and skills.

Offering support while providing education and skills seems to be more dependent on the skills of the group's leaders/facilitators than on the educational program itself. While allowing grandparents to disclose and share their personal stories, supportive facilitators can establish expectations of growth (Strom & Strom, 2000). It is widely accepted that sharing one's experiences with a group can be a healthy experience when a facilitator encourages constructive self-evaluation. Furthermore, disclosing personal stories about how they became custodial grandparents, discussing the details of their families, and comparing and contrasting the memories of raising their adult children with their current experiences can be likened to aspects of the life review process. This counseling intervention, proposed by Butler (1963), is recommended with older adults as they master the tasks of later life. The life review process can help reviewers bring closure to unfinished business (Waters, 1984) and work through the aspects of their lives that may be associated with guilt and regret (Nordhus & Nielsen, 1999). Because custodial grandparents often encounter such feelings as they reflect on their role as parent of their adult children, the life review process may provide some perspective.

While responding to grandparents' stories, questions, and comments, facilitators can offer support and growth experiences by focusing on the grandparents' unique strengths and by recognizing that each family is different (Chenoweth, 2000). In this sense, it is imperative that mental health professionals do not pathologize the families by implying dysfunction. Though many of these grandchildren come from less than ideal backgrounds, the constructive focus of facilitators should be on the family strengths and how grandparents can leverage these strengths to benefit the family.

Using these perspectives, the authors developed and facilitated a group intervention program for grandparents raising their grandchildren during the spring and summer of 2001. The groups yielded information that is consistent with the literature regarding their feelings of loss, anger, greater isolation, and multiple roles strain (Chenoweth, 2000; Emick & Hayslip, 1999; Fuller-Thompson & Minkler, 2000; Hayslip et al., 1998); however, other themes emerged that are important to address and use in future interventions with custodial grandparents.

CUSTODIAL GRANDPARENT PROGRAM

Three separate sets of custodial grandparent groups were held between April and September, 2001, at The University of North Texas in Denton, Texas. Each set of groups met for one and a half to two hours each Saturday morning for six consecutive weeks. Although the groups were originally planned for 90 minutes, we soon discovered that the grandparents wanted to continue talking with us and with each other for at least another 30–60 minutes. We also realized that these grandparents would have taken as much time as we would have been willing to give.

Before conducting the groups, the authors structured the program to include six topics of education and discussion: (1) parent training, (2) talking to kids about sex, (3) drugs & alcohol, (4) depression, grief, loss, and anger, (5) learning and attention difficulties, and (6) a question-and-answer session concerning legal and economic issues that was facilitated by a custodial grandparent. However, we found the groups to be most engaged and best helped when we minimally covered the topics, and used them only as a loose framework to generate discussion. We provided handouts with information and suggestions for the grandparents to read at their leisure, and focused more on facilitating interaction and sharing among the groups. Although we prepared a significant amount of material, we found the groups were more therapeutic when we did not push to cover all of the information.

The groups included custodial grandparents who ranged in age from 41 to 76 years, and came from all corners of the Dallas/Fort Worth/Denton area. Many drove at least 60 minutes to join us each of the six Saturday mornings for the sessions. All of the grandparents we worked with happened to be Caucasian, but varied widely in socioeconomic and education status, and the groups tended to be mostly female. The groups ranged in size from eight to twelve participants, some of which included married couples. Most grandparents who were married were joined by their spouses, but there were also many widowed or divorced individuals who attended. Some were seasoned veterans, having raised other grandchildren (and who were concurrently raising more than one) when the parents could no longer care for them, while others who had been planning their retirement had just received this new responsibility. One couple was now raising their young great-grandchild, having already raised one grandchild. In contrast, another couple was newlywed, having already raised their children from past marriages and were planning their new lives together in another state, only to have to stay in Texas to unexpectedly raise the woman's grandchild. While each grandparent had his or her own unique story and special situation, there was universality to their experiences as custodial grandparents.

Structuring the Groups

Over the course of the three sets of groups, it became clear that the custodial grandparents (much like their grandchildren) needed a safe, comfortable, structured environment in order to be open to discussing the topics and their own experiences. To facilitate this, we found it most helpful to set up a U-shaped formation of tables and chairs. The tables allowed the grandparents to take notes, comfortably have refreshments, and face one another so they could interact more easily. We also used table tent name cards that were made of card stock paper folded horizontally, and used a marker to write each grandparent's first name. The name cards helped us as facilitators, and also helped the grandparents connect with one another more readily.

When conducting these groups, we found that the room setup and the introduction seemed to set the tone for the remaining sessions. This was most evident in the second group, in which the facilitators spent less time warming up the group through introductions and instead began the content portion of the first session more quickly.

However, the group membership and resulting dynamics in this second group were also very different from the other two. This particular group was more resistant to receiving information and was somewhat more defensive during most of the sessions. This was best demonstrated in the anonymous comments provided on a questionnaire after the conclusion of the last session. One of the more vocal grandparents exemplified this best when he said, "The parenting skills 'lecture' was not what I had anticipated . . . this should have been more discussion-oriented with the grandparents sharing or asking questions." We did not hear these comments in other groups, and found grandparents from these other groups to be more receptive to the program. While the defensiveness that emerged in the second group was probably coincidental with the way in which the group was structured, we strongly recommend spending some time "warming up" future groups by allowing the grandparents to learn a little about one another, while still providing a structured program and education in the first session.

However, based on the themes that emerged in the groups, other factors appeared to contribute to grandparents' willingness to process their difficulties and to be open to education and support. Although each group differed in the ways members related to one another and to the facilitators, some consistent themes emerged from all three groups: most were systemic in nature, and primarily centered on feelings of loss and guilt. The difficulties encountered by most every grandparent we talked to can be divided into five categories: (1) relationships with others, (2) relationships with parents of grandchildren, (3) relationships with grandchildren, (4) relationship with self, and (5) multigenerational family patterns.

Relationships With Others

The most prominent theme that emerged from the groups is the feeling of isolation and invisibility. Although custodial grandparenting is becoming more common, one grandparent summed up the feelings of many when she said, "We're not a recognized nontraditional family." As a result, many grandparents are stuck in limbo: they are isolated and excluded not only from their birth cohort, but also from younger parenting cohorts. Grandparents in all three groups reported losing friends when they became custodial grandparents, mostly because the active parent role is no longer relevant to their friends' lives. One grandparent echoed the feelings of many when she said, "We lose our friends doing this . . . I've lost my support, my community." Finding support and friendship among active parents is also difficult, as both the real and perceived age difference between the custodial grandparents and traditional parents creates barriers to relationships. The grandparents reported feeling discounted and misunderstood by many traditional parents, from whom the grandparents feel blame for not raising their children "right" in the first place, as well as by their same-age peers who are not raising their grandchildren. Many grandparents sense that others hold them accountable for their situation and that others are quick to make erroneous assumptions about them. This is difficult for all of these grandparents, regardless of their situation, and leads to greater internalization of guilt and shame. Along with this guilt, however, often come feelings of anger and other conflicted emotions when the grandparents discuss their grandchild's parents.

Relationships With Grandchildren's Parents

It surprised us to hear most grandparents refer to their grandchild's parent as "the mother/father" rather than "my daughter/son." If the parent was living, it appeared these grandparents wanted to distance themselves from the parent, even though in almost every case the parent is the grandparent's adult child. This sharply contrasts the grandparents' references to their other children, whom they readily label as their sons or daughters. It appears the reasons for this emotional distancing are complex. One reason, as discussed above, is the shame and guilt the grandparents feel at having raised an irresponsible parent. Another contributing factor to this distancing is the anger the grandparents feel toward their child for sidetracking their lives. Another emotion that seems to create this need for distance may be the fear these grandparents experience when they realize the power their children hold over them. Many of the parents do not resign their parental rights, which can open the door for the child's parent to take the child from the grandparent, and/or generate expensive legal fees. One grandparent echoed the experiences of many when he said, "It's like a poker game with the custody issue—we need to bluff with the parents because they won't have resources to check [and call our bluff]." It is imperative for grandparents raising grandchildren to be well informed of their legal options, and especially to hear from other grandparents who have been able to work in or around the system to ensure their conservator or guardian status. As these groups progressed, we realized the importance of helping grandparents work through these complex feelings they have toward their adult child, and to provide advocacy and legal information to help them regain some sense of power and control in their situation. The threat of the parent reappearing and disrupting the grandchild's life looms constantly for these grandparents, and many feel the need to overprotect and pamper their grandchildren in response to this legitimate fear.

Relationships With Grandchildren

While almost all the grandparents expressed little regret about their decision to raise their grandchild, many feel pressure to "do things right" this time around. Many of the grandparents are very protective of their grandchildren, and take perhaps even greater responsibility for these children than they took with their own. One grandmother expressed this best when she explained, "She is my child, as if I gave birth to her . . . ain't nobody [sic] going to mess with that—ever." While most grandchildren being raised by their grandparents are contending with difficult issues that children from traditional families might not experience, these grandparents may feel pulled to engage in a pampering relationship with the child. These grandparents understand how much their grandchildren must cope with each day, and are at times reluctant to parent firmly and consistently. One grandmother articulated this conflict best when she said, "Emotionally, these kids are going through so much, I guess we do tread lightly . . . we don't want to be the bad guys." Having experienced enough pain from their relationships with others as well as with their adult children, many custodial grandparents cannot cope with the addition of their grandchildren's anger. We found it helpful to acknowledge this conflict and to help them feel less conflicted by encouraging them to engage in the pampering grandparent role, for example, on one specified day or time each week.

The multiple roles that custodial grandparents must assume also seemed to create difficulties in their relationships with their grandchildren. While some grandparents were comfortable with allowing their grandchildren to call them by whatever name they chose at a given moment, others were less sure about how to deal with this role confusion. This reflects some grandparents' difficulties with setting boundaries and limits with their grandchildren, because they, themselves, are unsure from moment to moment how far their boundaries extend. This appeared to be most difficult for grandparents who had just begun parenting their grandchildren. Discussing ways to navigate these multiple roles, acknowledging the complexity of their roles, understanding how their grandchildren sort out these roles through their own ways of categorizing experiences, and giving them permission to just be grandparents sometimes seemed to be most helpful. Much of the guilt the grandparents experience, in addition to the multiple responsibilities they face raising a grandchild, seems to affect their ability to care for themselves. Self-care was an issue that we found ourselves covering in every group, even though it wasn't a scheduled topic.

Relationship With Self

Many of the grandparents (particularly the older ones) expressed a need to be cared for at this time in their lives, and were somewhat resentful having to care for others instead. Yet, at the same time, many reported feeling unable to take the time to engage in self-care, and even reported feeling guilty when they make the effort to take time for themselves. The idea of self-care is so foreign to these overworked caretakers that many had difficulty even generating a wish list of self-pampering activities during one of the groups. This issue is critical to caregivers of any age, but is especially important for caregivers who assume multiple roles and whose health may need greater attention with age. We found it helpful to reframe self-care in terms of child care: the grandparents could more readily understand that if they did not care for themselves first, they may not be able to effectively care for their grandchildren. The greatest barrier to caring for self, however, is finding adequate child care. Groups like these can help grandparents network and perhaps trade child care responsibilities with one another so that each can have some time for self.

As most of the grandparents reported feeling as if the group provided the care and support they had been missing, we also encouraged the grandparents to continue using the standard group meeting time as their self-care time after our final group meeting. Presenting this option provided a therapeutic bind for many of the grandparents who insisted they could not find time for themselves: if they could make our group every Saturday, then they could certainly continue to reserve that time for self-care once the groups ended. It appears the issue of self-care is an important component to deliberately include in future custodial grandparenting interventions.

Multigenerational Family Patterns

Feeling guilty about self-care seemed to arise during discussions in which grandparents brought up their own family-of-origin issues and the patterns of caretaking in their families. We were surprised to find how many of these grandparents had parents or other relatives who had also raised grandchildren. In fact, our last group included a grandmother raising her grandchild who attended with her daughter who was also raising her own grandchild. Grandmother, mother, grandchild/nephew, and grandchild/great-grandchild had pooled their resources, and seemed to be coping fairly well with their situation. It occurred to us that approaching custodial grandparenting from a family systems perspective might be helpful for many of these grandparents. Using genograms (McGoldrick & Gerson, 1985) might allow grandparents to gain perspective and some distance from their situation in order to better assess systemic patterns of parenting (and other issues), which may help them make different choices. Furthermore, allowing grandparents to share their genograms with the group may be therapeutic as they share their history, and may also allow the other grandparents to feel effective in offering their perspectives or in seeing common experiences.

While many universal themes emerged from the grandparents in all three sets of groups, the membership in each set presented unique dynamics that suggest custodial grandparents may experience different tasks or phases during their process of coming to terms with their new role.

Phases of Custodial Grandparenting

Much like the process of grief (see Kübler-Ross, 1969), the process of parenting a grandchild seems to occur in phases. Like grief, many environmental variables contribute to the phases custodial grandparents will experience and how they will process the life changes. Because these grandparents are dealing with losses on many levels (e.g., loss of being a traditional grandparent, loss of financial independence, loss of leisure, loss of an age-appropriate retirement, perhaps the loss of raising responsible children, and perhaps the death of a child), it seems appropriate that coming to terms with custodial grandparenting very much resembles the grief process. Like the course of grieving, the emotions and, perhaps, the stages these grandparents encounter are not linear: they may emerge and reemerge throughout the process of custodial grandparenting. However, in each of the three groups, we found their processes revealed three separate dynamics that can be used to perhaps better structure future grandparenting groups.

Overwhelmed/Frustrated

Some of the grandparents, particularly the ones we encountered in our first set of groups, were overwhelmed with the responsibility of raising their grandchild and readily admitted to needing help. One of the grandparents summed up the feelings of many in the group when she said, "How do I deal with the situation that I'm in . . . that's where I need answers." Another grandparent in this same group revealed her frustrations when she admitted feeling "handicapped" in the education and legal systems because "I don't know enough." These feelings are exacerbated when the grandchild has special emotional or learning needs, or when the custodial arrangement is unclear and is not legally binding.

Although these grandparents are in need of help, being in a constant state of need may be the best way they've learned to cope with their difficulties. Much like these grandparents experience from the multiple systems they encounter, we experienced many "yes, buts" from them when we suggested some possible solutions to their concerns. Helping these grandparents explore and process their "blind spots" (Egan, 1994) seemed to be the most effective way to assist them in our groups. Despite their requests, grandparents in this phase of the process are not ready for solutions. However, they are open to hearing alternatives, unlike some of the grandparents we encountered in our groups.

Resistant/Denying

Others, particularly grandparents in our second group, were much more resistant to the alternatives we offered. They wanted to present the image of having everything together and under control, and tended to deny any difficulties with their situation or their ability to cope with it. The most effective approach we found to reach these grandparents was to address issues (particularly anger) relevant to their relationships with the parents of their grandchildren. These grandparents did not believe they needed help with their grandchildren, but instead with handling the parent of the grandchild. One of the grandparents emphasized the salience of this issue when he provided feedback suggesting we include "something on dealing with our adult children—how we could help them to be more responsible for their children . . . or how to stop wishing for the impossible." A family systems approach that uses genograms (McGoldrick & Gerson, 1985) or the life review intervention (Butler, 1963) in group sessions may be useful in helping grandparents who present with much unresolved and, perhaps, unexpressed anger toward the parent of their grandchild. However, some custodial grandparents have been able to cope with their multiple losses, and have been able to balance their emotions with their ability to problem solve in their new role.

Accepting

Finally, in our third group, we found grandparents who could appropriately express anger and sadness, were willing to admit their struggles, and, despite some having multiple losses, seemed to have come to terms with their situation. Although these grandparents were present in the first and second groups, we found that this dynamic more readily emerged in our third and final group. These grandparents were willing to ask for help, were able to accept what we provided, and were able to work with the issues more readily on their own. Many openly admitted to still feeling overwhelmed and frustrated, and were at times resistant, but seemed to have better coping strategies in place.

FUTURE DIRECTIONS

Although we found that many grandparents want to share their experiences in the hope of gaining and giving support, we also found that the structure of an educational program can provide safety and can facilitate more frank discussion. In conducting these groups, we realized that the grandparents need much of the same safety and containment that we encourage caregivers to provide children who lose a parent.

This is consistent with others' (e.g., Chenoweth, 2000; Strom & Strom, 2000) recommendations to combine support and education when conducting custodial grandparenting groups. Many of these grandparents experience multiple stressors in their lives, and may find it difficult to separate their emotional from their intellectual needs. In this respect, Cox (2000) suggests conducting support and education groups separately. Based on our experiences with these groups, it seems we professionals can easily create this dichotomy, but the grandparents' experiences are not so neatly divided. Nonetheless, we believe it is beneficial to provide some structure to the groups both in education and with support and process.

Although the educational component is easy to structure, professionals must be flexible within this structure to provide grandparents with the necessary support and process elements. As mentioned earlier, we strongly recommend allowing grandparents to introduce themselves at the beginning of the first session, and to encourage them to share a little about their situation (number of grandchildren, names, ages, how they came to care for grandchildren). In our last session, we also found it helpful to allow the grandparents to offer suggestions about the topics that had most interested them over the course of the program. Although we had already planned the next topics and sessions, it was helpful for us to learn what was most salient to them, and it was therapeutic in showing the grandparents that we valued their input.

Although we were able to structure the educational topics, it was much more difficult to provide some structure and direction for the support and process component. As mentioned earlier, one of the ways to provide a flexible structure to this important element may be including a session midway or late in the program in which grandparents bring their genograms (McGoldrick & Gerson, 1985) or engage in a life review exercise (Butler, 1963). Grandparents could work on either of these a week or two before the scheduled session by gathering information from family members, or bringing in photos and other mementos from their children, grandchildren, or from their own lives to share with the group.

In the same vein, it might be useful to emphasize more strongly in future sessions a focus on grandparents' emotional health and ways to improve their relationships with others and with themselves. This might be achieved by educating and facilitating skills in group such as sharing feelings; learning to separate emotion from intellect (Bowen, 1978) so people can tolerate opinions and experiences that are different from their own; learning to stop, think, and brainstorm to solve problems; and learning healthy skepticism. A cognitive-behavioral component may also be useful in helping grandparents focus on positive events and positive behaviors from their grandchildren and others, and to help them generate alternative thoughts about situations. These grandparents seemed especially vulnerable to blaming themselves and engaging in negative feedback loops. Learning these skills is also part of learning better self-care, which we find to be a critical component for future groups. We recommend planning a self-care component that focuses on creating space for oneself (e.g., finding relaxation and enjoyment in activities such as music, reading, exercise, massage, being with friends, and perhaps focusing on self through counseling) in future groups, which could be easily included in a "Relating to Others/Relating to Self" session.

When we asked the groups to provide anonymous feedback about what was most helpful to them about the sessions, many grandparents reported that being with similar others was most therapeutic for them. The grandparents clearly experienced many of Yalom's (1995) eleven therapeutic factors through the group experience, as best evidenced by many who said the groups helped them experience "the feeling of unity" and "just knowing you are not alone." Being able to interact with similar others and share their experiences was critical to the success of these groups. What many grandparents found especially powerful was not only finding similar others in the group, but hearing another custodial grandparent facilitate one of the groups in which she provided legal, economic, and practical information. Based on the feedback received from the groups, we strongly recommend finding a custodial grandparent advocate (especially one who is a custodial grandparent) to provide at least one session in such programs.

Providing resources for legal and financial help and trusted referrals for counseling and psychological assessment are essential to helping these grandparents deal with their complex roles. Many grandparents are overwhelmed, and providing a short list of local resources and services as well as some guidance (and personal recommendations when appropriate) on finding these resources is necessary when conducting these programs. The grandparents seemed to appreciate specific information about the warning signs of depression from APA's National Depression Screening Day Presentation. Providing information like this is helpful to grandparents who are unsure about when to seek professional help. Grandparents also found information that detailed childhood problems to be useful (such as the signs of "normal versus complicated grief" listed by child's age group in Cox, 2000).

The grandparents seemed to benefit significantly from these groups; however, the greatest barriers to grandparents' attendance in future groups are scheduling and childcare. Because more than 56% of grandparents raising grandchildren work outside the home (U.S. Census Bureau, 2000), these groups typically must be scheduled on a weekend or on a weeknight. We found the most success scheduling a Saturday morning group with these grandparents. However, they still struggled with obtaining childcare for their grandchildren during this time. One suggestion for future groups might be arranging a simultaneous group for the grandchildren (depending on their ages), or providing someone who can care for the children on-site during the grandparents' group sessions.

Finally, because isolation from others and loss are key issues for these grandparents, many of these topics were reactivated at the end of each group program. Perhaps future programs could extend to twelve instead of six weeks, and could include or more strongly emphasize the additional components suggested above. Twelve weeks may also allow facilitators to work simultaneously with loss issues by discussing and processing the ending of the group as the sessions progress. In addition, with permission from the group, we found it helpful to pass around a voluntary contact sheet for members to provide their names, e-mail addresses, and phone numbers if they wished to connect with other members outside of the group. While this is typically discouraged in many process-oriented groups, these grandparents are in desperate need of continued support from one another to help them maintain connections and decrease their isolation.

REFERENCES

Bowen, M. (1978). *Family therapy in clinical practice.* New York: Aronson.

Butler, R. N. (1963). The life review: An interpretation of reminiscence in the aged. *Psychiatry, 26,* 65–76.

Chenoweth, L. (2000). Grandparent education. In B. Hayslip & R. Goldberg-Glen (Eds.), *Grandparents raising grandchildren: Theoretical, empirical and clinical perspectives* (pp. 307–326). New York: Springer.

Cox, C. B. (2000). *Empowering grandparents raising grandchildren: A training manual for group leaders.* New York: Springer.

Egan, G. (1994). *The skilled helper* (5th ed.). Belmont, CA: Wadsworth.

Emick, M. A., & Hayslip, B. (1996). Custodial grandparenting: New roles for middle-aged and older adults. *International Journal of Aging and Human Development, 43,* 435–454.

Emick, M. A., & Hayslip, B. (1999). Custodial grandparenting: Stresses, coping skills, and relations with grandchildren. *International Journal of Aging and Human Development, 48,* 35–61.

Fuller-Thomson, E., & Minkler, M. (2000) America's grandparent caregivers: Who are they? In B. Hayslip & R. Goldberg-Glen (Eds.), *Grandparents raising grandchildren: Theoretical, empirical and clinical perspectives* (pp. 3–21). New York: Springer.

Hayslip, B., & Shore, R. J. (2001). Custodial grandparenting and mental health services. *Journal of Mental Health and Aging, 6,* 367–384.

Hayslip, B., Shore, R. J., Henderson, C. E., & Lambert, P. (1998). Custodial grandparenting and the impact of grandchildren with problems on role satisfaction and role meaning. *Journals of Gerontology: Social Sciences, 53B,* S164–S173.

Haywood, E. M. (1999). Custodial grandparents and their grandchildren. *The Family Journal: Counseling and Therapy for Couples and Families, 7,* 367–372.

Kübler-Ross, E. (1969). *On death and dying.* New York: Macmillan.

McGoldrick, M., & Gerson, R. (1985). *Genograms in family assessment*. New York: Norton.

Minkler, M., Fuller-Thomson, E., Miller, D., & Driver, D. (1997). Depression in grandparents raising grandchildren. *Archives of Family Medicine, 6,* 445–452.

Nordhus, I. H., & Nielsen, G. H. (1999). Brief dynamic psychotherapy with older adults. *Journal of Clinical Psychology, 55,* 935–947.

Pinson-Millburn, N. M., Fabian, E. S., Schlossberg, N. K., & Pyle, M. (1996). Grandparents raising grandchildren. *Journal of Counseling and Development, 74,* 548–554.

Shore, R. J., & Hayslip, B. (1994). Custodial grandparenting: Implications for children's development. In A. Gottfried (Ed.), *Redefining families: Implications for children's development* (pp. 171–218). New York: Plenum.

Strom, R. D., & Strom, S. K. (2000). Goals for grandparents and support groups. In B. Hayslip & R. Goldberg-Glen (Eds.), *Grandparents raising grandchildren: Theoretical, empirical and clinical perspectives* (pp. 289–303). New York: Springer.

U.S. Bureau of the Census. (2000). *Current populations survey*. Washington, DC: U.S. Government Printing Office.

Waters, E. B. (1984). Building on what you know: Techniques for individual and groups counseling with older adults. *The Counseling Psychologist, 12,* 63–74.

Yalom, I. D. (1995). *The theory and practice of group psychotherapy*. New York: Basic Books.

CHAPTER 14

Grandparents Raising Grandchildren: Guidelines for Family Life Educators and Other Family Professionals

Megan L. Dolbin-MacNab and Dena B. Targ

INTRODUCTION

In the last two decades, there has been a notable increase in the number of families in which grandparents are the primary caregivers for their grandchildren (Casper & Bryson, 1998). Concurrent with this demographic increase, these grandparent-headed families have received attention from academic sources representing a variety of professions and disciplines, including family life education, family therapy, and social work. Within academic journals and books across these disciplines, reports of research about grandparent-headed families and discussions of the topic of custodial grandparents have become more common (Cox, 2000b; Hayslip & Goldberg-Glen, 2000). In addition to empirical and scholarly information, many articles and books on grandparents raising grandchildren also include sections dedicated to implications for a variety of educators and human service professionals (e.g., Bartram, 1996;

Bonecutter & Gleeson, 1997; Cox, 2000a; Hayslip & Goldberg-Glen, 2000; Strom & Strom, 1993; Thaxton, 1995).

Across disciplines such as family life education, marriage and family therapy, and social work, many authors highlight similar themes for professionals who work with grandparents raising grandchildren. Besides these common suggestions for effective practice, specific disciplines also offer suggestions that could inform and assist family professionals working within other disciplines. This chapter compiles predominant themes from within and across disciplines on providing effective education and service to grandparent-headed families into a list of guidelines for family professionals. At this time, the information on issues facing grandparents raising grandchildren and implications for practice strategies for grandparent families has not been integrated into one concise source that cuts across disciplines. This chapter fills that gap by synthesizing the major issues facing grandparents who are caring for their grandchildren and guidelines for practice that a variety of family professionals can use when interacting with this population.

SUMMARY OF ISSUES FOR GRANDPARENTS RAISING GRANDCHILDREN

Since 1980, there has been a dramatic increase in the number of children who are living with a grandparent (Casper & Bryson, 1998). In 1980, 4% (2.3 million) of children under the age of 18 were living with at least one grandparent. By 1997, this number had increased to 4 million or 6% (Casper & Bryson). The majority of grandparents who are raising their grandchildren are between the ages of 50 and 64 (Vines-Collins, 1997). Forty-six percent of grandparent-headed homes are maintained exclusively by grandmothers. Finally, demographic data on grandparent-headed families also suggest that these families, compared to other families with children, are more likely to be poor and reside in or around urban areas (Casper & Bryson).

The major reason for this increase in the number of grandparents raising their grandchildren is widespread problems associated with the parent(s) of the grandchildren. Specifically, as a result of substance abuse, divorce, incarceration, child abuse and neglect, abandonment, teenage pregnancy, HIV/AIDS, unemployment, or psychological problems, many grandparents assume the major responsibility of caring for their grandchildren (Burnette, 1997; Roe & Minkler, 1998). In addition to these problems, some grandparents become primary caregivers for their grandchildren following the death of the parent(s) due to accident, illness, murder, or suicide.

For many grandparents, raising their grandchildren is associated with a number of difficult problems. Legal issues, including guardianship, school enrollment, and obtaining medical care are at the forefront of grandparent concerns. Additionally, raising children is expensive. Many grandparents have low incomes and, moreover, are poor. Others who have incomes sufficient for supporting themselves do not have the extra economic resources needed to care for their grandchildren and still live comfortably. Therefore, the cost of raising grandchildren can create a major strain (Roe & Minkler, 1998).

In order for grandparents to discern if a grandchild is developing appropriately and to effectively respond to a grandchild's behavior, they need current information on typical child and adolescent development (Strom & Strom, 1993). Becoming a primary caregiver for young children may raise other important parenting issues for grandparents, such as how to control behavior, whether to be indulgent or firm, how to adapt to changing times, how to divide child care responsibilities (between men and women), and how to cope with being viewed as "old reliable" by other relatives in the family (Stokes & Greenstone, 1981). Basic parenting skills that can assist grandparents include self-care, effective communication, guidance, and advocacy (Chenoweth, 2000).

Grandparents raising grandchildren may need exceptional knowledge and skills related to development and parenting because their grandchildren are often struggling with a variety of physical and emotional problems that are related to the circumstances that brought them to the care of their grandparents (Emick & Hayslip, 1996; O'Reilly & Morrison, 1993). For example, children who were exposed to drugs or who have suffered from abuse and neglect may have physical and/or emotional difficulties that make it especially challenging to care for them (Burton, 1992; Hirshorn, Van Meter, & Brown, 2000; Minkler & Roe, 1993). More specifically, many children have strong feelings of loss, rejection, abandonment, guilt, anger, embarrassment, and divided loyalties (Crumbley & Little, 1997). Additionally, many of these children also exhibit behavior problems such as acting out or aggression (Shore & Hayslip, 1994; Baker, 2000).

Finally, with the addition of grandchildren to their daily lives, grandparents must also deal with a loss of time for themselves, social isolation, and anger for having to assume a parenting role after "being finished" (Jendrek, 1993; Pinson-Millburn, Fabian, Schlossberg, & Pyle, 1996). Other issues include grief and loss, a redefinition of roles, and feelings of guilt or embarrassment (Crumbley & Little, 1997). In addition, the grandparents may have health problems that limit their stamina and mobility (Roe & Minkler, 1998). Therefore, many grandparent caregivers are likely to experience a great deal of stress. Learning a spectrum of coping strategies is essential if grandparents are to successfully manage their responsibilities. Three general approaches to coping are changing the situation, reframing the experience, and managing reactions to stress.

Despite the difficulties that grandparents face, the experience can also be positive. Many grandparents view caring for their grandchildren as resulting in a greater purpose for living (Jendrek, 1993). Burton, Dilworth-Anderson, and Merriweather-DeVries (1995) suggest that other rewards associated with being a grandchild's caregiver include the chance to raise a child differently from the way the child's parent was raised, the opportunity to nurture family relationships, the ability to maintain some family history, and to provide love and companionship to the grandchild. Thus, although the experience can be stressful, many grandparents still find raising their grandchildren to be a very satisfying experience.

When grandchildren are placed in the care of their grandparents, there are also benefits for the children. For many children, going to live with a grandparent represents a transition to a safer and more stable environment. Additionally, by going to live with someone they know instead of a nonkin foster placement, grandchildren may have fewer traumas in relation to adjusting to their new living arrangements (Bell & Garner, 1996). Furthermore, by staying in contact with other extended family members and siblings, grandparent-headed households have the unique advantage of maintaining family ties (Bell & Garner).

Clearly, both grandparents and their grandchildren face stressors and rewards when it comes to adjusting to living in a grandparent-headed household. However, because being a grandparent caregiver means engaging in roles that are totally unexpected, because solutions to their problems are just emerging, and because issues may be compounded by life course location, stressors are often magnified. By acknowledging the complexity of the needs of grandparent-headed families and learning how to apply principles of good practice to this population, family professionals will be more prepared to assist these families through education, enrichment, and intervention.

GUIDELINES FOR FAMILY PROFESSIONALS

As illustrated in the summary of issues facing these families, grandparent-headed families are very complex and require attention to a variety of levels of functioning and social influence. Because the ecological perspective (Bronfenbrenner, 1979) acknowledges complexity and multiple levels of influence, it is the unifying theoretical framework for the guidelines in this chapter. The ecological perspective focuses on individuals and families developing in the social environment, including the community, state, and nation. Risks and opportunities within the individual, family, or the larger world can impede or encourage successful development (Garbarino, 1992).

The ecological perspective is relevant to the situations of grandparent-headed families because they are influenced by factors located both inside and outside the family. Specifically, grandparent families face economic, legal, psychological, and educational risks. As a result, solutions to their problems, for example, in the form of social support, education, therapy, social services, and public policies, must come from a variety of sources. Furthermore, the ecological perspective asserts that the social environment itself needs to be strengthened. Therefore, social issues, which may create individual or family problems, can and should be addressed by people working together to create change. For example, grandparent caregivers, the professionals who work with them, and others interested in the issues, can work together to influence the passage of legislation to make it more relevant to families composed of grandparents and grandchildren. Thus, with respect to the population of grandparent-headed families, the ecological perspective is especially relevant because it addresses both individual and family functioning and the social contexts that impact these families. This integrated view supplies the foundation necessary so that family life educators and other family professionals can provide excellent support to grandparent-headed families.

Family professionals are an important component of the social environment for grandparent-headed families. Despite an increase in dissemination of information about grandparents raising grandchildren, many educators and practitioners are not yet aware of the existence of this population because it has not been part of their professional training or experience. Even if they are aware of this population, many family professionals do not fully grasp the complexity and scope of the multiple social factors that influence these families. Therefore, they may not recognize the value of considering strategies from other disciplines. Furthermore, although many family professionals implement guidelines for "good practice" with every population with whom they have contact, they may have not considered how they might need to tailor their education and practice strategies to grandparents raising their grandchildren. This chapter takes common guidelines for "good practice," within and across family professions, and discusses them from the standpoint of grandparent-headed families. These guidelines are intended to help family life educators and other family professionals from a variety of disciplines think about how to transform their "good practice" with this population into "best practice."

Guideline 1: Consider Multiple Issues

As discussed previously, there are a variety of issues that grandparents face including legal, financial, child and adolescent development, parenting skills, and adult stress and coping. Similarly, Burton (1992) states that physical, social, spiritual, mental, and parental issues are common concerns of grandparent-headed families. However, depending on the professional context, the presenting problem may differ. For example, grandparents who see a therapist may prioritize behavioral and emotional problems with their grandchildren. In contrast, grandparents in a support group more often want legal or financial questions addressed first. No matter what is presented, however, grandparents often need assistance with a variety of concerns. Furthermore, for many grandparents, the first professional they contact becomes the person they trust and go to for a variety of concerns. Therefore, it is important that family professionals offer information and support so that grandparents can obtain appropriate assistance for all of their concerns, not just the concerns that the professional is trained to handle.

Guideline 2: Network With Other Professionals

As further needs become apparent that the professional cannot meet, he or she should be prepared to network in order to gain information either to address these additional needs or to refer grandparents to the appropriate resources (Burton, 1992; George & Dickerson, 1995; Strom & Strom, 1993; Thaxton, 1995). For example, a major legal issue for many grandparents is that of custody or guardianship. Many grandparents do not know the possible types of custody and the ramifications of each. It would be helpful if human service professionals were aware of some of these custody options or were knowledgeable about another source of information. Similarly, many grandparents who are raising grandchildren are concerned about having the financial resources to support themselves and their grandchildren (O'Reilly & Morrison, 1993). A family life educator or family therapist should be aware that members of grandparent-headed families might be eligible for Temporary Assistance to Needy Families (TANF) benefits, Supplemental Security Income (SSI), Food Stamps, Medicaid, and specialized school services. Through networking with others and providing referrals, family professionals can ensure that grandparents are receiving needed information and support in all areas of their lives.

Guideline 3: Remove Barriers

When beginning the process of working with custodial grandparents, professionals should consider the numerous barriers that grandparents raising grandchildren face when attempting to obtain assistance. One of the biggest barriers for many grandparents is time. The grandparents may be very busy with all of their responsibilities and are not likely to have a great deal of time or emotional energy to "shop around" for assistance or for the most appropriate assistance. Other barriers to obtaining appropriate assistance include limited financial resources, physical impairment or disability, lack of experience with human service agencies, unreliable transportation, lack of child care, and unfamiliarity or negative history with services (Burnette, 1997).

Family professionals should be aware of these barriers and should do their part to manage them by being responsive, prompt, and responsible in service delivery (Miller & Sandberg, 1998; Thaxton, 1995). For example, most grandparents do not have much experience dealing with human service professionals and may not understand what they should expect and what is expected of them. Therefore, it is important to explain the structure and functioning of an agency to the grandparent and to be flexible with grandparents as they learn how to negotiate human service agencies (Miller & Sandberg). Additionally, because many grandparents have difficulty with obtaining childcare, finding reliable transportation, and coping with the restrictions caused by health problems, professionals should be open to changes in schedules and other pressing concerns. Finally, family professionals could also assume the role of advocate by helping the grandparent make telephone calls and arranging appointments with other professionals. In this case, grandparents can be empowered to be in charge of their situation and can feel more confident in their ability to obtain the services they need. That is, the more professionals can be available and responsive in their service to grandparents, the easier it is for grandparents to overcome many of the barriers that prevent them from obtaining assistance.

Guideline 4: Create a Respectful Helping Environment

Because there are many ways of creating families, most family professionals realize that it is important to acknowledge and accept diverse family makeup as valid and to recognize the circumstances that formed the family (Bonecutter & Gleeson, 1997; Thaxton, 1995). In the case of grandparent-headed families, grandparents have stepped in to help solve difficult family problems with a range of levels of success (Burton, 1992; Jendrek, 1993; Minkler, Roe, & Price, 1992; Thaxton, 1995). As a result, many grandparents need time to adjust to their new family structure and may be experiencing a wide range of feelings. For example, many grandparents feel embarrassed or angry about their family situation (O'Reilly & Morrison, 1993). They may also worry that professionals and other people are judging them. Because of these and many other feelings, it can take some grandparents a long time to approach a professional for assistance. Therefore, when grandparents do seek professional assistance, it is most likely because they have tried everything they can think of to solve their problems and have realized that they cannot do it alone. For example, the grandparent may have tried repeatedly to manage a grandchild's behavior at school. Or, the grandparent might have tried a variety of tactics for working with the grandchild's parents. By recognizing and respecting their family structure as a type of resourcefulness and not viewing it or help seeking as a sign of weakness or dysfunction, professionals can create an environment that will show the grandparents that their expertise is valued and that someone cares about them. Furthermore, by communicating respect for a grandparent's knowledge, experience, strength, and role, professionals are likely to enhance their own effectiveness when working with grandparents raising their grandchildren (Bonecutter & Gleeson, 1997). This respectful stance is also essential for improving grandparents' self-esteem and mental health (Thaxton, 1995). As Thaxton states, "take time to listen to the grandparents' stories."

Guideline 5: Utilize a Collaborative Style

In most family-serving professions, there are models of practice that are more or less directive. These can be broadly classified into a continuum from an expert stance to a collaborative stance (Nichols & Schwartz, 1998; Verduin, Miller, & Greer, 1977). In choosing a stance to use when working with grandparents raising grandchildren, professionals should consider a variety of factors. These include the professional's own experience and comfort level with the stance, the presenting problem, family characteristics, and the culture or setting of the profession. Although no one stance is best, for the purposes of creating an atmosphere of respect and empowering these grandparents to solve their own problems, a collaborative stance is recommended (Bonecutter & Gleeson, 1997; Stokes & Greenstone, 1981; Thaxton, 1995).

One of the major reasons a collaborative stance is recommended for working with grandparents who are raising their grandchildren is its focus on strengths and resources. That is, this strength-based stance allows grandparents to feel a sense of pride in themselves and ownership of their situations. Many grandparents report that their lives feel totally out of control, they have no power to change their circumstances, and they are taxed to their emotional limit (Cox, 2000a; Minkler, Roe, & Price, 1992). Therefore, if professionals can work collaboratively to allow grandparents to reinforce their successes, to devise their own goals, and to make decisions about what is best for them, it is more likely that the grandparents will feel in control of their lives and their family situation. This feeling is often very powerful and new for grandparents. Other ways professionals can work collaboratively with grandparents include reinforcing the solutions that the grandparents have already devised, asking the grandparents to share their suggestions and expertise, and asking them to serve as consultants or mentors to other grandparents (Chenoweth, 2000; Cox, 2000a).

Guideline 6: Provide a Context of Safety

As mentioned earlier, many grandparents are apprehensive about asking for help. They may not have much experience with human service agencies (Cox, 2000a).

Or, they may have had negative experiences with human service agencies. Most grandparents also do not understand what will happen if they enter a program, join a support group, or begin therapy. They may be afraid that unless they say the "right thing," they will get into trouble. Or, they may be embarrassed or ashamed of their feelings.

Because of these concerns, a critical step in the helping process is to create a context of safety. A safe context is an environment in which the grandparent understands all aspects of the intervention/program, knows what is expected of him or her, and feels comfortable sharing opinions. When meeting with a grandparent, the professional should explain all of these things and should give the grandparent an opportunity to ask questions, make comments, and express concerns (Thaxton, 1995). The professional should also ask about previous experiences with human service agencies. If the grandparent has had negative experiences, the professional should do his or her best to address these concerns.

Another facet of a safe environment is helping grandparents feel that they can be open and honest about their genuine feelings without fear of criticism. Many grandparents are angry with their children for putting them in the position of caring for their grandchildren (O'Reilly & Morrison, 1993). However, the grandparents may be afraid that the professional will think they are cruel for having such negative feelings toward their child. By showing empathy toward the grandparents and their feelings, professionals can create this context of safety.

Whether working with the family as a whole or with a group of grandparent caregivers, in order for family professionals to create a safe environment, it is essential to establish ground rules. Sometimes, there is a great deal of conflict and chaos in grandparent-headed families. Therefore, ground rules can be very useful in helping family members feel that they can safely talk and express their opinions and feelings. Ground rules outline expectations for the behavior and interactions of participants (Strom & Strom, 1993). Examples of ground rules are, "listen while others are talking" and "do not call each other names." By discussing the ground rules and having all members of the group agree to follow them, participants and professionals together can create a constructive and safe environment.

Although safety is important in any human service or educational setting, these suggestions are helpful in addressing the specific needs and concerns of grandparent-headed families. By adapting these suggestions into their practice with grandparents who are raising their grandchildren, family professionals can ensure that grandparents feel understood and comfortable. When grandparents feel comfortable, they are more likely to benefit from the instruction and services provided them.

Guideline 7: Facilitate Effective Group Interaction

Although grandparent-headed families are becoming more common, many grandparents are still very isolated and feel that there is no one who truly understands their situation. For this reason, an environment where groups of grandparent caregivers can meet and discuss their feelings, concerns, and solutions, is often extremely helpful. For professionals who want to incorporate group meetings into their services, an important consideration for working with groups of grandparents or their grandchildren is attention to group interaction. Generally, developing a strong sense of mutuality and cohesion among group members is critical for a positive group experience (Stokes & Greenstone, 1981). Within groups, mutuality is often demonstrated by nonjudgmental expressions of support and active participation in group discussion and activities. Some examples of this in practice include having grandparents introduce themselves to new members by sharing their stories or having grandparents work together to use their expertise to devise solutions to their problems and concerns. As a result of having a sense of mutuality, grandparents often feel that they are understood and that they have a support network, both of which are critical for grandparent well-being and the success of their families.

Unfortunately, a sense of mutuality and support is often compromised by irregular attendance or complete withdrawal which, in the case of grandparents raising their grandchildren, is often caused by health issues, family burdens, transportation problems, and difficulty in accepting help (Stokes & Greenstone, 1981). Professionals should be alert to breakdowns in mutuality and do whatever they can to keep grandparents engaged in the group. Some ways of helping grandparents stay engaged include having attendance/participation contracts, asking grandparents to provide feedback about each group meeting, allowing grandparents to plan upcoming meetings, offering suggestions for transportation and child care, and addressing the grandparents' needs.

Guideline 8: Recognizing the Broader Family Context

In terms of grandparent-headed families, professionals should be cognizant that a child is embedded in a larger system of familial relationships beyond the household. For many professionals, it is easy to become focused on one aspect of the family's situation. Therefore, in the context of the family, professionals should ask about and try to include other relatives and fictive kin, for example, in discussions or as a focus of intervention (Strom & Strom, 1993). It is particularly important to consider the role of the middle generation (Bonecutter & Gleeson, 1997; Burnette, 1997). Many grandparents report that it is difficult to communicate with their children and that there is often conflict over visitation with the grandchildren (O'Reilly & Morrison, 1993). Therefore, if the grandchildren's biological parents are accessible, they should be invited to participate whenever appropriate and possible. However, even if the middle generation is absent, they are still likely to have some level of influence on family dynamics and issues. Even in situations such as these, family professionals should raise the issue of the absent middle generation. No matter what the situation, by recognizing the broader context of the family and its impact on the grandparents and grandchildren, professionals providing education and service will be more effective in meeting the needs of these families.

Guideline 9: Remain Cognizant of Cultural Differences

Professionals should recognize the multiple layers of differences that exist among grandparent-headed families. There may be some similarities across these families, but there may also be major differences based on contextual factors. Some of the bases of these layers of difference can be seen in racial or ethnic background, gender expectations and roles, socioeconomic status, as well as timing of and reasons for becoming a grandparent-headed family. Because of these differences in context and background, professionals should ask grandparents about their beliefs and values. Assuming these families are similar is risky because grandparents are likely to feel that the professional does not understand them or is being disrespectful.

Grandparent-headed families from different racial/ethnic groups often have varied traditions, expectations, and experiences. Racial and ethnic groups can also differ in terms of the role men and women play as parents and grandparents. Further, the level of cultural assimilation will impact how grandparents perceive and enact a surrogate parent role. Taken together, these factors then interact with socioeconomic status, which influences resource mobilization and acquisition (Burton et al., 1995; George & Dickerson, 1995). It should be noted, however, that although there may be some similarities within racial and ethnic groups, there is also much diversity. Within the broader categorization of a racial group, families may have vastly different cultural traditions.

As an example of the diversity that exists within a larger grouping, Apfel and Seitz (1991) interviewed black grandmothers who were caring for their grandchildren. They found four models that could describe the relationship between the grandmothers and their adult children: replacement, supplement, supported-primary, and parental apprentice. In the replacement model, the grandmother fully assumes the parenting role for her adult child. In the supplement model, the grandmother and the adult child share the parenting role. The supported-primary parent model suggests that the adult child takes the primary responsibility for the care of the child with the some assistance from the grandmother. Finally, the parental apprentice model involves the grandmother as a mentor assuming more responsibility when the grandchild is young and less responsibility as the mother becomes increasingly confident in the parenting role. Taken together, these models highlight the importance of attending to differences in subgroups within larger populations.

Guideline 10: Consider Family Interaction Patterns

For family professionals who provide education or services to grandparents raising their grandchildren, an important consideration is the interaction patterns within the families (Bartram, 1996). At some point, the majority of grandparents experience some type of difficulty within their families. For example, the grandparent may have difficulty getting the grandchild to follow family rules. Or, there may be high levels of conflict between grandchildren. Another problem may be that grandchildren get caught in the middle of conflict between the grandparent and the middle generation parent. No matter what the problem, these family interactions can lead to a great deal of stress for the whole family.

Although most often used in the context of family therapy, other family professionals can address these concerns by exploring the relationships between the various subsystems within these families (Bourdeau & Dolbin, 2001). According to this conceptualization, all families have subsystems and those subsystems interact with one another. They can be composed of members within the same generation or of members across generations. In grandparent-headed families, important subsystems include combinations of the grandparents, the grandchildren, and the biological parents (Bartram, 1996).

Another tenet from family therapy that could be helpful to family life educators and other professionals is the idea that clear boundaries between the various subsystems in a family are critical for healthy family functioning (Bartram, 1996). That is, the boundaries between subsystems should be clear and flexible enough that the subsystems can adapt to changes, work together, and communicate with each other. Problems arise when the boundaries between subsystems become too rigid or too diffuse. When boundaries are too rigid, families and subsystems often have difficulty adapting to life changes or stressors. However, when boundaries are too diffuse, the family often becomes chaotic because there is no generational hierarchy in the family. Bartram discusses how, in order to facilitate healthy family functioning, generational hierarchy should be maintained by having a firm and powerful grandparent subsystem in charge of the family. It is when problematic boundaries and interaction patterns (e.g., coalitions, alliances, and triangulation) disrupt this generational hierarchy that conflict arises and disruptive behavior often occurs (Bartram).

Although a focus on family interaction is often associated with family therapy, its concepts may be helpful to practitioners in other arenas. Families, and especially grandparent families, are complicated. Sometimes it can be difficult to understand what is going on within a family, which makes service provision very challenging. Therefore, in order to help understand why a grandparent-headed family might be functioning a certain way, it might be useful to consider the boundaries, interaction patterns, and subsystems within the family. For example, are the grandchildren "in charge" of what happens in the family? Does the grandparent have a favorite grandchild? Is the grandparent too rigid about rules? Whatever the interaction patterns and boundaries, in order to help such families function more effectively, it could be helpful to design interventions for helping the grandparents solidify and establish their generational hierarchy. For example, in an educational setting, professionals can take steps to reinforce generational hierarchy by including the grandparents in educational decision making and by respecting the grandparents as the primary caregivers. In support groups, meetings can be devoted to refreshers in parenting skills and updates on issues facing today's children (e.g., drugs, gangs, sex).

CONCLUSION

The ecological framework includes the social environment as a significant influence on the well-being of families. For grandparent-headed families, professionals are an important component of that environment. This chapter presents guidelines for successful practice with grandparents who are raising their grandchildren. Because the guidelines reflect common practice principles, the suggestions are applicable to a diverse range of professionals working with custodial grandparents. No matter what the discipline, recognizing multiple issues, creating an atmosphere of respect, developing grandparents' sense of agency, and acknowledging cultural diversity are crucial for successful intervention. By incorporating the guidelines suggested in this chapter in their work with grandparents raising grandchildren, professionals can empower grandparents with the tools to resolve their own dilemmas. In addition, empowered grandparents can help to educate individuals in similar situations about sources of support as well as cooperate with others to influence public policy (Cox, 2000a).

The stories of grandparent-headed families often exemplify strength and resourcefulness. However, as indicated by the ecological model, a broader issue still remains. Many of the problems facing grandparents who are parenting their grandchildren are likely to be solved only as a result of initiatives at local, state, and national levels that are sensitive to grandparent caregivers. Possible initiatives include local support groups, state laws to facilitate school enrollment, and national financial assistance policies that recognize grandparent-headed families. Although working with grandparent-headed families on a case-by-case basis will continue to be very important, professionals also need to give serious consideration to education and advocacy, in other words to impacting the social environment. Family professionals could educate other professionals, such as attorneys and doctors, as well as community members, about the situation of grandparent caregivers, provide advice to policy makers, and organize community groups to support grandparents.

Finally, family professionals should consider that it is not enough to help these families once they have formed but that they also should address contributing risk factors such as poverty, drug abuse, AIDS, and violence (Minkler, 1998). Without a broader focus on the societal problems underlying the phenomenon of grandparents raising grandchildren, the number of grandparent caregivers in need of assistance is likely to continue to grow.

REFERENCES

Apfel, N. H., & Seitz, V. (1991). Four models of adolescent mother–grandmother relationships in Black inner-city families. *Family Relations, 40,* 421–429.

Baker, D. B. (2000). Custodial grandparenting and ADHD. In B. Hayslip, Jr. & R. Goldberg-Glen (Eds.), *Grandparents raising grandchildren: Theoretical, empirical and clinical perspectives* (pp. 145–160). New York: Springer.

Bartram, M. H. (1996). Clarifying subsystem boundaries in grandfamilies. *Contemporary Family Therapy, 18*(2), 267–277.

Bell, W., & Garner, J. (1996). Kincare. *Journal of Gerontological Social Work, 25,* 11–20.

Bonecutter, F. J., & Gleeson, J. P. (1997). Broadening our view: Lessons from kinship foster care. In G. R. Anderson, A. S. Ryan, & B. R. Leashore (Eds.), *The challenge of permanency planning in a multicultural society* (pp. 99–119). New York: Haworth.

Bourdeau, E., & Dolbin, M. L. (2001). The only true constant in life is change: Therapy with the Bradleys. *Reflections,* 7(2), 63–72.

Bronfenbrenner, U. (1979). *The ecology of human development: Experiments by nature and design.* Cambridge, MA: Harvard University Press.

Burnette, D. (1997). Grandparents raising grandchildren in the inner city. *Families in Society: The Journal of Contemporary Human Services, 78*(5), 489–501.

Burton, L. M. (1992). Black grandparents rearing children of drug-addicted parents: Stressors, outcomes, and social service needs. *The Gerontologist, 32*(6), 744–751.

Burton, L. M., Dilworth-Anderson, P., & Merriwether-DeVries, C. (1995). Context and surrogate parenting among contemporary grandparents. *Marriage and Family Review, 30*(3/4), 349–366.

Casper, L. M., & Bryson, K.R. (1998). Co-resident grandparents and their grandchildren: Grandparent maintained families. Retrieved August 15, 2001, from http://www.census.gov/population/www/documentation/twps0026/twps0026.html.

Chenoweth, L. (2000). Grandparent education. In B. Hayslip, Jr. & R. Goldberg-Glen (Eds.), *Grandparents raising grandchildren: Theoretical, empirical and clinical perspectives* (pp. 307-326). New York: Springer.

Cox, C. B. (2000a). *Empowering grandparents raising grandchildren.* New York: Springer.

Cox, C. B. (Ed.). (2000b). *To grandmother's house we go and stay: Perspectives on custodial grandparents.* New York: Springer.

Crumbley, J., & Little, R. L. (1997). *Relatives raising children: An overview of kinship care.* Washington, DC: CWLA Press.

Emick, M. A., & Hayslip, B. (1996). Custodial grandparenting: New roles for middle-aged and older adults. *International Journal of Aging and Human Development, 43*(2), 135–154.

Garbarino, J. (1992). *Children and families in the social environment.* New York: Aldine de Gruyter.

George, S. M., & Dickerson, B. J. (1995). The role of the grandmother in poor single-mother families and households. In B. J. Dickerson (Ed.), *African American single mothers: Understanding their lives and families* (pp. 146–163). Thousand Oaks, CA: Sage.

Hayslip, B., & Goldberg-Glen, R. (Eds.). (2000). *Grandparents raising grandchildren: Theoretical, empirical and clinical perspectives.* New York: Springer.

Hirshorn, B. A., Van Meter, M. J., & Brown, D. R. (2000). When grandparents raise grandchildren due to substance abuse: Responding to a uniquely destabilizing factor. In B. A. Hayslip & R. Goldberg-Glen (Eds.), *Grandparents raising grandchildren: Theoretical, empirical, and clinical perspectives* (pp. 269–288). New York: Springer.

Jendrek, M. P. (1993). Grandparents who parent their children: Effects on lifestyle. *Journal of Marriage and the Family, 55,* 609–621.

Miller, R. B., & Sandberg, J. G. (1998). Clinical interventions in intergenerational relations. In M. Szinovacz (Ed.), *Handbook on grandparenthood* (pp. 217–229). Westport, CT: Greenwood.

Minkler, M. (1998). Intergenerational households headed by grandparents: Demographic and sociological contexts. In Generations United (Ed.), *Grandparents and other relatives raising children: Background papers from Generations United's expert symposium* (pp. 3–18). Washington, DC: Generations United.

Minkler, M., & Roe, K. M. (1993). *Grandmothers as caregivers: Raising children of the crack cocaine epidemic.* Newbury Park, CA: Sage.

Minkler, M., Roe, K. M., & Price, M. (1992). The physical and emotional health of grandmothers raising grandchildren in the crack cocaine epidemic. *The Gerontologist, 32*(6), 752–761.

Nichols, M. P., & Schwartz, R. C. (1998). *Family therapy: Concepts and methods.* Boston: Allyn and Bacon.

O'Reilly, E., & Morrison, M. L. (1993). Grandparent-headed families: New therapeutic challenges. *Child Psychiatry and Human Development, 23*(3), 147–159.

Pinson-Millburn, N. M., Fabian, E. S., Schlossberg, N. K., & Pyle, M. (1996). Grandparents raising grandchildren. *Journal of Counseling and Development, 74*(6), 548–554.

Roe, K. M., & Minkler, M. (1998). Grandparents raising grandchildren: Challenges and responses. *Generations, Winter 1998–1999,* 25–32.

Shore, J. R., & Hayslip, B. (1994). Custodial grandparenting: Implications for children's development. In A. E. Gottfried & A. W. Gottfried (Eds.), *Redefining families: Implications for children's development.* New York: Plenum.

Stokes, J., & Greenstone, J. (1981). Helping Black grandparents and older parents cope with child rearing: A group method. *Child Welfare, 60*(10), 691–701.

Strom, R. D., & Strom, S. K. (1993). Grandparents raising grandchildren: Goals and support groups. *Educational Gerontology, 19,* 705–715.

Thaxton, S. M. (1995). Grandparents as parents: Understanding the issues. *Child Care Information Exchange, 104,* 18–21.

Verduin, J. R., Miller, H. G., & Greer, C. E. (1977). *Adults teaching adults.* Austin, TX: Learning Concepts.

Vines-Collins, L. (1997). Census facts for Grandparent's Day. Retrieved August 15, 2001 from http://www.census.gov/Press-Release/fs97-09.html.

CHAPTER 15

Behavioral Content of Grandmother-Grandchild Dyadic Interactions

Julie Hicks Patrick and Jennifer Pickard

OVERVIEW

Much of what we know about the grandparent-grandchild relationship has been derived from retrospective accounts from college students (Wiscott & Kopera-Frye, 2000), anecdotal accounts from adults (Hansen, 1996; Torres-Gil, 1996) and self-reports of current relationship quality offered by a single member of the dyad (Matthews & Sprey, 1985; Peterson, 1999; Uhlenberg & Hammill, 1998). These studies attest to the long-lasting and positive effects of interaction accruing to both grandchildren and grandparents. However, grandparent-grandchild relationships are marked by interdependence between members of the dyad, as well as the uniqueness of individual relationships within multigenerational families (Cherlin & Furstenberg, 1985; Datan, Rodeheaver, & Hughes, 1987; Matthews & Sprey, 1985). In order to move beyond anecdotal and descriptive evidence, it may be necessary to apply different research methodologies to the study of grandparent-grandchild relationships. Given that these relationships are dynamic and multifaceted, examination of what actually transpires within the dyad and the effects of these interactions is necessary (see Fingerman & Bermann, 2000).

Examining the behavioral content of grandparent-grandchild interactions has the potential to provide important information to custodial grandparents and the service providers with whom they work. Many custodial grandparents, and indeed, noncustodial grandparents, struggle with the cohort differences in child-rearing practices (Strom & Strom, 2000) and with challenging behaviors presented by the grandchildren (Hayslip, Shore, Henderson, & Lambert, 1998; Silverthorn & Durant, 2000). Specifically, children today are reared within a more open and flexible cultural environment that offers more permissive behavioral norms than those that were in place when the grandparents were initially parenting young children. An in-depth analysis of the kinds of behaviors that occur within the dyadic unit could prove helpful to grandparents, as clinicians could target specific behavioral patterns on which to intervene. Thus, in this chapter, we present data that suggests that adapting methodologies used to study parent-child interactions can be adapted to study grandparent-grandchild relationships. Moreover, our approach allows us to examine how behaviors of grandparents and grandchildren interact to affect task performance.

CONCEPTUAL FRAMEWORKS FOR STUDYING GRANDPARENT-GRANDCHILD INTERACTIONS

For decades, researchers have called for a shift from self-reports by one member of a dyad to a more complete focus on dyadic processes (Dunham & Bengtson, 1986; Jackson & Hatchett, 1986). In the grandparenting literature, Block (2000) provides one of the few studies of grandparent-grandchild dyadic process. Using data from 40 grandparent-grandchild pairs, Block examined dyadic consensus regarding frequency of contact and satisfaction with the relationship. Although paired t-tests showed that grandparents reported more frequent contact than grandchildren did, similar levels of relationship quality were reported by the dyad members. Block's work is noteworthy for focusing on the dyad as the unit of analysis. However, additional aspects of grandparent-grandchild interactions should be considered. Specifically, studies need to examine what actually occurs during grandparent-grandchild interactions. Especially for children who present "difficult" behaviors, the strategies grandparents use to guide and maintain positive interactions may be especially critical and may be amenable to interventions promoting constructive dyadic interactions (Hayslip et al., 1998; Silverthorn & Durant, 2000; Strom & Strom, 2000).

One reason the study of grandparent-grandchild relations has not progressed is the relative ease of collecting individual self-reports in comparison to the difficulties of collecting dyadic measures. An equally significant barrier, however, is the lack of a conceptual framework in which to examine these relationships and interactions. The family systems approach, which recognizes family relationships as reciprocal causal sequences, may provide an appropriate framework within which to examine such interactions. With its focus on interconnected lives, the family systems approach embodies many of the components of the life-span developmental approach (Fingerman & Bermann, 2000).

The family systems approach also provides several specific methods to examine reciprocal influences between partners (Smyer & Qualls, 1999). In the standard approach, partners work together in either a free play or structured task situation; the behaviors of each participant are coded according to underlying affective and behavioral components (Leaper, 1992; Stone, 1998). Most studies focus on behavioral control and the affective tone with which these behaviors are enacted. High control-high positive affect is generally observed in guidance and feedback behaviors. In a recent study, Fagot (1998) examined parent-child collaboration on a social problem-solving task. Parents offered substantial guidance to their children, with 32% to 43% of their interaction time spent providing instruction and feedback. Evidence shows that children benefit both socially and cognitively from interactions characterized by high levels of guidance (Leaper, 2000; McKay, Pickens, & Stewart, 1996; Radziszewska & Rogoff, 1991).

In contrast, high control-low positive affect interactions (or negative control) are characterized by criticism and physical dominance on the task. Children experiencing high levels of negative control are at risk for poor behavioral and cognitive outcomes (Borrego & Urquiza, 1999; Fagot, 1998; McKay et al., 1996; Stone, 1998). Interestingly, high positive affect during interactions may not be sufficient for promoting social and cognitive benefits for children. Rather, positive outcomes may depend on at least moderate levels of adult control during the interaction. Whether grandparents effectively provide such control to young grandchildren has not been examined extensively.

In accord with the mutual influences addressed by the family systems approach (Maccoby, 2000; Smyer & Qualls, 1999), there is good evidence that the child's behavior influences the levels of guidance or control enacted by adults. In an early study of parent-child interactions, Humphries, Kinsbourne, and Swanson (1978) compared the control behavior of mothers and sons interacting on a collaborative task. Mothers of children with and without hyperactivity disorders were asked to reproduce several figures using an Etch-a-Sketch® drawing board. Each member of the dyad could control only a single knob, one of which made vertical lines and the other of which made horizontal lines. Figures included those in which vertical and horizontal lines alternated, requiring the dyad to appropriately coordinate their moves. Some figures also included diagonal lines. To draw diagonal lines, collaborators had to turn the knobs simultaneously. When working with their own sons, mothers of children with hyperactivity used more control than mothers whose children did not exhibit hyperactivity. To determine whether high control was characteristic of the mothers of boys with hyperactivity or was a reaction to the child's behavior, Humphries et al. paired the women with a child from the contrast group. When paired with a child who did not exhibit hyperactivity, mothers of children with hyperactivity exhibited far less control. Likewise, when paired with a child with hyperactivity, mothers whose sons did not have the disorder exhibited high levels of control. Thus, the women appropriately altered their behavior to accommodate that of the child.

The ability to alter one's behavior according to the characteristics of one's partner has also been noted among older women. Gould and Shaleen (1999) found that older women changed their interaction styles when working with young adults with or without mental retardation, being more explicit when collaborating with adults with mental retardation. Although each grandparent-grandchild pair is considered to be a unique relationship (Uhlenberg & Hammill, 1998), the behavioral flexibility of grandmothers collaborating with different grandchildren has yet to be examined empirically.

We argue that the kinds of interaction tasks used by Humphries et al. (1978) may provide a means to examine such interactions. In addition, the tasks certainly have face validity, being highly similar to the kinds of tasks grandparents and grandchildren may enjoy together. For custodial grandparents, these tasks may also be similar to the types of at-home projects or homework that school-aged grandchildren are assigned.

Whether grandmothers exhibit high levels of control and whether there is a relation between grandmothers' and grandchildren's behaviors has yet to be determined. In fact, many questions regarding grandmother-grandchild interactions remain unanswered. Thus, the current study addressed the following research questions:

1. What is the nature of grandmother-grandchild interactions in terms of affiliation and control behaviors?
2. Do dyadic behaviors influence task performance?
3. Do grandmothers exhibit behavioral flexibility when working with different grandchildren?

METHOD

Sample

Data for these analyses were provided by 12 grandmother-grandchild dyads who participated in a pilot study examining the behavioral content of grandparent-grandchild interactions. Dyads were recruited through a variety of sources, including press releases, flyers, and word-of-mouth referrals. Families received a $20 honorarium for their participation. Participation was limited to women over age 50 who were able to participate with a grandchild between the ages of 6 and 12 years. The children, on average, were 8.4 years old ($SD = 2.3$, range 6 to 12). Seven boys and five girls were included. Although five of the dyads were co-residing, no grandchild gender by residence status interaction was observed (X^2 (1) = 1.66). Of note, residence status did not interact with any of the variables examined in the present analyses; therefore, the grandmothers' data were combined to form a single group.

The grandmothers were, on average, 58.2 years old ($SD = 5.6$; range 50 to 68). All had completed high school (M = 13.0; $SD = 1.5$). Most (91.7%) had more than one grandchild, with the age range from 1 to 12 ($M = 5.0$, $SD = 4.2$).

Procedure

Each pair completed a battery of interaction tasks, which were videotaped for later transcription and coding. Following the tasks, each person completed questionnaires measuring task performance perceptions, and subjective assessments of relationship quality, and noting demographics. Grandmothers also completed several scales related to child behaviors, caregiving duties, and grandparent perceptions. Only the tasks and measures used in the present analyses are described in detail here.

All data were collected during a single interview session, which lasted approximately 45 minutes. Most (10/12) of the interviews took place in the home of the grandmother; two interactions occurred on the campus of a large mid-Atlantic university. Experimental tasks were completed prior to the completion of individually administered surveys.

Collaborative Figure Copying

To assess dyadic interactions, we modified the task used by Humphries et al. (1978). Dyads were seated next to each other and presented with a single Etch-a-Sketch® drawing board. Dyads were instructed that each member could operate only a single knob while working together to reproduce specific figures. Two practice trials were administered, with each dyad having unlimited opportunity to complete these figures. The first practice trial involved producing a square. To accomplish this task, dyad members had to alternate moves, coordinating the creation of the two vertical and two horizontal lines. All dyads successfully completed this trial in a single attempt. The second preexperimental stimulus was an isosceles triangle, which allowed the dyad to practice making diagonal lines. Dyads were instructed that to complete a diagonal line, both knobs must be turned simultaneously, in the appropriate direction and at the same speed. Although the task was more challenging, all dyads produced an acceptable figure within two attempts, and all indicated that they were ready to proceed to the experimental tasks.

As shown in Figure 15.1, the first experimental collaboration involved the reproduction of a simple step figure. The second experimental figure, which resembled a house, was significantly more challenging. Dyads were encouraged to work together, to communicate freely, and to use as much time as they needed.

Dyadic Interaction Measures

Based on common behavioral coding schemes used in the parent-child literature (Fagot, 1998; Leaper, 1992, 2000), behaviors were selected to index guidance, affiliation, and negative control. *Guidance* was operationalized by three behaviors, including physical help giving (i.e., pointing), verbal directions (i.e., repeating procedures), and verbal help giving (i.e., making suggestions). *Negative control* included critical or negative statements made to the dyad partner (e.g., "You're stupid"), verbally controlling statements offered with a negative tone (e.g., "I said you have to go *up*"), and physical control behaviors (i.e., obstructing the partner's access to the materials or taking control of the partner's directional knob). *Affiliation* was indexed using four behaviors (following the other's directions, agreements, smiling/laughing, verbal praise). Following a two-week joint training period, two people (J.H.P. and a research assistant) independently scored four protocols (28.5% of the

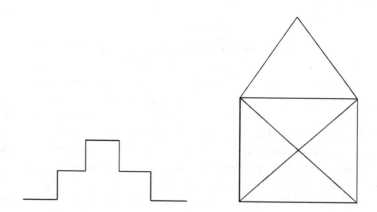

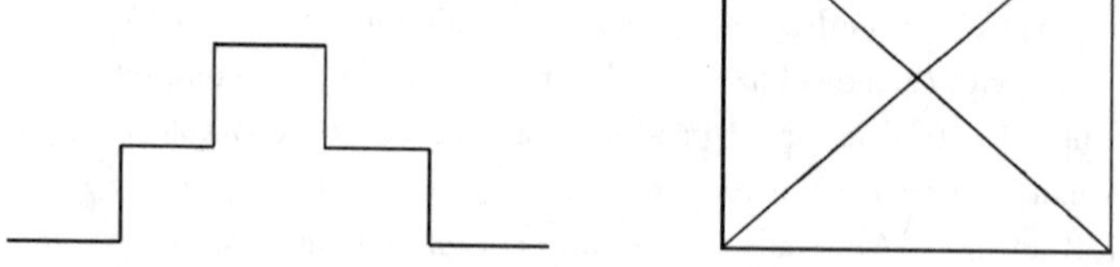

FIGURE 15.1 Stimulus figures.

tapes). A frequency count of each of the target behaviors was taken based on both the video and the transcripts. Coding criteria were set to a minimum of 90% agreement for each behavior; kappa ranged from .91 to .98 (average kappa = .94). The research assistant scored the remaining protocols.

Behavioral coding used both the videotapes and the transcriptions. The following excerpt from Mrs. A. and her grandson collaborating on the "house" illustrates the kinds of statements and behaviors that were coded.

Speaker	Comment	Behavior
Mrs. A.	OK, *ready*? You know what, we're up so high, *how do you get this thing down? We're way up here (pointing). How do we get it down here (pointing)?* Is that me? (moves knob)	6 guidance
Grandson	Now *stop*! OK, *go down*. OK, *now stop* (hand *motion*) . . . There!	4 control
Mrs. A.	OK, now *how do we get it over there (pointing)?*	2 guidance
Grandson	*Go back* the maze way.	1 guidance
Mrs. A.	*Do we have to go back (pointing)?*	2 guidance
Grandson	Yeah (quietly, but doubtfully). *Let's go, go up!*	1 guidance

Task Performance

Task performance measures included the total time on task, the number of words spoken during the interaction, the proportion of words uttered by each partner, and the quality of the collaborative products. As shown in Table 15.1, the average length of time to complete the "steps" was 55.8 seconds (SD = 20.4). Dyads exchanged an average of 74.6 words while collaborating on this figure (SD = 39.9). In terms of which partner was providing more verbal interaction, the grandmothers contributed 62.9% of the spoken words.

The "house" required more time to complete than did the "steps" (M = 140.33, SD = 59.45). Likewise, dyads uttered more words during the collaboration on the "house" (M = 256.9, SD = 131.0), with grandmothers contributing the majority (61.6%) of these.

Criteria for rating the quality of the figures were developed and included a focus on the integrity of the diagonals, the precision of the angles, and the presence of all the required lines. Two coders independently rated five figures obtained during pilot testing and achieved an average of 92% agreement. In the current sample, most dyads produced acceptable "steps," with 16.7% rated as excellent, 58.3% as

TABLE 15.1 Sample Means and Group Differences

Variable	Grandmothers	Grandchildren	Wilcoxon (z)
Number of Words	207.20 (114.5)	124.30 (95.0)	1.89+
Affiliation	12.55 (7.4)	8.42 (6.7)	1.88+
Follow direction	1.00	0.67	
Agreements	3.09	1.42	
Laugh/smile	6.00	5.00	
Praise	2.45	1.33	
Guidance	17.64 (12.2)	11.75 (9.9)	1.89+
Give direction	7.82	6.17	
Verbal help	5.36	3.58	
Physical help	4.45	2.00	
Control	6.00 (4.8)	17.50 (14.2)	2.27*
Criticisms	1.09	10.67	
Verbal Control	3.55	3.42	
Physical Control	1.36	3.42	

+ $p = .06$; *$p < .05$

"good," 0% as "fair," and 16.7% as "poor." For the "house," no dyad produced an excellent figure, 16.7% received a rating of "good," 41.7% were rated as "fair," and 16.7% produced a poor figure. For both tasks, the work of one dyad could not be coded, due to videotape damage occurring prior to when this measure was derived.

Analytical Procedures

To address our research questions regarding the nature of grandmother-grandchild interactions, we collapsed across conditions to yield a single score for each construct, as shown in Table 15.1. We computed frequencies and conducted a series of linear association tests between members of the dyad. Because of our limited sample size, we used the Wilcoxon Signed-Ranks test, a nonparametric procedure that compares the distributions of two variables from related samples (Siegel & Castellan, 1988). It takes into account information about the size of differences within pairs of variables; the test statistic (z) is based on the ranks of the absolute values of the differences between the two variables. It is appropriate for continuous variables.

RESULTS

We examined the levels of affiliation, guidance, and control among the grandparent-grandchild dyads to address our first research question. As shown in Table 15.1, there were wide variations in the levels of behaviors exhibited by the dyads. To test whether members of the dyad differed, we conducted Wilcoxon Signed-Rank tests and cross-tabulations. Grandchildren exhibited significantly more control behaviors than did grandmothers ($z = 1.96$, $p < .05$). A trend existed for grandmothers to exhibit more affiliation behaviors ($z = 1.42$, p = .06) and more guidance behaviors ($z = -0.45$, p = .06), although these effects did not reach statistical significance.

To examine our second research question, whether dyadic behavior influenced task performance, we dichotomized the dyadic behavior measures and computed cross-tabulations with the ratings of task quality. We interpreted the gamma coefficient for ordinal data and the phi for nominal data. We chose to test the dichotomized behavioral variables at both the nominal and ordinal level because there is some debate in the field about how best to treat dichotomized variables in dyadic research (Leaper, 2000) and because no norms are available to guide dichotomization.

Task quality was the average rating across both figures, with dyads rated as consistently poor, consistently acceptable, or consistently good. Results of these cross-tabulations demonstrate that higher levels of grandmother control were associated with better quality performance (*phi* = .83, $p < .05$; *gamma* = .20). In no case was low grandmother control associated with acceptable or good task performance. In addition, neither grandmother affiliation (*phi* = .15; *gamma* = .22), grandchild control (*phi* = .40; *gamma* = .73), nor grandchild affiliation (*phi* = .46; *gamma* = .67) was related to the quality of task performance.

Our third research question concerned the behavioral flexibility of the grandmothers. To examine whether grandmothers would demonstrate flexibility when working with different grandchildren, we observed two grandmothers with multiple grandchildren. In order to minimize practice effects, we asked each grandmother to use the opposite directional knob from that used in her first session.

Mrs. A. worked with two grandchildren. With her first grandchild, about 43% of her behaviors were guidance-related and 0% were control; about 15% of the grandson's behavior were guidance-related and 24% were negative control. In her second session, Mrs. A. worked with the 11-year-old brother of her first partner. In this second session, Mrs. A. exhibited no guidance behaviors and about 39% of her behaviors were control-oriented. The older grandson was very different from the first, with 21% of his behaviors guidance-related and 15% negative control.

Mrs. B. also worked with a second grandchild. In her first interaction, this 60-year-old traditional grandmother worked with her 7-year-old maternal grandson. A few weeks later, she participated with her 6-year-old paternal granddaughter. Large differences in the interactions were observed, with 29% of the grandmother's interactions with the grandson and 66% of her interactions with the granddaughter guidance-related. Mrs. B. used more control behaviors with her grandson (17%) than with her granddaughter (10%). The children also differed, with control means of 17% and 0%, for the grandson and granddaughter, respectively. The children differed in guidance, with 48% of the grandson's and 16% of the granddaughter's behavior guidance-related. The following excerpts demonstrate the high level of flexibility shown by Mrs. B.

Grandson	(Child pulls materials away as grandmother tries to touch them). OK, first we'll start out doing the square (slides materials back to grandmother, who engages in task). Now, I go up, first. Now, you go that way. Good! You're making a rectangle (sarcastically). Now, I've done this one before, it's extremely hard. Now, to make, to form the "X," we're gonna have to work together again, count of 1, 2, 3. Whoopsey (whispering to self: wrong direction). Do this (points). Grandma we're supposed to . . .
Mrs. B.	(laughs) I think we . . .
Grandson	We messed up. We messed up. This time, I do the down at least (sarcastically to grandmother as he moves material out of reach).

Her interaction with her 6-year-old granddaughter differed markedly from the session with her grandson. Rather than receiving guidance statements from her grandchild, Mrs. B. effectively provided verbal and physical guidance to her granddaughter.

Mrs. B.	OK, let's see (pointing), you bring yours across.
Granddaughter	Uh-huh. Wait, where is it?
Mrs. B.	It's (pointing) it's right above this "E." Just, keep, just, start turning, see? OK. Bring it across. OK, that's far enough, (to self) I do it this way. OK, take it back over. Oops, we're not. No, we're gonna mess it up. Go ahead, take it back over. Grandma's the one who's not doing well (in response to child's grimace). OK, now, now we have to . . .

Thus, these two dyads' interactions suggest that grandmothers may be highly flexible when collaborating with different grandchildren.

DISCUSSION

Despite the valuable insights that descriptive studies have provided, the empirical knowledge base regarding grandparent-grandchild relationships is limited by a near-exclusive focus on a single member of the dyad. The current study sought to advance the field by examining the nature and quality of interactions between grandmothers and young grandchildren. Furthermore, we focused on dyadic interactions at a stage in the family life cycle during which grandparent-grandchild relations are especially important to both parties (Cherlin & Furstenberg, 1985). Additionally, we obtained direct measures of dyadic behavior during a structured play task that was similar to the kinds of activities grandparents and grandchildren often enjoy together. As mentioned, we chose our experimental tasks with an eye toward previous research as well as a consideration of the kinds of games and school work the children were likely to be encountering. Many grade-school homework assignments focus on joint projects, word searches, mazes, and other similar materials that have an educational component.

Although the women who participated in the study seem to be similar to other grandmothers, certain characteristics of our sample limit our interpretation of the results. First and foremost, our sample is small. A second limitation to generalizability is the fact that our sample includes only grandmothers and school-age grandchildren. Thus, we are not able to generalize our findings to grandfathers or to dyads in which the child is an adolescent. Future studies need to address these important groups as well.

With these limitations in mind, an examination of the frequency data suggests two clear trends regarding grandmother-grandchild interactions. First, these interactions are marked by a high level of affiliation, guidance, and control. Especially noteworthy is the frequency of laughter and other signs of obvious enjoyment that were present in these brief interactions. This enjoyment was mutual. Dyads also exchanged a high volume of verbal communication, with grandmothers generally speaking more during the interactions. A nonsignificant trend for grandmothers to exhibit more affiliative behaviors and more guidance behavior was observed. We interpret these trends as demonstrating the positive and supportive context that these grandmothers were trying to create.

High levels of control behaviors were also observed in the interactions. Across both tasks, grandchildren exhibited significantly more control behaviors than did grandmothers. In fact, given that the interaction tasks were approximately one and three minutes in duration, the grandchildren exhibited twice as many control behaviors as did the grandmothers. Some of the control behaviors were comparatively mild, such as touching the other's knob but not turning it. However, a few grandchildren exhibited particularly negative control behaviors, such as using profanity in anger, using potentially offensive slang words, and making disparaging remarks to the grandmother. Such behaviors may be particularly challenging for grandparents who raised their own children in a less permissive society than that in which the children are developing (Strom & Strom, 2000).

The second trend in the data involves the marked variation among dyads. Examining the standard deviations of the target behaviors shows that dyads exhibited a wide range on virtually every measure under investigation. Yet few related to the quality of the finished product. The only significant effect was observed for grandmother control behaviors. This trend speaks to the subtle complexities of modern grandparenting, namely, that there may not be a "right" way to grandparent, despite currently held stereotypes (Williams & Nussbaum, 2001). The effective grandmother is the one who is responsive to the uniqueness of each of her grandchildren and who provides appropriate levels of guidance and control.

IMPLICATIONS FOR CUSTODIAL GRANDPARENTS

For custodial grandparents who are reentering active child rearing, the implications are clear: affectionate guidance may be an especially useful approach to building a warm environment in which their grandchildren can thrive. Frequently, custodial grandparents struggle with questions related to when and how much guidance and control to provide to young grandchildren (Strom & Strom, 2000). Our data suggest that moderate levels of control, exerted in response to the child's behavior, may be necessary in order to improve the child's performance.

Efforts to assist custodial grandparents who are experiencing interaction difficulties with their young grandchildren may benefit from an in-depth assessment of the behavioral patterns within the dyad. Such individual assessments may allow grandparents to more effectively establish and maintain an atmosphere in which they are able to facilitate the grandchild's growth and development. Although at the group level the grandmothers in the current study were highly and appropriately engaged with the child, there were wide variations in the tone of the interactions. Given that each grandparent-grandchild relationship is unique and that these relationships are shaped by the personal characteristics of each partner and the environmental context in which the interactions occur, these brief but in-depth observations may facilitate behavioral change in either or both partners. For those working with families facing relationship difficulties, viewing videotaped interactions may provide both grandparents and grandchildren an opportunity to observe and understand the antecedents of negative behavioral sequences. Such images may be powerful tools for members of the dyad to alter the ways in which they interact without the impetus for change being suggested by someone outside the dyad.

REFERENCES

Best, D. L., House, A. S., Barnard, A. E., & Spicker, B. S. (1994). Parent–child interactions in France, Germany, and Italy: The effects of gender and culture. *Journal of Cross-Cultural Psychology, 25,* 181–193.

Block, C. E. (2000). Dyadic and gender differences in perceptions of the grandparent–grandchild relationship. *International Journal of Aging and Human Development, 51,* 85–104.

Borrego, J., & Urquiza, A. J. (1999). Parent–child interaction therapy with a family at high risk for physical abuse. *Child Maltreatment, 4,* 331–342.

Cherlin, A. J., & Furstenberg, F. F. (1985). Styles and strategies of grandparenting. In V. L. Bengtson & J. F. Robertson (Eds.), *Grandparenthood.* California: Sage.

Datan, N., Rodeheaver, D., & Hughes, F. (1987). Adult development and aging. *Annual Review of Psychology, 38,* 153–180.

Dunham, C. C., & Bengtson, V. L. (1986). Conceptual and theoretical perspectives on generational relations. In N. Datan, A. L. Greene, & H. W. Reese (Eds.), *Life-span developmental psychology: Intergenerational relations.* Hillsdale, NJ: Erlbaum.

Fagot, B. I. (1998). Social problem solving: Effect of context and parent sex. *International Journal of Behavioral Development, 22,* 389–401.

Fingerman, K. L., & Bermann, E. (2000). Applications of family systems theory to the study of adulthood. *Aging and Human Development, 51,* 5–30.

Gould, O. N., & Shaleen, L. (1999). Collaboration with diverse partners: How older women adapt their speech. *Journal of Language & Social Psychology, 18,* 395–418.

Hansen, J. C. (1996). Grandfather Chin. *Generations, 20,* 75–76.

Hayslip, B., Shore, R. J., Henderson, C. E., & Lambert, P. L. (1998). Custodial grandparenting and the impact of grandchildren with problems and role meaning. *Journals of Gerontology: Social Sciences, 53B,* S164–173.

Humphries, T., Kinsbourne, M., & Swanson, J. (1978). Stimulant effects on cooperation and social interaction between hyperactive children and their mothers. *Journal of Child Psychology and Psychiatry and Allied Disciplines, 19,* 12–22.

Jackson, J. S., & Hatchett, S. J. (1986). Intergenerational research: Methodological considerations. In N. Datan, A. L. Greene, & H. W. Reese (Eds.), *Life-span developmental psychology: Intergenerational relations.* Hillsdale, NJ: Erlbaum.

Leaper, C. (1992). Psychosocial Processes Rating Scale [on-line]. Available: http://www2.ucsc.edu/people/cam/research/pprs.html.

Leaper, C. (2000). Gender, affiliation, assertion, and the interactive context of parent–child play. *Developmental Psychology, 36,* 381–393.

Maccoby, E. E. (2000). Perspectives on gender development. *International Journal of Behavior Development, 24,* 386–406.

Matthews, S., & Sprey, J. (1985). Adolescents' relationships with grandparents: An empirical contribution to conceptual clarification. *Journal of Gerontology, 40,* 621–626.

McKay, J. M., Pickens, J., & Stewart, A. L. (1996). Inventoried and observed stress in parent–child interactions. *Current Psychology, 15,* 223–234.

Peterson, C. C. (1999). Grandfathers' and grandmothers' satisfaction with grandparenting: Seeking new answers to old questions. *Aging and Human Development, 49,* 61–78.

Radziszewska, B., & Rogoff, B. (1991). Children's guided participation in planning imaginary errands with skilled adult or peer partners. *Developmental Psychology, 27,* 381–389.

Siegel, S., & Castellan, N. J. (1988). *Nonparametric statistics for the behavioral sciences* (2nd ed.). New York: McGraw-Hill.

Silverthorn, P., & Durant, S. L. (2000). Custodial grandparenting of the difficult child: Learning from the parenting literature. In B. Hayslip & R. Goldberg-Glen (Eds.), *Grandparents raising grandchildren: Theoretical, empirical, and clinical perspectives* (pp. 47–63). New York: Springer.

Smyer, M. A., & Qualls, S. H. (1999). *Aging and mental health*. Malden, MA: Blackwell.

Stone, C. A. (1998). The metaphor of scaffolding: Its utility for the field of learning disabilities. *Journal of Learning Disabilities, 31,* 344–364.

Strom, R. D., & Strom, S. K. (2000). Meeting the challenge of raising grandchildren. *Aging and Human Development, 51,* 183–198.

Torres-Gil, F. M. (1996). Andrea Arrendondo Raya. *Generations, 20,* 73–74.

Uhlenberg, P., & Hammill, B. G. (1998). Frequency of grandparent contact with grandchild sets: Six factors that make a difference. *The Gerontologist, 38,* 276–285.

Williams, A., & Nussbaum, J. F. (2001). *Intergenerational communication across the life span.* Mahwah, NJ: Erlbaum.

Wiscott, R., & Kopera-Frye, K. (2000). Sharing culture: Adult grandchildren's perceptions of intergenerational relations. *Aging and Human Development, 51,* 199–215.

Wood, D., & Wood, H. (1996). Vygotsky, tutoring, and learning. *Oxford Review of Education, 22,* 5–16.

CHAPTER *16*

Lessons Learned From Custodial Grandparents Involved in a Community Support Group

Karen Kopera-Frye, Richard C. Wiscott, and Ana Begovic

INTRODUCTION

Due to increased longevity and improved health among older adults, the experience of grandparenting is very commonplace. However, what has changed dramatically is the meaning and functions of grandparenting for many older adults today. While traditional grandparenting roles have typically involved a significant formal, noncaretaking component (Neugarten & Weinstein, 1964), current trends are suggesting the increased prevalence of another function of grandparenthood: that of custodial grandparenting. The 1990 Census Bureau data indicate a 44% increase over the 1980 Census data in the number of children living with grandparents or other relatives. By 1997, approximately 4 million children lived in homes where the grandparent was the head of the household (Lugailia, 1998). Szinovacz (1998) asserts these numbers may be an underestimate as they only represent current caregiving households, and are not inclusive of those custodial grandparents who may have been caregiving in the past, but are not currently doing so at survey time.

So who are these custodial grandparents? Several large sample studies (e.g., Fuller-Thomson & Minkler, 2000; Giarrusso, Feng, Wang, & Silverstein, 1996) indicate that typically they are less likely to be married, are often female, are of African-American or Latino ethnicity, have other children living in their home, and have experienced the loss of a child in the past. Other studies have found them to report higher rates of depression (versus the norm) (Minkler, Fuller-Thomson, Miller, & Driver, 1997; Strawbridge, Wallhagen, Sherma, & Kaplan, 1997), poorer health (Emick & Hayslip, 1999; Minkler, Roe, & Price, 1992; Smith, 1994; Solomon & Marx, 1998), greater social isolation (Jendrek, 1993, 1994; Shore & Hayslip, 1990), decreased marital satisfaction (Jendrek, 1993), higher rates of stress and role overload (Burton, 1992; Jendrek, 1996), and almost a quarter of these households live below the poverty line (Chalfie, 1994; Fuller-Thomson, Minkler, & Driver, 1997). Solomon and Marx (2000) found the physical, mental, and social health of custodial grandparents to be poorer than that of their age peers who were noncustodial grandparents. The importance of this research is that it identifies older adults who may be vulnerable to the stresses of custodial grandparenting, thereby having special needs beyond the traditional grandparenting role.

COMMUNITY SUPPORTS FOR CUSTODIAL GRANDPARENTS

An important first step in identifying potential community supports for custodial grandparents is to examine the characteristics of the grandchildren being cared for. While research in this area is limited, several findings suggest common patterns. Shore and Hayslip (1990, 1994) found that custodial grandparents often obtain therapy for their male grandchildren (Hayslip, Shore, Henderson, & Lambert, 1998) because of behavior problems; of those grandparents raising grandchildren with psychological problems, higher reported personal distress, diminished role satisfaction and meaning, and less optimal grandparent-grandchild relationships were evident. Additionally, Solomon and Marx (1995) found grandchildren living with their grandparents were physically healthier and had reportedly fewer behavior problems than children living with only one biological parent (single/remarried); however, they were at significantly greater risk of experiencing school problems than children in two-parent households.

Characteristics of the custodial grandparents also offer insight toward future community interventions. Minkler, Roe, and Price (1992), in a smaller study of African-American grandparents raising grandchildren, found 65% to be concerned or very concerned about their own health, with a third indicating worsened health since assuming caretaking responsibilities. A common theme across the participant interviews indicated that they did not have the "luxury" of being sick and that the health of the grandchild came first over theirs. Burton (1992) found that despite 60 primary caregiving grandparents finding emotional satisfaction in their role, a number of contextual (e.g., neighborhood crime), familial (e.g., caregiving for other family members while at the same time caring for prenatally exposed crack cocaine children), and individual factors (e.g., role strain/role overload, no time for self) resulted in severe negative economic, health-related, and psychological costs to them. Similarly, Emick and Hayslip (1996) and Shore and Hayslip (1994) found that custodial grandparents were more likely to seek professional help for their grandchildren rather than themselves, despite experiencing poorer well-being, greater social isolation, and more disrupted relationships than their grandchildren. An important source of stress for the grandparents without legal custody was uncertainty about whether the grandchildren's parents would return and take the grandchildren away.

A limited amount of previous work aids in the understanding of the state of supportive services available for those in the custodial grandparenting role. An important study by Minkler, Driver, Roe, and Bedeian (1993) investigated 124 existing multiservice support programs for caregiving grandparents. Based on the first year results, some striking patterns emerged. Three quarters of the programs consisted solely of support groups for custodial grandparents, with 40% lacking formal sponsorship such as in-kind support in the form of meeting space and mailings. Lack of financial support was the most frequently mentioned barrier facing such programs, with 80% of the programs reporting no funding.

The unfunded status of these programs often resulted in severe difficulties, including program instability and ineffectiveness. Because of a lack of child care provisions, many grandparents could not leave home to attend support group meetings. Additional factors such as frequent changes in meeting schedules, infrequent meetings offered, and lack of transportation to the meeting sites (the most frequently cited reason for poor attendance), often resulted in a lack of group participation.

Twenty-four comprehensive programs, however, pointed to a brighter situation. Individual counseling, help in accessing medical care, respite care, transportation, a "warm line," and didactic support characterized these programs. For example, a program run by staff members and volunteer grandparents, the Grandparents as Second Parents (GASP) warm line, located in California, received more than 1,000 calls during its first six months of operation and was able to assist 750 callers with emotional and/or tangible forms of assistance. This effort blossomed to include support groups, a newsletter, a speakers bureau, peer training, and a resource directory. While this example demonstrates what one program with committed and supported staff can accomplish, programs such as these cannot substitute for the need of farther reaching policies and programs backed by legislative power that recognize and respond to the needs of increasing numbers of custodial grandparents.

Other demonstration grant or pilot projects such as "Grandma's Kids," arising out of Temple University and funded by the Center for Substance Abuse Prevention (Rogers & Henkin, 2000); or the 10-week Core Learning Program for primarily African-American caregivers who are caring for grandchildren from substance abusing parents, funded by W. K. Kellogg Foundation (Hirshorn, Van Meter, & Brown, 2000); plus projects funded by the Brookdale Foundation via their Relatives as Parents Programs (RAPP initiatives), and AARP's Grandparent Information Center (GIC), serving as a national clearinghouse for support information since 1993, have all shown some positive and intriguing results. However, they have two problems: either they are short-lived or they simply provide informative resources and not the tangible assistance that is critical for custodial grandparents.

Although these programs offer some promise on optimizing the custodial caregiving experience, they suffer from a host of deficits in meeting the widespread needs of large numbers of custodial grandparents. For example, while custodial grandparents are often encouraged to gain emotional support from such local and national support groups and organizations, these entities are often unstable due to lack of formal financial resources. In our experiences with local custodial grandparent support groups in northeastern Ohio such as Grandparents As Parents Again (GAPA), AARP's GIC initially listed four such support groups existing in Ohio; two of these groups did not exist six months after beginning and had folded when we attempted to contact them. Therefore, the purpose of the present study was to better understand the needs and challenges faced by a small group of custodial grandparents belonging to GAPA.

PARTICIPANTS AND PROCEDURE

In-depth interviews were conducted with 14 custodial grandparents ranging in age from 49 to 76 years (M age = 56.6 years). Eleven of the grandparents were female, all but one Caucasian. Seven of the grandparents earned less than $2,000 per month, three earned between $2,500 and $4,000 per month, and one earned over $10,000 per month. The majority (N = 9) had a high school education or less, with two grandparents indicating some college, two graduated college, and one holding a master's level degree.

A comprehensive, primarily qualitative, survey instrument was designed to better understand the experiences of grandparents providing care for grandchildren. In addition to demographic information, participants answered in-depth questions in eight general domains. They were first asked to answer questions about themselves and, when applicable, about the grandchildren they provided care for. The domains queried included: (1) the caregiving experience (e.g., what types of caregiving functions were performed, grandchild status), (2) financial issues, (3) legal issues, (4) social relationship issues (e.g., level of social activity with friends, both self and grandchild), (5) physical health concerns (both self and grandchild), (6) mental health status (both self and grandchild), (7) service utilization/needs, and (8) general concerns and comments. Each interview lasted approximately two hours and was performed by the study authors after attendance at a local area support group meeting.

RESULTS

The interview protocols were reviewed by one study author with the help of a student assistant blind to the participants' identities and demographic characteristics. Because of the small sample size, data was coded for predominant themes. The results that follow highlight the experiences shared by this sample regarding grandparents' caregiving for grandchildren.

The Caregiving Experience

Participants reported having an average of 4.2 grandchildren (range 1 to 12). Three of the grandparents indicated providing primary care for a single grandchild while the majority ($N = 11$) stated they were providing primary care for two grandchildren. Six of the grandparents cared for a grandchild over the age of 10 years (age range = 11 to 15 years), six reported caring for a young school-aged child (5 to 9 years), and eight provided primary care for a preschool-aged child (age range 2.5 month to 4 years). Seven of these grandparents reported that they held permanent custody of their grandchildren. Five had been granted temporary custody and were unsure of whether permanent custody would be sought (e.g., too expensive, did not want to hurt parents of child). Two grandparents had no formal custody status of their grandchildren. When asked for the reason grandparents were caring for grandchildren, the predominant theme uncovered was parents' drug and alcohol abuse (N = 8). Other reasons noted included abandonment and neglect and/or abuse.

Grandparents were presented with a list of 22 functions of care (e.g., preparing meals, driving grandchildren to activities, protecting child from family of origin conflict) and were asked to tell whether they did these activities with their dependent grandchild. For the sample as a whole, an average of 17.6 functions were endorsed (range = 13 to 20 functions). Respondents also had the opportunity to list additional functions not included on the list. One grandparent indicated a significant time spent teaching moral values, and two grandparents indicated a significant amount of time spent dealing with welfare agencies.

Financial Issues

The majority of grandparents (N = 12) reported receiving some monies from state or local agencies to help in the raising of their grandchildren. However, in no case was this supplement more than $300 per month. When asked how much more money was needed per month to properly rear grandchildren, the average response was $800 (range = $200 to $2,000 per month).

Legal Issues

Grandparents expressed many concerns over legal issues surrounding the custody and care of grandchildren. Participants incurred an average of $6,500 in legal expenses since assuming primary caregiving responsibility (range $1,000 to $15,000). Only two of the respondents qualified for any type of legal aid assistance. A very important legal matter noted by the majority of grandparents was guardianship status in the event of the grandparents' incapacitation or death. Almost all of the grandparents ($N = 12$) noted no available relative or friend to assume guardianship responsibilities. For those grandparents with temporary custody or no formal legal recognition of caregiving status, adoption was also a concern (mainly because parent would not relinquish rights).

Social Issues

Grandparents reported spending an average of 2.5 hours per week engaged in social activities. Importantly, five of the respondents noted no time at all to engage in hobbies or spend time with friends.

Participants were asked about the number of people available for emotional support and the relationship of these people if any were listed. Five grandparents said that they had no friends or family that they could talk to about the caregiving situation or other personal concerns. Three grandparents listed only one person, while six listed between two and five people available for support. Interestingly, when asked who they rely on for support most, all grandparents who indicated at least one support person said it was their spouse whom they relied on most.

Grandparents were also asked about the social activities of their grandchildren. All respondents noted that grandchildren engaged in some type of social recreation and added that this usually took up a great deal of time. When asked what they would like to provide in terms of social activities that currently were not available, all grandparents indicated that more time for activities (e.g., play games, go to the movies, take children to museums) with the grandchild as a grandparent (as opposed to a parental figure) was desired.

Physical Health Concerns

Only two grandparents indicated no health-related problems. Three grandparents noted one health problem, while the remainder ($N = 9$) said they experienced two or more health related concerns. Common health problems noted included arthritis, diabetes, asthma, and heart conditions. Nine of the respondents said that these health problems interfere with their ability to provide care for grandchildren to a moderate degree.

Grandparents also reported a range of health-related problems experienced by grandchildren. In this small sample, nine grandparents reported at least one custodial grandchild who had health problems. These conditions ranged from irritable bowel syndrome to asthma to side effects from mother's crack cocaine usage; five children were identified by grandparents as having ADHD. Eleven grandparents were able to obtain some type of medical coverage to help deal with these problems.

Mental Health Status

In an open-ended question, eleven grandparents said that they experienced some type of emotional problems since beginning care for their grandchildren. Common emotional problems noted included stress, depression, and anxiety. When asked specifically about common symptoms of depressions, grandparents indicated significant distress. In the past week, ten grandparents said they felt depressed, ten said they were sad, nine felt lonely, seven had crying spells, and four said they felt like failures.

Importantly, nine of these grandparents said that emotional problems interfered with their ability to provide adequate care to grandchildren at least to a moderate degree. However, only three of the grandparents sought any type of professional counseling for these problems. Reasons for not seeking professional help for mental health needs included lack of time, lack of financial resources, or both.

Grandparents also talked about the mental health of their grandchildren. Common mental health problems experienced by grandchildren included depression, rejection, feelings of worthlessness, and anxiety over missing parents. All grandparents believed that the mental health needs of their grandchildren were being met through individual counseling (e.g., social service agency, school-based programs).

Service Utilization

During this part of the interview, grandparents responded to three different question areas. First, they ranked the three most important issues (from a list of seven) facing them in providing care to their grandchildren. The three most important issues (ranked first, second, or third by all respondents) were financial issues (endorsed by 79% of the sample), legal issues (endorsed by 50% of the sample), and the physical health status of their grandchildren (endorsed by 50% of the sample). Six grandparents (42%) also said the mental health of their grandchildren was an important issue they faced. Areas deemed relatively unimportant by this sample of caregiving grandparents included their own personal social needs, mental health needs, and physical health needs.

Grandparents were then asked whether they knew how to obtain resources to deal with each of these important issues. A large range of responses were obtained across respondents and across issue domains. For example, although most grandparents indicated that financial issues were one of their most important concerns, only one grandparent indicated that she knew who to contact to obtain help in this area. In no category were there more than three grandparents who understood where they could turn for help in a particular area. Importantly, there were no grandparents who knew whom to contact in all seven domains.

Finally, grandparents were given a list of 11 potential services (e.g., affordable day care, support group for grandchild, written information) that could help in the caregiving situation and asked to rate how likely they would be to use each if the service were available (using a four-point Likert scale ranging from "0 = never would use it" to "3 = very likely to use it"). Grandparents said it was not likely they would use job counseling ($M = 1.0$), affordable day care ($M = 1.6$), and information about parenting ($M = 1.9$). Services that were identified as "somewhat" to "very likely" to use included support groups for grandchildren ($M = 2.9$), legal advice ($M = 2.7$), health care services ($M = 2.5$), and hotline availability ($M = 2.4$).

General Concerns and Comments

When asked what their most pressing worries or concerns were, the majority of respondents talked about the future. A general theme that emerged was worry about being able to live long enough to provide care for grandchildren. Many were also worried about whether the grandchildren would grow up to be responsible adults. Interestingly, no themes of regret were uncovered, as no grandparent talked about making the same mistakes with grandchildren that they may have made with their own children. Only three grandparents indicated an immediate concern: one talked about the grandchild's problems in school and two talked about worries over the grandchild's parents taking them away.

Finally, each protocol was reviewed for issues of positive caregiving experiences. No grandparent spontaneously talked about the benefits of caring for their grandchildren.

DISCUSSION

Data gathered from our in-depth qualitative interviews with grandparents raising grandchildren provided insight into many important lessons to be learned about these types of caregiving situations. Mr. B., the president of the GAPA support group from which our participants were sampled, is a typical custodial grandparenting case.

> *Mr. B., aged 63 years, Caucasian, and his wife, Mrs. B., aged 62, care for two grandchildren, aged 4 and 6 years. Mrs. B. is the sole financial supporter of the household, working as a secretary for 35 years in the same small industrial company and bringing home a modest income. Mr. B., a skilled professional, had to retire on disability due to back problems and has been unemployed for 40 years; he receives a nominal monthly check for disability. They assumed care for their two grandchildren three years ago when their daughter developed a drug problem and abandoned the children on Mr. and Mrs. B.'s doorstep. The daughter lives nearby, and despite their repeated attempts to help her get substance abuse treatment, she never remains longer than the intake in therapy. They have assumed all caretaking responsibility for their grandchildren, taking the kindergartner to school every day and watching the 4-year-old at home. Mr. B. is worried about the future as his wife's health is failing and he is unable to work. Together, they are financially responsible for both grandchildren and provide total care daily. Mr. B. has petitioned the Ohio courts for legal custody of both grandchildren repeatedly, but to no avail as the courts refuse to terminate maternal rights and their mother will not voluntarily consent. She drops in about once every six months to see the children, after which Mr. and Mrs. B. have to deal with excessive acting-out behaviors in the children for days after the visit.*
>
> *Mr. B. initially sought resources for his new caregiving responsibility only to find that the six existing support groups in his area had folded within four months time. He started GAPA seven years ago when he took out an ad in the local newspaper for other resources and received 100 calls within a month from custodial grandparents in the same situation. He continues to receive approximately 12 new calls weekly, and a local union organization has offered its union hall as a monthly meeting place for the group. Mr. B. currently sends out 60 newsletters, assumes all preparation of the newsletters, mailing costs, and authorship, entirely out of pocket without owning a computer himself or receiving financial support. He has formed links with local community social service agencies that sporadically*

provide in-kind contributions to the group, but in an unpredictable fashion. Mr. B. continues to provide monthly meetings for the group, in-kind on-site childcare during the meetings, legislative lobbying and advocacy for the caregivers, informational newsletters, speakers, refreshments, and legal/medical/social service referral contact information, solely at his own expense of time and money. The state of Ohio is one of the many states that lack a formal network service for nonparental caregivers, despite having an estimated 66,000 grandchildren having grandparents as their primary caregivers during 2000.

More Needs Than Resources?

The issues and needs raised by these custodial grandparents are similar to those voiced by custodial grandparents in large samples. In fact, our grandparents were quite representative in terms of those studied in larger projects. As demonstrated by the case of Mr. B., custodial grandparents are typically caring for more than one younger-aged grandchild with minimal resources. Does it take a village to raise a child? Presumably, it does. When examining the themes noted across the group, we see several key issues. A considerable amount of care is often provided by the grandparent, despite concurrent nonoptimal life circumstances. The fact that our grandparents reported social isolation; financial, legal, and health constraints; emotional distress; and a lack of awareness of how to access resources, while still providing an average of 17 (of 22) daily caregiver functions, is amazing. However, they reported their role to be nonideal; the majority instead indicated they would rather do "grandparent activities" like going to the theater with the grandchild instead of "parental" functions.

Lesson 1: What Types of Needs Are We Looking At?

The utility of the needs and issues raised in our study lies in the types of potential pathways for intervention that are suggested by the findings. Although Mr. B.'s providing information via the Grandparent Information Center may be considered a potential resource, it did not meet the types of needs raised by this group and others. Most of our group's needs were for tangible assistance—financial and legal aid or concern for the health status and welfare of their grandchildren, especially future custody—needs that are not being met by existing programs to date. Simply providing a national information source on local services (information which was outdated) cannot address the critical, tangible services these caregivers need.

Attention in the literature has focused on the education of custodial grandparents regarding parenting. Is this an ultimate need? While education programs are certainly noble pursuits, they are just one small part of the picture. A large gap in needed services involves assessment and outreach. The fact that Mr. B. and other GAPA members had no awareness of potential resources (e.g., through schools), hence created their own support group because of an absence of outreach efforts by professionals in the community, speaks volumes about our communication efforts with caregiving grandparents. An ideal avenue in which to reach custodial grandparents, given their time demands, is through the grandchildren's school. Early interventionists and school counselors, often aware of children who are cared for by people other than parents, could be extremely beneficial in aiding such caregivers, involving them in the decision-making process for the child's future, and providing helpful information. Temple University's Grandma's Kids program is just that type of program and is showing promising findings. However, this is but one program, which has had its challenges, and is restricted to a particular geographic region.

Lesson 2: What Can We Do?

A second "lesson" learned from Mr. B. and GAPA involves the high degree of stress experienced by these individuals as they rapidly transition from the grandparenting role to the parenting role. Interventions aimed at reducing some of the emotional distress they experience could include readily available, free legal advice to address their custody concerns and rights. Further, since many of our grandparents were emotionally distressed, and research indicates that psychotherapy can be just as beneficial for older adults as younger adults (Knight, 1996), a community outreach mental health service providing "mental health check-ups" could be ideal for these caregivers. A program such as this could also address the social isolation reported by Mr. B. and others; most felt they had nobody to turn to in times of distress.

As strongly expressed by Mr. B. and GAPA members, a promising intervention could address their need to be more than caregivers, but grandparents as well. By recognizing that grandparents often have strengths in maintaining family connections, as kinkeepers, or culture keepers, culturally based intergenerational sharing programs could support their value, thereby potentially ameliorating some of their distress. By drawing on the research indicating the positive effects of grandparents as culture keepers or as an intergenerational bridge between the young and old (Kopera-Frye & Wiscott, 2000; Wiscott & Kopera-Frye, 2000), this aspect of their role as keeper of the family history can be made manifest. A study by Wiscott and Kopera-Frye (2000) indicated that adult grandchildren reported significantly positive influences on their values, beliefs, and so on through the mechanisms of shared general and cultural activities. This could provide the context in which to explore and address custodial grandparenting needs such as role definition and positive mental health.

Lesson 3: How Can We Help More Efficiently?

Overall, the most important lesson Mr. B. and GAPA members learned is that current programs are woefully inadequate in meeting the diverse needs reported by today's custodial grandparents. Caregiving trends in the United States are markedly changing. It is vital that program service delivery systems adapt to meet these new challenges. The most common flaws identified in existing programs are that they are often regionally specific, short-lived, and not comprehensive enough to address the diverse needs experienced by those in the grandparent–grandchild caregiving situation. Until community professionals and researchers make a concerted effort to listen to the needs of this group and commit to integrating these concerns into programs and services for custodial grandparents, there will not be much change.

It is our hope that more professionals will engage in meaningful dialogue with grandparents who are raising their grandchildren. These types of exchanges vividly illustrate the frustrations and barriers commonly experienced. More important, by talking with the individuals currently in these situations, professionals can suggest new and innovative routes of intervention. Programs and services created through the mutual interaction of provider and recipient hold promise in improving the quality of life for all involved.

REFERENCES

Burton, L. M. (1992). Black grandparents rearing children of drug-addicted parents: Stressors, outcomes, and social service needs. *Gerontologist, 32,* 744–751.

Chalfie, D. (1994). *Going it alone: A closer look at grandparents parenting grandchildren.* Washington, DC: American Association of Retired Persons, Women's Initiative.

Emick, M. A., & Hayslip, B. (1996). Custodial grandparenting: New roles for middle-aged and older adults. *International Journal of Aging and Human Development, 43,* 135–154.

Emick, M. A., & Hayslip, B. (1999). Custodial grandparenting: Stresses, coping skills, and relationships with grandchildren. *International Journal of Aging and Human Development, 48,* 35–61.

Fuller-Thomson, E., & Minkler, M. (2000). America's grandparent caregivers: Who are they? In B. Hayslip Jr. & R. Goldberg-Glen (Eds.), *Grandparents raising grandchildren: Theoretical, empirical, and clinical perspectives* (pp. 3–21). New York: Springer.

Fuller-Thomson, E., Minkler, M., & Driver, D. (1997). A profile of grandparents raising grandchildren in the United States. *Gerontologist, 37,* 406–411.

Giarrusso, R., Feng, D., Wang, Q., & Silverstein, M. (1996). Parenting and co-parenting of grandchildren: Effects on grandparents' well-being and family solidarity. *International Journal of Sociology and Social Policy, 16,* 124–156.

Hayslip, B., Shore, R. J., Henderson, C., & Lambert, P. (1998). Custodial grandparenting and the impact of grandchildren with problems on role satisfaction and role meaning. *Journals of Gerontology: Social Sciences, 53B,* S164–S173.

Hirshorn, B. A., Van Meter, M. J., & Brown, D. R. (2000). When grandparents raise grandchildren due to substance abuse: Responding to a uniquely destabilizing factor. In B. Hayslip Jr. & R. Goldberg-Glen (Eds.), *Grandparents raising grandchildren: Theoretical, empirical, and clinical perspectives* (pp. 269–287). New York: Springer.

Jendrek, M. P. (1993). Grandparents who parent their grandchildren: Effects on lifestyle. *Journal of Marriage and Family, 55,* 609–621.

Jendrek, M. (1994). Grandparents who parent their grandchildren: Circumstances and decisions. *Gerontologist, 34,* 206–216.

Knight, B. (1996). *Psychotherapy with older adults.* Thousand Oaks, CA: Sage.

Kopera-Frye, K., & Wiscott, R. (2000). Intergenerational continuity: Transmission of beliefs and culture. In B. Hayslip Jr. & R. Goldberg-Glen (Eds.), *Grandparents raising grandchildren: Theoretical, empirical, and clinical perspectives* (pp. 65–84). New York: Springer.

Lugailia, T. (1998). *Marital status and living arrangements: March 1997. Current Population Reports.* Washington, DC: U.S. Bureau of the Census.

Minkler, M., Driver, D., Roe, K. M., & Bedeian, K. (1993). Community interventions to support grandparent caregivers. *Gerontologist, 33,* 807–811.

Minkler, M., Fuller-Thomson, E., Miller, D., & Driver, D. (1997). Depression in grandparents raising grandchildren. *Archives of Family Medicine, 6,* 445–452.

Minkler, M., & Roe, K. (1993). *Grandmothers as caregivers: Raising children of the crack cocaine epidemic.* Newbury Park, CA: Sage.

Minkler, M., Roe, K. M., & Price, M. (1992). The physical and emotional health of grandmothers raising grandchildren in the crack cocaine epidemic. *Gerontologist, 32,* 752–761.

Neugarten, B. L., & Weinstein, K. K. (1964). The changing American grandparent. *Journal of Marriage and the Family, 11,* 199–205.

Rogers, A., & Henkin, N. (2000). School-based interventions for children in kinship care. In B. Hayslip Jr. & R. Goldberg-Glen (Eds.), *Grandparents raising grandchildren: Theoretical, empirical, and clinical perspectives* (pp. 221–238). New York: Springer.

Shore, R. J., & Hayslip, B. (1990, November). *Comparisons of custodial and noncustodial grandparents.* Paper presented at the annual meeting of the Gerontological Society of America, Boston.

Shore, R. J., & Hayslip, B. (1994). Custodial grandparenting: Implications for children's development. In A. E. Gottfried & A. W. Gottfried (Eds.), *Redefining families: Implications for children's development* (pp. 171–218). New York: Plenum.

Smith, A. (1994). African-American grandmothers' war against the crack cocaine epidemic. *Arete, 19,* 22–36.

Solomon, J. C., & Marx, J. (1995). "To grandmother's house we go": Health and school adjustment of children raised solely by grandparents. *Gerontologist, 35,* 386–394.

Solomon, J. C., & Marx, J. (1998). The grandparent–grandchild caregiving gradient: Hours of caring for grandchildren and its relationship to grandparent health. *Southwest Journal of Aging, 14,* 31–39.

Solomon, J. C., & Marx, J. (2000). The physical, mental, and social health of custodial grandparents. In B. Hayslip Jr. & R. Goldberg-Glen (Eds.), *Grandparents raising grandchildren: Theoretical, empirical, and clinical perspectives* (pp. 183–205). New York: Springer.

Strawbridge, W. J., Wallhagen, M. I., Sherma, S. J., & Kaplan, G. A. (1997). New burdens or more of the same? Comparing grandparent, spouse, and adult child caregivers. *Gerontologist, 37,* 505–510.

Szinovacz, M. E. (1998). Grandparents today: A demographic profile. *Gerontologist, 38,* 37–52.

Wiscott, R., & Kopera-Frye, K. (2000). Sharing of culture: Adult grandchildren's perceptions of intergenerational relations. *International Journal of Aging and Human Development, 51,* 199–215.

CHAPTER 17

Strategies for Solving Everyday Problems Faced by Grandparents: The Role of Experience

JoNell Strough, Julie Hicks Patrick, and Lisa M. Swenson

Grandparenthood is an important and frequently occurring role for most middle-aged and older adults (Kornhaber, 1986; Williams & Nussbaum, 2001). The grandparent-grandchild relationship can be beneficial for both the grandparent and grandchild (Block, 2000; Peterson, 1999). However, when grandparents take on responsibility for raising young grandchildren, grandparenting also can present challenges and problems (Hayslip, Shore, Henderson, & Lambert, 1998; Jendrek, 1994; Pruchno, 1999). For example, custodial grandparents may give up travel and leisure-related retirement plans to raise their children's children, effectively engaging in parenthood for a second time. Cohort differences in norms for appropriate child-rearing (Williams & Nussbaum) and grandchildren with behavior problems (Jendrek) can be especially troublesome for custodial grandparents. Given the frequency and importance of grandparenting, along with recent increases in custodial grandparenthood (Minkler & Fuller-Thomson, 2000), information on how people deal with grandparenting problems is needed. It is particularly important to understand how individuals deal with everyday problems that may serve as gateways to parallel problems faced by custodial grandparents. Success or failure in solving such problems may have implications for understanding whether or not a grandparent successfully copes with the custodial role. To examine how individuals deal with problems associated with the grandparent role, we drew from research and theory on everyday problem solving.

Problems faced by grandparents reflect many of the defining features of everyday problems. For example, everyday problems are encountered in day-to-day life on a somewhat regular basis (Denney, 1989; Willis, 1996). Everyday problems range in severity (Berg, Strough, Calderone, Meegan, & Sansone, 1997; Sansone & Berg, 1993). Grandparenting problems could range in severity from minor hassles (e.g., scheduling a grandchild's birthday party) to major life events (e.g., actually raising one's grandchild). Another defining feature of everyday problems is that they are ill-structured; there is no one "best" solution, instead a variety of solutions may suffice (Berg, Strough, Calderone, Sansone, & Weir, 1998; Denney, 1989; Sinnott, 1989). For example, a grandmother who finds repeated requests to babysit for her grandchildren burdensome could either discuss the situation with the parents, or refuse to babysit the next time she is asked. Both strategies might effectively solve the problem.

Everyday problems are also defined by the social context in which they occur (Meacham & Emont, 1989). Other people are often present either because they are central to the problem (Strough, Berg, & Sansone, 1996), or because individuals' problem-solving strategies involve other people (Berg et al., 1998). With grandparents' everyday problems, the social context is likely to be represented by intergenerational relationships between grandparents and grandchildren, between grandparents and their adult children (parents of the grandchildren), and between adult children (parents) and children (Williams & Nussbaum, 2001). In this chapter, we present data pertaining to the problem-solving strategies that older adults suggest for dealing with two everyday problems associated with intergenerational relationships and the grandparent role.

Previous research often has focused on the demographic correlates of entry into custodial grandparenting. Research based on large-scale national data sets indicates that lower levels of education, female gender, African-American race, and at least good subjective health are associated with a greater likelihood of custodial grandparenting (Minkler & Fuller-Thomson, 2000). Large-scale national data sets, however, do not address how aspects of the larger social context contribute to a grandparent's decision to assume a custodial role. A recurrent theme among custodial grandparents is that their peers do not understand or support their decisions to raise their grandchildren (Generations United, 2000). Despite the lack of perceived social support, and regardless of their own personal beliefs and health, grandparents do step in to care for grandchildren when they are needed (Minkler & Fuller-Thompson, 2000).

The situations that are associated with grandparents assuming a custodial role have begun to be addressed. Szinovacz (1998) suggests that characteristics of the adult child are important, wherein parental characteristics associated with grandparents adopting a custodial role include incarceration (Dressel & Barnhill, 1994) and substance abuse (Minkler & Roe, 1993; Pruchno, 1999). Indeed, such situations may serve as gateway problems to the role of custodial grandparent. Grandparents who become actively involved in a grandchild's life believe that they set positive examples for avoiding substance use and abuse (King & Elder, 1998). Active involvement in a grandchild's life also may occur when adult children are employed and in need of child care (Jendrek, 1994; Szinovacz & Roberts, 1998). Although there is a developing understanding of the problems that may precede custodial grandparenting, little research has addressed how older adults deal with such problems.

To investigate how older adults deal with grandparenting issues, we focused on the problem-solving strategies they suggested others should use to solve such difficulties. We were particularly interested in the role that experience with grandparenting problems might play in understanding the strategies older adults suggested. Our interest in the role of experience was motivated both by theoretical concerns within the everyday problem-solving literature, and practical concerns within the literature on custodial grandparenting.

The theoretical importance of problem-solving experience is apparent when the origins of the everyday problem-solving literature are considered. Everyday problem solving research arose from dissatisfaction with standardized measures of intelligence (Berg & Sternberg, 1985; Denney, 1984; Labouvie-Vief, 1982; see Berg & Klaczynski, 1996 for a review). Constructs such as practical intelligence (Sternberg & Wagner, 1986), optimally exercised potential (Denney, 1989), and wisdom (Baltes & Staudinger, 1993; Smith & Baltes, 1990) were proffered as more relevant for understanding intellectual development in later life. These constructs encompass experiential aspects of intelligence that correspond to cognitive skills used in daily life. Such skills may improve or be maintained with age (Berg & Sternberg, 1985; Denney, 1989). Given the frequency of grandparenting in later life, grandparenting may be an everyday domain in which problem-solving skills are maintained or improved.

Research examining the effect of experience on problem-solving strategies—often operationalized as safe and effective problem solutions—typically rests upon one of two hypotheses. The first hypothesis is that experience with solving specific kinds of everyday problems is akin to expertise. Those with experience might generate fewer strategies because they disregard those that they have found to be ineffective for dealing with the problem. This pattern of results would parallel findings from the decision-making literature (e.g., Scribner, 1986). From this perspective, a number of different strategies are not needed; rather, a single strategy that effectively solves the problem is sufficient. For example, a grandmother who is repeatedly asked to baby-sit may determine that establishing limits on her availability does not deter her children from repeating their requests; hence, she may decide that the only feasible strategy is to decline all requests.

The second hypothesis is that experience might be associated with generating a greater number of strategies. This is thought to indicate good problem solving because it indicates flexibility in how a person approaches the problem and the potential to deal with obstacles (Spivack & Shure, 1982). From this perspective, generating a greater number of strategies is more effective than a single strategy because if one strategy fails, an alternative can be readily employed. For example, the grandmother in the baby-sitting scenario described above could set limits on her availability, discuss the situation with the parents, solicit support from her spouse in declining requests, or decide that the time with the grandchildren is not a burden but a pleasant activity.

Despite the theoretical importance of experience, research addressing the role of experience on problem-solving strategies is scant and inconclusive. Cornelius and Caspi's (1987) work indicated that experience was unrelated to problem-solving strategies. Based on a series of studies, Denney and colleagues concluded that experience was related to generating a greater number of safe and effective problem solutions, with these experience benefits peaking in middle age (Denney & Pearce, 1989; Denney, Tozier, & Schlotthauer, 1992). In contrast, Berg, Meegan, and Klaczynski (1999) did not find effects of experience on the number of strategies, but trends in their data indicated that experience was associated with fewer strategies.

The inconclusive results on experience and strategies may be due to issues of definition and measurement of both experience and strategies. In Denney and colleagues' (1989, 1992) work, experience was not assessed directly; rather, experience was inferred by using problems that were created with input from the population of interest (older adults). Berg et al. (1999) and Cornelius and Caspi (1987) assessed experience via self-report ratings of how often individuals had experienced problems similar to those they were asked to solve. These measures assess experience in terms of the frequency of one's personal experience. It may be the case, however, that a single experience can change one's views of how best to solve a problem.

Definitions of experience used in previous research focus on personal experience. Because everyday problem solving occurs in a social context, individuals may benefit not only from personal experience, but also vicariously from the experience of others. This may be particularly true for problems involving the grandparent role, given that most older adults eventually become grandparents (Kornhaber, 1986). Those who are not grandparents may be able to draw from the experience of their peers to assist other people in solving problems associated with the grandparent role, or if they are presented with a hypothetical problem related to grandparenting. In the current investigation we considered both personal experience and vicarious experience with grandparenting problems.

Most investigations of experience and problem-solving strategies focus on the number of strategies that individuals generate when they are asked for problem solutions (Berg et al., 1999; Denney & Pearce, 1989; Denney et al., 1992). These investigations overlook a key dimension of strategies, namely, strategy type. As is suggested by the expertise approach, knowledge of the types of strategies that are most and least effective for solving certain kinds of everyday problems may differ as a function of experience. Experience is unrelated to the likelihood of using problem-focused (e.g., taking action to alter the situation) and emotion-focused (e.g., reinterpreting the situation) strategies (Cornelius & Caspi, 1987). However, selection of problem-focused and emotion-focused strategies does vary according to problem domain (e.g., family, work) as well as the specific problem within a domain (Blanchard-Fields, Jahnke, & Camp, 1995; Cornelius & Caspi, 1987; Watson & Blanchard-Fields, 1998).

Strategies can vary not only in the extent to which they focus on the problem as opposed to one's emotions, but also in the extent to which they involve changing aspects of the self versus changing aspects of the problem context (Berg et al., 1998). Like problem-focused and emotion-focused strategies, strategies focused on changing the self and context vary according to problem domain (e.g., family, health), as well as the specific problem within each domain (Berg et al., 1998). In the current investigation, we examined whether experience with grandparenting problems was related to strategies that involved changing aspects of the self or the social context of the problem. We also investigated whether such strategies varied according to the specific type of grandparenting problem.

We considered two problems. Both involved an intergenerational conflict between the grandparent and the parent that affected the grandchild. We thought that the first problem, a grandmother who was faced with repeated requests to baby-sit for three grandchildren and felt she was being taken advantage of, might be fairly common and thus allow us to gain insight into the role of grandparenting. The second problem involved an adult daughter with a serious drug and alcohol problem; the grandparents were afraid their grandchild was being neglected and wanted to help their daughter and grandchild. We selected this problem because such situations often lead to custodial relationships among grandparents and grandchildren (Hayslip et al., 1998; Jendrek, 1994; Minkler & Fuller-Thomson, 1999). Together, the two problems represented grandparenting problems that ranged in severity.

We investigated the extent to which older adults reported personal and vicarious experience with these two problems and whether experience was related to strategies for solving these problems. We examined three dimensions of problem-solving strategies. First, we considered number of strategies in order to address the expertise and flexibility perspectives on the role of problem-solving experience. Second, we distinguished the total number of strategies from the number of unique types of strategies to better understand the roles of flexibility and expertise. Third, we examined whether experience was related to the types of strategies older adults generated in response to grandparenting problems. We also considered whether strategies varied as a function of the specific type of grandparenting problem.

METHOD

Participants

Participants were 112 older adults (*M* age = 71.86 yrs., *SD* = 5.92 yrs., 52 men, 59 women) from a mid-Atlantic state in the U.S. Ninety-seven percent of the sample was Caucasian; 75% were married (88% of males, 64% of females), 17.6% were widowed (6% of males, 29% of females), 3.7% were divorced, and 3% were never married; 74% were retired, 12% were homemakers, 4% worked full-time, and 4% worked part-time.

Procedure

A random list of potential participants aged 65 and older was generated by Survey Sampling Inc. A written questionnaire and consent form were mailed to the residences of potential participants. The return rate of the questionnaires was approximately 10%. Participants were volunteers and did not receive an honorarium. The questionnaire assessed numerous aspects of older adults' everyday problem solving; only the data relevant to the current report are described here (for other reports see Patrick & Strough, 2001; Strough, Cheng, & Swenson, in press; Strough, Patrick, Swenson, Cheng, & Barnes, in press).

The questionnaire was self-administered. Instructions informed participants that they could skip any questions they did not want to answer. The number of participants who responded to each question varied slightly. Rather than using estimates to replace missing data, we report results based on cases where valid responses were present.

The order of the measures in the questionnaire was as follows. First, participants were presented with problem scenarios that involved the grandparent role. Second, they were asked what the problem solvers should do to solve the problem. Third, they assessed vicarious and personal experience with the problem. Finally, they provided demographic information.

Problem Scenarios

Participants were presented with nine hypothetical everyday problems; of these, two involved the grandparenting role (see Patrick & Strough, 2001, for results for problems dealing with relocation decisions). The first problem involved a woman who was always being asked to baby-sit for her three grandchildren. The woman enjoyed the children but felt that their mother and father were taking advantage of her. The second problem involved an older married couple whose adult daughter had a serious drug and alcohol problem. The couple felt that their daughter had neglected her two-year-old and they wanted to help their grandchild and daughter.

Strategies

After each vignette, strategies were assessed by asking participants what the grandmother/grandparents should do. Participants wrote their responses.

Participants' responses were classified into one of nine mutually exclusive and exhaustive categories. The coding scheme was adapted from previous research that distinguished strategies for changing aspects of the self from strategies for changing the context of the situation (Berg et al., 1998); it was modified to distinguish among types of strategies aimed at changing the social context.

Three categories contained strategies for changing aspects of the self. *Cognitive self-regulation* involved regulating how the problem solver thought about the problem (e.g., decide what to do). *Emotional self-regulation* focused on changing emotional responses (e.g., stop worrying). *Behavioral self-regulation* was self-initiated action to make the problem solver's own behavior conform to the demands of the problem (e.g. decline all baby-sitting requests).

Three strategy categories included efforts to change the social context. Strategies for *controlling others* were active attempts by the problem solver to change other people's behaviors, beliefs, or feelings (e.g., place the daughter in a drug and alcohol treatment program). *Discussion* strategies were attempts to engage other people in a discussion of the problem (e.g., talk with the parents about imposing on the grandmother's time). *Seeking assistance* involved getting advice or professional help, or seeking services (e.g., call child protective services).

The remaining three categories contained responses that were not strategies. *Other* responses included comments such as "I did not know what to do to solve the problem." If the participant wrote "nothing" or "I did not do anything," a code of *nothing* was given. If no response was given, a code of *missing* was assigned. When participants indicated multiple strategies, multiple strategy codes were used.

Experience

After participants responded to the strategy question, experience with the problem was assessed. To assess vicarious experience, participants were asked, "Besides yourself, has someone you know faced this problem?" and then participants indicated either yes or no. To assess personal experience, participants were asked, "Have you ever faced this problem?" and then participants indicated either yes or no.

Variables and Reliability

Strategies

Three indices of strategies were used. The first was the *total number of strategies*; this index reflected either different types of strategies or multiple instances of the same type of strategy. The second index was the *number of unique strategies*. For example, if there was one controlling strategy and one discussion strategy, there were two unique strategies; if there were two discussion strategies, there was only one unique strategy. The third index was the proportion of the total number of strategies of a particular *strategy category*. For example, if three strategies were given and two of the strategies were in the same category and the third was different, the participant's response was scored as .66 for the first strategy category, and .33 for the second. If only one strategy was given, the proportion score was 1.0 for that category. These three indices of strategies were used for each of the two problems.

Reliability

Two coders placed strategies into the above categories. Eight questionnaires were used to refine the coding categories and to train coders to 80% agreement. Reliability was then established between these two coders based on their joint coding of 22% of the data. Interrrater agreement was 82% for strategy category, 91% for number of strategies, and 92% for number of unique strategies. Disagreements between coders were resolved through discussion. One of the two reliable coders then completed the coding independently.

Experience

Responses to the questions pertaining to personal and vicarious experience with the problem were combined to create one index of experience for each of the two problems. Personal and vicarious experience were combined because the number of individuals who had personal versus vicarious experience was too small for meaningful comparisons. For the baby-sitting problem, 52.8% of the participants had some experience with the problem (2.2% personal experience only, 32.3% vicarious experience only, 18.3% both personal and vicarious experience). For the grandchild neglect problem, 31.1% of participants had some experience with the problem (1.1% personal experience only, 23.3% vicarious experience only, 6.7% personal and vicarious experience).

RESULTS

Problem Scenario: Baby-sitting

One-way analysis of variance (ANOVA) was used to investigate the effect of experience on strategies. Experience with the problem (experience, no experience) was the between-subjects variable. The total number of strategies, number of unique strategies, and proportion of each strategy category were the dependent measures.

We first examined the problem of the grandmother who was repeatedly asked to baby-sit and felt like her children were taking advantage of her. There were no significant differences between those with experience (M = 2.02, SD = 1.0) and those without experience (M = 2.23, SD = 1.41) in the total number of strategies. Similarly, there were no significant differences between those with experience (M = 1.35, SD = .53) and those without experience (M = 1.40, SD = .54) in the number of unique strategies.

When we examined the strategy category, the most prominent strategies were changing one's own behavior (M = .51, SD = .42) and strategies for controlling other people's behavior (M = .39, SD = .42), followed by discussion strategies (M = .07, SD = .21) (see Figure 17.1). For discussion strategies, a nonsignificant trend was found in proportions by experience, F (1,89) = 3.38, p = .07. When older adults had experience with the baby-sitting problem, a lesser proportion of their strategies involved discussion (M = .04, SD = .12) as compared to older adults without experience (M = .12, SD = .28) (Figure 17.1). No significant differences were found by experience for any of the other types of strategies.

Problem Scenario: Grandchild Neglect

For the problem that involved the adult daughter with a drug and alcohol problem who was suspected of neglecting her child, there were no significant differences in the total number of strategies with experience (M = 2.52, SD = 1.31) and those

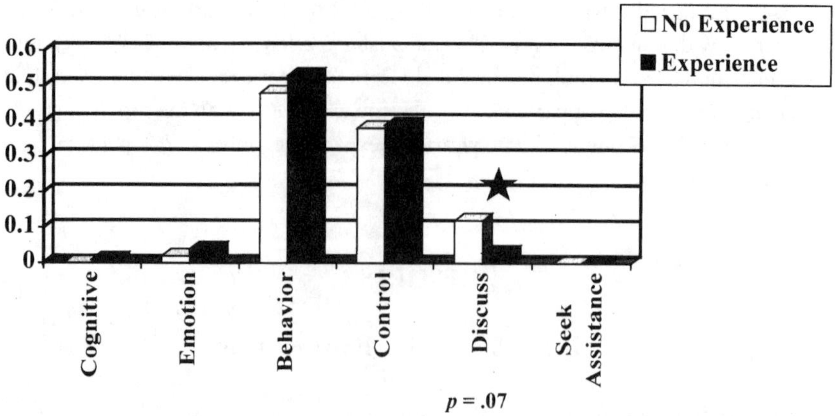

FIGURE 17.1 Proportion of strategy type by experience: Baby-sitting problem.

without experience ($M = 2.20$, $SD = 1.05$) with the problem. There was a nonsignificant trend for number of unique strategies $F\ (1,83) = 3.16$, $p = .08$. Older adults who had experience with this problem ($M = 1.44$, $SD = .58$) tended to report a somewhat lesser number of unique types of strategies than those without experience ($M = 1.69$, $SD = .60$).

For strategy category, strategies that involved changing one's own behavior ($M = .40$, $SD = 35$) and strategies for controlling others ($M = .39$, $SD = .34$) were again very prominent (see Figure 17.2). Strategies for seeking assistance from others also emerged as a prominent category ($M = .17$, $SD = .35$).

Strategies that involved seeking assistance from others varied significantly by experience. When older adults had experience with a grandchild neglect problem, a greater proportion of their strategies involved seeking assistance ($M = .30$, $SD = .44$), than did the strategies of older adults who did not have experience with this type of problem ($M = .12$, $SD = .29$), $F\ (1,84) = 5.93$, $p < .05$.

Strategies that involved controlling others varied significantly by experience $F\ (1,85) = 3.81$, $p \leq .05$. When older adults had experience with a grandchild neglect problem, a lesser proportion of their strategies ($M = .26$, $SD = .35$), as compared to older adults without experience ($M = .42$, $SD = .33$), involved controlling others (see Figure 17.2). None of the other types of strategies (cognitive regulation, emotional regulation, behavioral regulation, discussion) varied by experience with the grandchild neglect problem.

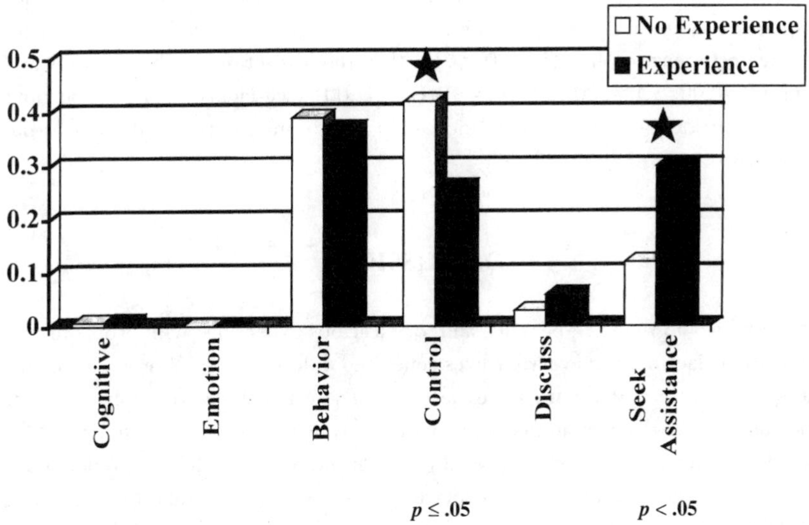

FIGURE 17.2 Proportion of strategy type by experience: Grandchild neglect problem.

Strategies by Problem Scenario

Next, we addressed whether or not the severity of the problems was associated with differences in strategies. We used paired sample *t*-tests to examine whether the two scenarios differed in the number of unique strategies, total number of strategies, and proportion of each type of strategy that was generated.

The total number of strategies generated in response to the baby-sitting (M = 2.12, SD = 1.19) and grandchild neglect (M = 2.29, SD = 1.11) problems did not differ significantly.

The number of unique types of strategies differed significantly across the two problem scenarios t (89) = 3.46, $p < .001$. Older adults reported a greater number of unique types of strategies for the more serious grandchild neglect problem (M = 1.63, SD = .61) than for the less serious baby-sitting problem (M = 1.37, SD = .55).

For the proportion of each strategy category, significant differences were found between the two problem scenarios. Strategies that involved changing one's own behavior comprised a significantly greater proportion of strategies for the less serious baby-sitting problem scenario than the more serious grandchild neglect scenario (M = .52, SD = .42) than the more serious grandchild neglect scenario (M = .40,

SD = .35), *t* (91) = −2.26, $p < .05$ (see Figure 17.3). Strategies for seeking assistance comprised a significantly greater proportion of strategies for the more serious grandchild neglect scenario (*M* = .17, *SD* = .35) than the less serious problem with babysitting (*M* = .00, *SD* = .00), *t* (90) = 4.64, $p < .001$ (see Figure 17.3). Proportions of the other strategy categories did not differ significantly between the two problem scenarios.

DISCUSSION

Older adults who reported personal and/or vicarious experience with problems that grandparents face in their everyday lives generated different types of problem-solving strategies than those without such experience. These findings have implications for understanding how older adults cope with gateway problems associated with the major life event of becoming a custodial grandparent, as well as for how older adults deal with relatively minor hassles associated with the grandparent role. Moreover, by placing grandparenting research within an everyday problem-solving framework, a greater understanding of the role that experience plays within the domain of grandparenting is made possible.

"Insiders," namely, older adults who reported some experience with problems associated with the grandparent role, differed from "outsiders" (those without such

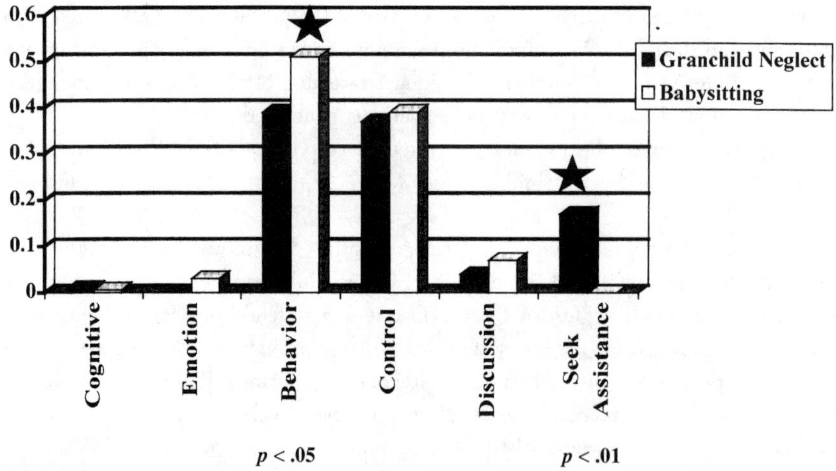

FIGURE 17.3 Proportion of strategy type by problem scenario.

experience) in terms of the types of strategies they viewed as viable options for dealing with grandparenting problems. In addition, in comparison to those without experience, older adults who had experience with the grandchild neglect problem suggested a somewhat smaller number of unique strategies. These findings are in accord with the theory that suggests that expertise limits the types of strategies that are viewed as viable. This has implications for understanding how to provide support to grandparents who may be facing problems associated with the custodial role. Custodial grandparents report that other people's opinions of child-rearing norms and the "proper" role of a grandparent are difficulties associated with raising their grandchildren (Generations United, 2000). This may reflect the fact that experienced grandparents' views of viable strategies for dealing with problems may be more limited than those of their peers. Service providers could target this issue.

Experienced older adults were more likely than those without experience to suggest seeking assistance from others to deal with a case of suspected grandchild neglect. Moreover, the assistance sought was usually from a social services agency (e.g., child protective services). These findings suggest that grandparents who have experience with cases of suspected child neglect are aware of the resources and agencies present in their communities. These findings are encouraging, given that awareness and use of available social services can contribute to successful grandparenting (Strom & Strom, 2000).

Substance abuse by a grandchild's parents is one gateway problem associated with a grandparent assuming a custodial role (Minkler & Roe, 1993; Pruchno, 1999). Although experienced older adults appeared to be willing to recruit outside assistance to target the aspect of the problem pertaining to suspected neglect, they were less willing to intervene to control the daughter's substance abuse problem. Compared to those without experience, older adults who had some experience (personal, vicarious, or both), were less likely to suggest controlling the parent's behavior, for example, by committing the parent to a treatment center. Older adults who have experience with adult offspring who abuse drugs and alcohol may understand the difficulty of changing patterns of such abuse when the abuser does not want to change. If so, they may choose to focus their problem-solving attempts on intervening to protect the well-being of the grandchild, rather than changing the child's parent. A greater focus on the grandchild as compared to the adult child may be a contributing factor in becoming a custodial grandparent. Indeed, King and Elder (1995) found that grandparents' reasons for becoming actively involved in a grandchild's life often involved helping the grandchild to avoid substance use and abuse.

In contrast to the findings for the grandchild neglect problem, few experience-related differences were found in problem-solving strategies for the baby-sitting problem. Older adults with and without experience with the baby-sitting problem were most likely to suggest strategies for changing one's own behavior and for controlling other people. There was some indication that those with experience viewed discussion strategies as less viable for dealing with the baby-sitting problem, as compared to those without experience. This is consistent with the notion that expertise limits the types of strategies that are viewed as effective. Older adults with experience may have learned that discussing their concerns about repeated requests to baby-sit with the grandchild's parents is not an effective way of solving the problem.

The seemingly different influence of experience on the types of strategies across the two problem scenarios may reflect the fact that the problems varied in their severity. We could not conduct a statistical test to examine the potential interaction among experience, problem, and strategy, due to the small number of participants who had experience with both problems. However, we did find that the problem scenarios were associated with differences in the types of strategies that were generated. Changing one's own behavior was relatively more likely to be suggested for the less serious baby-sitting problem than for the grandchild neglect problem. This relative difference must be understood in light of the fact that changing one's own behavior was the most prominent type of strategy for both types of problems when experience with the problem was not taken into account. Seeking assistance was more likely to be suggested for the grandchild neglect problem than for the baby-sitting problem. Indeed, not a single participant suggested seeking assistance as a strategy for dealing with the baby-sitting problem. Moreover, older adults offered a greater number of unique strategies in response to the grandchild neglect problem as compared to the baby-sitting problem. Taken together, these findings suggest that older adults may be more willing to recruit outside assistance when problems have potentially serious consequences for a grandchild and that older adults engage in flexible thinking when faced with a problem with potentially serious consequences (cf., Willis, Dolan, & Bertrand, 1999).

Across both problem scenarios, strategies that involved regulating or including others (i.e., seeking assistance, controlling others, discussion) were most likely to show differences by experience. This may reflect the interpersonal nature of the problems. Both problems involved intergenerational relationships among grandparents, adult children, and grandchildren. Strategies that involved only one's self, such as changing one's own behavior, were frequently suggested as ways to deal with both types of problems. These strategies, however, did not vary by experience. Thus, experience may be particularly likely to be associated with the use of interpersonally oriented strategies when problems in intergenerational relationships arise.

Our findings highlight the need for an increased understanding of the prevalence of problems that may serve as gateways to custodial grandparenting within the general population. As might be expected, the baby-sitting problem was relatively more common (53% reported some experience) than the grandchild neglect problem (31% reported some experience). Moreover, of those with experience, personal experience with the problem was relatively more common for the baby-sitting problem (20.5%) than the grandchild neglect problem (7.8%). Although a sizable portion of our participants knew someone who had faced a problem that involved grandchild neglect, relatively few had personally faced this problem. Moreover, it is likely that even among those who face this problem, not all go on to assume a custodial role. For example, approximately 10% of grandparents reported that they had ever assumed responsibility for a grandchild and approximately 6% are currently raising a grandchild (Minkler & Fuller-Thomson, 1999; Szinovacz, 1998).

Previous research has conceptualized experience as both a domain-general (e.g., Cornelius & Caspi, 1987) and a domain-specific (e.g., Berg et al., 1999) phenomenon. Our results suggest that experience may be best conceptualized at the level of specific problems. If so, our findings indicate the need for models to explain how experience might transfer across different problems. In doing so, it will be important to consider individuals' problem-solving goals. Experience with problems may shape goals; goals in turn may guide strategy selection (Berg et al., 1998). Individuals' goals for solving everyday problems vary in the extent to which they focus on their own needs and the needs of others (Strough et al., 1996). For example, the grandchild neglect problem allowed for a variety of goals to be pursued, including those related to self-interest (e.g., not getting involved) and the interests of others (e.g., child's well-being, parent's well-being). If a grandmother knows from experience that she cannot change her daughter's alcohol abuse, she may focus on the grandchild's well-being rather than on her daughter's well-being. Grandparents whose goals focus exclusively on the grandchild's well-being may select strategies that differ from grandparents whose goals focus on the well-being of both the grandchild and the child's parent. Moreover, when grandparents have similar goals for solving different kinds of problems, they may use similar strategies. For example, a grandparent whose goals focus on her grandchild's well-being may select strategies that promote the child's well-being regardless of whether the problem involves a conflict between her own leisure time and baby-sitting, or between her daughter's privacy and potential neglect of the grandchild.

Considering how experience may shape grandparents' goals and strategies may be useful in designing support services for custodial grandparents. Strom and Strom (2000) suggest that a good fit between grandparents' goals and their circumstances is important for successful grandparenting. Service providers may benefit from identifying and clarifying grandparents' goals for solving intergenerational problems. In addition, questioning grandparents about their previous experience, if any, and the strategies they view as viable solutions may help service providers to better understand the custodial situation as it is perceived by the grandparent.

LIMITATIONS AND FUTURE DIRECTIONS

Our findings must be understood in light of the methods used to examine everyday problem-solving strategies and experience. First, the size of our sample was insufficient to distinguish between older adults who had personal versus vicarious experience with the grandparenting problems. Research is needed to address whether personal and vicarious experience have similar effects on problem-solving strategies. For instance, custodial grandparents may suggest different problem-solving strategies than those who have only vicarious experience with the custodial role. Second, our measure of experience differs from previous research, not only in the inclusion of vicarious experience, but also because we assessed experience as a categorical variable rather than as a continuous variable. Grandparents who deal repeatedly with the consequences of their offspring's alcohol abuse may use different strategies than grandparents who have experienced this problem only once, or who have witnessed someone else deal with this problem. Third, we presented older adults with hypothetical problems and asked them what the person should do. The strategies generated in response to this prompt may not be indicative of what they themselves would do if solving a problem with their own child and grandchildren. Finally, caution should be exercised in generalizing our results to other cultural and ethnic groups because these groups' experiences with grandparenting problems may differ from those of our participants.

CONCLUSION

In sum, the findings of the current investigation contribute to a greater understanding of the strategies older adults view as viable for coping with grandparenting challenges and problems. The findings begin to suggest how to best provide support for custodial grandparents by emphasizing that *who* a potential or current custodial grandparent consults for advice might influence the type of advice they receive. Further investigations of linkages among grandparents' experiences, strategies, and goals may lead to a better understanding of the interpersonal processes that contribute to successful grandparenting.

REFERENCES

Baltes, P. B., & Staudinger, U. M. (1993). The search for a psychology of wisdom. *Current Directions in Psychological Science, 2,* 75–80.

Berg, C. A., & Klaczynski, P. A. (1996). Practical intelligence and problem solving: Searching for perspectives. In F. Blanchard-Fields & T. M. Hess (Eds.), *Perspectives on cognitive change in adulthood and aging* (pp. 323–357). New York: McGraw Hill.

Berg, C. A., Meegan, S. P., & Klaczynski, P. (1999). Age and experiential differences in strategy generation and information requests for solving everyday problems. *International Journal of Behavioral Development, 23,* 615–639.

Berg, C. A., & Sternberg, R. J. (1985). A triarchic theory of intellectual development during adulthood. *Developmental Review, 6,* 334–370.

Berg, C. A., Strough, J., Calderone, K. S., Meegan, S. P., & Sansone, C. (1997). Planning to prevent everyday problems from occurring. In S. L. Friedman & E. K. Scholnick (Eds.), *Why, how, and when do we plan? The developmental psychology of planning* (pp. 209–236). Hillsdale, NJ: Erlbaum.

Berg, C. A., Strough, J., Calderone, K. S., Sansone, C., & Weir, C. (1998). The role of problem definitions in understanding age and context effects on strategies for solving everyday problems. *Psychology and Aging, 13,* 29–44.

Blanchard-Fields, F., Jahnke, H. C., & Camp, C. (1995). Age differences in problem-solving style: The role of emotional salience. *Psychology and Aging, 10,* 173–180.

Block, C. E. (2000). Dyadic and gender differences in perceptions of the grandparent–grandchild relationship. *Aging and Human Development, 51,* 85–104.

Cornelius, S. W., & Caspi, A. (1987). Everyday problem solving in adulthood and old age. *Psychology and Aging, 2,* 144–153.

Denney, N. W. (1984). A model of cognitive development across the life span. *Developmental Review, 4,* 171–191.

Denney, N. W. (1989). Everyday problem solving: Methodological issues, research findings, and a model. In L. W. Poon, D. C. Rubin, & B. A. Wilson (Eds.), *Everyday cognition in adulthood and late life* (pp. 330–351). New York: Cambridge University Press.

Denney, N. W., & Pearce, K. A. (1989). A developmental study of practical problem solving in adults. *Psychology and Aging, 4,* 438–442.

Denney, N. W., Tozier, T. L., & Schlotthauer, C. A. (1992). The effect of instructions on age differences in practical problem solving. *Journal of Gerontology: Psychological Sciences, 47,* 142–145.

Dressel, P. L., & Barnhill, S. K. (1994). Reframing gerontological thought and practice: The case of grandmothers with daughters in prison. *The Gerontologist, 34,* 685–691.

Generations United. (2000). *Grandparents and other relatives raising children: Challenges of caring for the second family.* Generations United Fact Sheet. Retrieved October 3, 2001 from http://www.gu.org/Files/gpgeneral.pdf.

Hayslip, B., Shore, R. J., Henderson, C. E., & Lambert, P. L. (1998). Custodial grandparenting and the impact of grandchildren with problems and role meaning. *Journals of Gerontology: Social Sciences, 53B,* S164–S173.

Jendrek, M. P. (1994). Grandparents who parent their grandchildren: Circumstances and decision. *The Gerontologist, 34,* 206–216.

King, V., & Elder, G. H. (1995). American children view their grandparents: Linked lives across three rural generations. *Journal of Marriage and the Family, 57,* 165–178.

Kornhaber, A. (1986). Grandparenting: Normal and pathological—A preliminary communication from The Grandparent Study. *Journal of Geriatric Psychiatry, 19,* 19–37.

Labouvie-Vief, G. (1982). Dynamic development and mature autonomy: A theoretical prologue. *Human Development, 25,* 161–191.

Meacham, J. A., & Emont, N. C. (1989). The interpersonal basis of everyday problem solving. In J. D. Sinnott (Ed.), *Everyday problem solving* (pp. 7–23). New York: Praeger.

Minkler, M., & Fuller-Thomson, E. (1999). The health of grandparents raising grandchildren: Results of a national study. *American Journal of Public Health, 89,* 1384–1389.

Minkler, M., & Fuller-Thomson, E. (2000). Second time around parenting: Factors predictive of grandparents becoming caregivers for their grandchildren. *Aging and Human Development, 50,* 185–200.

Minkler, M., & Roe, K. M. (1993). *Grandparents as caregivers: Raising children of the crack cocaine epidemic.* Newbury Park, CA: Sage.

Patrick, J. H., & Strough, J. (2001). *Everyday problem solving: Experience, strategies, and behavioral intentions.* Manuscript submitted for publication.

Peterson, C. C. (1999). Grandfathers' and grandmothers' satisfaction with grandparenting: Seeking new answers to old questions. *Aging and Human Development, 49,* 61–78.

Pruchno, R. (1999). Raising grandchildren: The experiences of Black and White grandmothers. *The Gerontologist, 39,* 209–221.

Sansone, C., & Berg, C. A. (1993). Adapting to the environment across the life span: Different process or different inputs? *International Journal of Behavioral Development, 16,* 215–241.

Scribner, S. (1986). Thinking in action: Some characteristics of practical thought. In R. J. Sternberg & R. Wagner (Eds.), *Practical intelligence: Origins of competence in the everyday world* (pp. 143–162). New York: Cambridge University Press.

Sinnott, J. D. (1989). A model for solution of ill-structured problems: Implications for everyday and abstract problem solving. In J. D. Sinnott (Ed.), *Everyday problem solving* (pp. 72–99). New York: Praeger.

Smith, J., & Baltes, P. B. (1990). Wisdom related knowledge: Age/cohort differences in responses to life planning problems. *Developmental Psychology, 26,* 494–505.

Spivack, G., & Shure, M. B. (1982). The cognition of social adjustment. In B. B. Lahey & A. E. Kazdin (Eds.), *Advances in child psychology* (pp. 323–372). New York: Plenum.

Sternberg, R. J., & Wagner, R. K. (Eds.). (1986). *Practical intelligence: Nature and origins of competence in the everyday world.* New York: Cambridge University Press.

Strom, R. D., & Strom, S. K. (2000). Meeting the challenge of raising grandchildren. *International Journal of Aging and Human Development, 51,* 183–198.

Strough, J., Berg, C. A., & Sansone, C. (1996). Goals for solving everyday problems across the life span: Age and gender differences in the salience of interpersonal concerns. *Developmental Psychology, 32,* 1106–1115.

Strough, J., Cheng, S., & Swenson, L. M. (in press). Preferences for collaborative and individual everyday problem solving in later adulthood. *International Journal of Behavioral Development.*

Strough, J., Patrick, J. H., Swenson, L. M., Cheng, S., & Barnes, K. A. (in press). Collaborative everyday problem solving: Interpersonal relationships and problem dimensions. *International Journal of Aging and Human Development.*

Szinovacz, M. E. (1998). Grandparents today: A demographic profile. *The Gerontologist, 38,* 37–52.

Szinovacz, M. E., & Roberts, A. (1998). Programs for grandparents. In M. E. Szinovacz (Ed)., *Handbook on grandparenthood* (pp. 247–256). Westport CT: Greenwood.

Watson, T. L., & Blanchard-Fields, F. (1998). Thinking with your head and your heart: Age differences in everyday problem-solving strategy preferences. *Aging, Neuropsychology, and Cognition, 5,* 225–240.

Williams, A., & Nussbaum, J. F. (2001). *Intergenerational communication across the life span.* Mahweh, NJ: Erlbaum.

Willis, S. (1996). Everyday problem solving. In J. E. Birren & K. Warner Schaie (Eds.), *Handbook of the psychology of aging* (4th ed., pp. 287–307). San Diego, CA: Academic Press.

Willis, S. L., Dolan, M. M., & Bertrand, R. M. (1999). Problem solving on health-related tasks of daily living. In D. C. Park, R. W. Morrell, & K. Shifren (Eds.), *Processing of medical information in aging patients: Cognitive and human factors perspectives* (pp. 199–219). Hillsdale, NJ: Erlbaum.

CHAPTER *18*

Epilogue: The Next Stage in Helping Custodial Grandparents

Julie Hicks Patrick and Bert Hayslip, Jr.

During the past few decades, significant progress has occurred in helping custodial grandparents adapt to the challenges of raising grandchildren. First and foremost has been the increased attention to these issues from the popular media and the scientific community. Grandparents, service providers, and researchers have succeeded in raising public awareness about the prevalence and challenges of custodial grandparenting. While remaining nonnormative, raising one's grandchildren is now viewed as a relatively common occurrence among middle-aged and older adults. In addition, our knowledge regarding grandparent-headed families has increased exponentially. We have learned that "family" is a broad and dynamic term that encompasses a variety of constellations; that custodial grandparents come in all ages, races, and income levels; that entry to the custodial grandparent role is precipitated by an amalgam of events that directly influence grandparents and grandchildren; and that grandchildren living with grandparents present a variety of rewarding and challenging behaviors. This descriptive knowledge has been useful, although in terms of helping custodial grandparents, it has not been applied to its full advantage.

Currently, support groups are the most common approach for helping custodial grandparents. As detailed in the preceding chapters, both the mechanics and the content of such groups are important considerations. Support group leaders have been careful to remove barriers to participation, including concerns about transportation, childcare, and scheduling (Kolomer et al.). Such attention to removing barriers results in better use of support groups. We know that groups are more effective when the support groups are focused in content, flexible in scheduling, and jointly led by custodial grandparents and professionals (Smith; Wohl et al.). Although it may not always be preferable to tie support groups to the formal service network, some expertise in navigating the formal service system may be advantageous (Kelley & Whitley; Smith).

Despite the improved delivery of support group interventions, participation in grandparent support groups remains relatively low; Kopera-Frye et al. and Smith reported that approximately half of their respective samples had previously attended a support group. One reason for such underutilization may relate to a low level of perceived benefits. In the recent past, grandparent support groups have not been guided by theory, and custodial grandparents may have perceived few benefits (Smith; Wohl et al.). However, as support groups and other interventions begin to incorporate existing theoretical principles, the benefits ensuing to support group members are increasing. In fact, the data presented in these chapters demonstrates that custodial grandparents attending support groups experience a variety of positive effects. However, support groups vary widely in content. Some focus primarily on information (Kinney et al.) and parenting strategies (Dolbin-MacNab & Targ; Kern), whereas others focus on concrete behaviors that grandparents can enact to improve their coping and physical well-being (Crowther & Rodriguez). In addition to psychological benefits ensuing as a function of support group attendance, tangible rewards may result as well. Through contact with more experienced custodial grandparents and professionals working within the formal service network, custodial grandparents may access a wider array of formal supports (Kelley & Whitley; Kinney et al.). Thus, we need to do a better job publicizing the potential benefits of these interventions to grandparents and service providers. We need to take seriously what custodial grandparents themselves say they need and want from us (Baird).

Many successful interventions for grandparents are derived from the tenets of life span developmental theory, which hold that development: (1) is a lifelong and multidirectional process, (2) is influenced by multiple factors, (3) occurs within a dynamic context, and (4) is influenced by chronological age, historical period, and generational cohort. Thus, it is a powerful framework from which to develop, implement, and evaluate interventions for custodial grandparents. Despite the significant progress that has been made thus far, there is much work that remains. Guided by the richness of life span theory, we suggest several research and intervention questions to be pursued in the next decade.

Although science seeks to distill general principles that describe, explain, and predict various behaviors, the field is ready for increased precision in the design, implementation, and evaluation of support group effectiveness. We know that individual characteristics of both the grandparent and the grandchild affect mental and physical health outcomes. What remains unclear is which interventions hold promise for which grandparents, whether certain characteristics of the grandparent and/or grandchild interact with the effectiveness of the intervention, whether interventions promote growth in addition to decreasing negative outcomes, and whether indirect effects accrue to the grandchildren. Thus, it is necessary to further disentangle the effects of individual characteristics and outcomes by carefully examining different trajectories of adaptation. By explicitly noting the life context in which custodial grandparenting takes place, we can develop a more idiographic approach to interventions. Matching the intervention to the individual, although a daunting task, is likely to result in the best possible outcomes for that individual.

Specifically, the field needs highly targeted research that addresses the different needs of middle-aged and older grandparents raising grandchildren. As reviewed by Crowther and Rodriguez, the stereotypical custodial grandparent is a woman in her late 50s or early 60s. However, custodial grandparents vary widely in their ages. Few investigations have examined these age differences explicitly, despite theoretical predictions and some empirical support that age (Kelley & Whitley), role demands (Roberto & Qualls), and previous experience (Strough et al.) likely influence important outcomes. In addition, support from age peers, family members, the school system, and other exosystem entities (Conway & Stricker) may vary markedly as a function of grandparent age. Thus, grandparent age may well mediate the effects of interventions. Interestingly, however, it may be the younger custodial grandparents, perhaps more recent to the role, who report greater distress (Kelley & Whitley).

The different challenges inherent to the grandchild's developmental stage and level of psychological health must be considered as well (Keller & Stricker; Kern). Living with and loving toddlers presents a different set of demands than living with and loving teenagers. Although current research often controls for the age of the grandchild, we need to address more sharply the influence of the grandchild and other family members on grandparent well-being (Conway & Stricker; Patrick & Pickard). In addition, we need longitudinal studies that address the transitions from one stage of child development to the next while acknowledging interfamilial differences in the duration of coresidence. Given the dynamic nature of custodial grandparenting, it is reasonable to expect changes over time that correspond to the increasing age of both grandchild and grandparent, as well as length of coresidence. Support groups that are targeted for specific stages of child development might be especially helpful. In addition, acknowledging potential differences that covary with the gateway issue that was the impetus for coresidence (Strough et al.), duration of coresidence, and other situation-specific aspects might be useful.

Within a developmental context, support group interventions may need to be targeted to specific concerns. As described in the preceding chapters, grandparents come to support groups with a variety of issues and concerns (Smith; Wohl et al.); targeting the group toward those specific concerns is often helpful. As Smith's study shows, a large percentage of grandparents want information about child rearing. For grandparents who are distressed about the return to active child rearing, explicit training in current approaches to discipline and ways to promote a nurturing and supportive environment for the grandchildren may be especially helpful (Dolbin-MacNab & Targ; Kern). Targeted support groups may also help to avoid potentially negative effects. In a heterogeneous group, exposure to child-rearing issues that are outside of one's immediate concerns may temporarily increase grandparent distress (Hayslip; Kolomer et al.). This idea dovetails with Strough and colleagues' findings that adults with experience dealing with multigenerational problems approach such problems differently than do adults without such experience. Thus, by increasing group similarity, custodial grandparents may be better prepared to navigate the demands of the immediate environment. In those respects, data do show that grandparent caregivers can benefit in many ways from purposefully defined interventions (Hayslip), but these findings also indicate that with such gains come some emotional costs.

That is not to imply, however, that custodial grandparents do not need to plan for the future. Custodial grandparents who are living with a child, with or without disabilities, want and need to plan for the future (Kopera-Frye et al.; Smith). In this regard, the field can learn from other literatures examining the challenges facing older caregivers of adults with disabilities (Kinney et al.; Roberto & Qualls). In this literature, the importance of future planning is highlighted. Based on the adult caregiving literature, it is reasonable that custodial grandparents who are dealing with a grandchild's developmental disability (Kolomer et al.) may experience different challenges and concerns than those who are raising a grandchild who presents emotional or behavioral problems (Smith) in the absence of cognitive impairment. Differentiating the service needs and mental health effects on grandparents as a function of the nature of these disabilities is critical. Integrated service delivery and support systems may be especially important for these grandparents (Kinney et al.; Kolomer et al.). Interestingly, many grandparents articulate the desire to plan for the future and to secure helpful services for their grandchildren as major issues in their caregiving role (Kopera-Frye et al.; Smith).

We need to expand our field of view to focus on the grandchildren as well. The predominant approach to helping custodial grandparents has been to provide formal services to the family and support groups for the grandparents. Indeed, a large percentage of these children exhibit emotional and behavioral problems (Kern; Patrick & Pickard; Smith). Moreover, when asked what additional services they need, a large percentage of grandparents want support groups for the grandchildren (Keller & Stricker; Kopera-Frye et al.). For grandchildren exhibiting particularly problematic behaviors, a behavioral assessment may inform the intervention approach (Conway & Stricker).

An additional area to consider in intervention efforts includes the ways in which differences in relationships with the middle generation affect these families (Keller & Stricker). Although the literature is beginning to examine differences in affection and relationship quality within the grandparent-grandchild dyad (Conway & Stricker; Keller & Stricker; Patrick & Pickard), there are a host of unexamined individual difference variables that will likely affect the emotional relationship between custodial grandparents and grandchildren. Variables that will be important to consider in future studies include the impact of the middle-generation parent, sibling relationships within blended families, and household composition within the grandparent's home. To date, relatively few studies have included such family-specific variables. The nearest attempt has been to highlight the different contexts in which European-American and African-American grandparents raise their grandchildren (Crowther & Rodriguez; Kolomer et al.). Future research needs to examine the effects of raising multiracial grandchildren, particularly when the grandparent and grandchild have different racial backgrounds. Issues of social and peer acceptance may be especially salient for grandparents raising multiracial grandchildren.

LIFE-SPAN THEORY AND CUSTODIAL GRANDPARENTING: THE NEXT DECADE

By its very nature, custodial grandparenting is a dynamic and transactional role. The chapters presented here have significantly advanced the theoretical rigor present to interventions with grandparents. Indeed, armed with a theoretical framework, we are beginning to develop effective interventions that incorporate the complexities of individual lives. However, for continued progress, more sophisticated measures and designs will be needed. To properly evaluate the effects of interventions for specific individuals and over time, we need dyadic-specific measures within longitudinal methodologies.

Finally, an additional area that needs to be addressed involves systemic changes at the intersection of the research community and the broader society. As a research and clinical community, we have developed techniques to decrease negative physical and psychological outcomes associated with parenting, caregiving, and dealing with disabilities. What we have failed to do is to give this knowledge away. Although there are a few notable exceptions, many of which are included in the current volume, researchers must do a better job of communicating their theoretically sound and empirically derived results to the lay, service-delivery, and policy-making communities. Part of this effort requires that research inform policy. Difficulties dealing with schools, coordinating services, and obtaining appropriate housing compound the challenges of raising a grandchild. Just as the focused efforts of grandparents, service providers, and researchers have increased public awareness, these three forces must continue to raise awareness among policy makers. A second prong to systemic change involves making grandparent interventions more effective, more accessible, and more portable. Greater reliance on theory and greater specificity in the design, implementation, and evaluation of interventions will increase their effectiveness. To increase the accessibility and portability of interventions, researchers must assist community-based agencies and grassroots groups to obtain ongoing financial support for grandparent interventions. Researchers have the expertise to apply for, and obtain, funds that are available for community-based programs. Thus, "giving the science away" may involve leaving our labs and partnering with community-based groups. Such efforts, however, are likely to result in synergistic benefits for grandparents, the communities in which they raise their grandchildren, service providers, and researchers.

Index